THE UNIQUE UNITS

Other National Historical Society Publications:

THE IMAGE OF WAR: 1861-1865

TOUCHED BY FIRE: A PHOTOGRAPHIC PORTRAIT OF THE CIVIL WAR

WAR OF THE REBELLION: OFFICIAL RECORDS
  OF THE UNION AND CONFEDERATE ARMIES

OFFICIAL RECORDS OF THE UNION AND CONFEDERATE NAVIES
  IN THE WAR OF THE REBELLION

HISTORICAL TIMES ILLUSTRATED ENCYCLOPEDIA OF THE CIVIL WAR

CONFEDERATE VETERAN

THE WEST POINT MILITARY HISTORY SERIES

IMPACT: THE ARMY AIR FORCES' CONFIDENTIAL HISTORY
  OF WORLD WAR II

HISTORY OF UNITED STATES NAVAL OPERATIONS IN WORLD WAR II
  by Samuel Eliot Morison

HISTORY OF THE ARMED FORCES IN WORLD WAR II
  by Janusz Piekalkiewicz

A TRAVELLER'S GUIDE TO GREAT BRITAIN SERIES

MAKING OF BRITAIN SERIES

THE ARCHITECTURAL TREASURES OF EARLY AMERICA

For information about National Historical Society Publications, write:
The National Historical Society, 2245 Kohn Road, Box 8200,
Harrisburg, Pa 17105

THE ELITE
The World's Crack Fighting Men

THE UNIQUE UNITS

Ashley Brown, Editor

Jonathan Reed, Editor

Editorial Board

Brigadier-General James L. Collins, Jr. (Retd.)
Former Chief of Military History, US Department of the Army

Ian V. Hogg
Authority on smallarms and modern weapons systems

Dr. John Pimlott
Senior Lecturer in the Department of War Studies,
Royal Military Academy, Sandhurst, England

Brigadier-General Edwin H. Simmons (Retd.)
US Marine Corps

Lisa Mullins, Managing Editor, NHS edition

A Publication of
THE NATIONAL HISTORICAL SOCIETY

Published in Great Britain in 1986 by Orbis Publishing

Library of Congress Cataloging-in-Publication Data
The Unique units / Ashley Brown, editor, Jonathan Reed, editor.
   p.   cm.—(The Elite : the world's crack fighting men ; v. 10)
  ISBN 0-918678-48-X
   1. Special forces (Military science)—History—20th century.
2. Special operations (Military science)—History—20th century.
I. Brown, Ashley. II. Reed, Jonathan. III. National Historical
Society. IV. Series: Elite (Harrisburg, Pa.) ; v. 10.
U262.U54   1989
356'.167—dc20   89-12499
                                  CIP

CONTENTS

	Introduction		7
1	**Brandenburg Strike East**	Jean Mabire	8
2	**Beating the Bombers**	Peter Macdonald	14
3	**Sabotage!**	Nigel Foster	22
4	**Heroism at Ben Het**	Ian MacNeill	27
5	**War in the Hills**	Leroy Thompson	33
6	**Strike on Leros**	James Lucas	40
7	**V Force**	Anthony Robinson	45
8	**Nile Raiders**	James Lucas	52
9	**Canaris's Commandos**	Jean Mabire	57
10	**War in the Backyard**	David Esler	62
11	**Kidnapped**	Bernard Brett	70
12	**Son Tay**	Leroy Thompson	75
13	**GSG9**	Leroy Thompson	80
14	**Sting Ray**	Bernard Trainor	85
15	**Quit You Like Men**	Ian Dear	94
16	**Freedom Fighters**	Adrian Gilbert	100
17	**The Secret War**	Leroy Thompson	108
18	**Secret Reconnaissance**	Ahrom Lapidot	114
19	**Green Berets**	Leroy Thompson	119
20	**High Speed Spies**	Alfred Price	126
21	**Danger UXB**	David Esler	133
22	**Private Army**	Adrian Gilbert	140
23	**Special Hardware**	Ian Hogg	145
24	**Spetsnaz**	Ed Blanche	152
25	**Centcom**	Gregor Ferguson	161
26	**A Question of Security**	Nigel Foster	168
	Combat Skills of the Elite: Escape and Evasion		174

INTRODUCTION

For some reason they almost always seem to be known by acronyms—EOD . . . UXB . . . SOE . . . GSG9 . . . RSR . . . CENTCOM. Perhaps it is because of the often secret nature of their work, that their official names are abbreviated into a bewildering alphabet. When they are given names . . . the Brandenburgers, the Green Berets . . . it is only by association with their deeds. Whatever they are or have been called, these Unique Units stand at the forefront of THE ELITE.

One need only look at what they have done to see why. Consider the Brandenburgers, the German special forces organized in 1939 to infiltrate behind enemy lines. The Brandenburg Regiment specialized in deception, posing as Soviets in 1941, moving into the Dodecanese islands in 1943, trekking 2,000 miles across Africa to place secret agents in Cairo. The SOE—Special Operations Executive—went undercover in Norway to combat Germany for the British, and fought the Axis throughout Europe with so much cloaking of mystery that even today its operations are not entirely known. The UXB heroes in World War II and their counterparts today in Britain's EOD—Explosive Ordnance Disposal—risked their lives almost daily to defuze thousands of unexploded enemy bombs and booby traps.

Every nation has had their unique units, and so have would-be nations from the Spanish Republicans in the 1930's to the contras of the 1980's. The German GSG9—Grenzshutzgruppe 9—a crack antiterrorist squad, rescued the passengers aboard a Lufthansa 737 in Somalia in 1977 without losing one of them. Britain's Raiding Support Regiment—the RSR—marched with the slogan "Quit You Like Men," and so they acquitted themselves in Yugoslavia and the Mediterranean in World War II.

The requirements of Ulrich Wegener, creator of GSG9, might serve to describe all of the Unique Units in THE ELITE. They must have the best men, the best organization, the best weapons. They must be infinitely subtle, and at times extremely ferocious. Whether for Unique Units or any other special band of men, it is a prescription for THE ELITE.

STRIKE EAST

After the cancellation of Operation Sea Lion, the plan to invade Britain in mid-1940, the Brandenburg Regiment (whose cuff band is shown above) underwent a period of expansion and intensive training at Quenzsee.

New recruits learnt all the skills associated with special forces, but particular stress was placed on techniques of deception. The Brandenburgers were usually deployed in very small units in which stealth was as important as strength. Instructors developed the skill of deception by having recruits parade in foreign uniforms.

To foster a sense of camaraderie and trust, the recruits were permitted to shake hands with officers rather than salute, and encouraged to form small, cohesive detachments. The training at the camp was also specifically designed to test ingenuity.

Once, recruits were ordered to get the fingerprints of a local police chief without being discovered. Later, as the programme intensified and became more difficult, men were ordered to capture 10 Wehrmacht soldiers within five hours and bring them to Quenzsee.

The Brandenburgers' unusual training methods and relaxed attitude to discipline won them few friends in the regular army. Traditionalists argued that blind obedience and rigorous adherence to accepted military tactics won battles and not the initiative displayed by the Brandenburg Regiment. Their complaints would ultimately help to destroy the unit.

The unorthodox methods used by the German special forces proved very useful during the invasion of the Soviet Union in 1941

AT DAWN on 22 June 1941, German forces went onto the offensive against the Soviet Union along a line from the Baltic in the north to the Black Sea in the south. As in the offensive on the Western Front the previous year, the Brandenburgers were to play a crucial role in Germany's Blitzkrieg strategy. Their task was to seize key points, such as bridges, tunnels or road junctions, in front of the German advance, and hold them until the main armoured units arrived. If the Brandenburgers failed to achieve their objectives, the Russians would be able to blow up the vital communications centres and thus impede the German offensive.

By the summer of 1941, Admiral Canaris's Bran-

As the might of the German armed forces turned against the Soviet Union (above), the experience of Brandenburgers, such as Leutnant Gräbert (left), proved invaluable in the securing of positions behind Russian lines.

denburgers comprised three battalions and several autonomous companies. As had become traditional, they were distributed in small units, operating independently and with considerable initiative being exercised by the often low-ranking unit commanders.

Needing to reach their objectives before the main body of the German Army, many of the Brandenburgers moved into Soviet territory on the night before the offensive. Disguised in Soviet uniforms, pulled on over their German field-grey, and driving Soviet trucks obtained from the Finns who had captured them in the winter of 1939/40, they attempted to infiltrate Soviet border positions. There were strict instructions to avoid any exchange of fire before the official start of the offensive. Although each Brandenburg unit was led by a man speaking perfect Russian, they did not always manage to deceive the Soviet border guards, who were alert to the possibility of a German attack. The Brandenburgers did not know the Soviet passwords for the night. If challenged and unable to talk their way out of trouble, their only chance was to flee, since the order not to open fire had to be respected. A number were killed in such incidents, but others successfully approached their objectives during the night and were well placed to exploit the confusion of the following morning as Soviet troops fled in the face of the onslaught.

As they drove towards the bridge, they were hit by a shell from a Soviet anti-tank gun

Some of the events of that night became legendary. Perhaps the most daring enterprise was Sergeant Zoller's heroic act of indiscipline. Zoller had been left out of the action, assigned to his company's base in the rear. Unprepared to accept this passive role, he decided to capture a bridge anyway, without receiving orders to do so. He chose as his objective the bridge at Siolko, on the river Bobr, and persuaded two of his men to join him. They succeeded in commandeering a Soviet vehicle, but as they drove towards the bridge they were hit by a shell from a Soviet anti-tank gun. Both his companions were killed, but Zoller survived. When the vanguard of the German Army reached the bridge, they found the sergeant in sole command of the position but still in Soviet uniform. Zoller was in such a state of shock after his adventure that he could not identify himself to the Germans and was taken prisoner, only to be released some days later after the intervention of a Brandenburg officer.

More typical of operations in the first week of the offensive was the taking of a crucial bridge in the Pripet marshes on 27 June. This swampy area presented considerable problems to an armoured advance, greatly restricting the movement of tanks. If the Russians destroyed key road bridges, the advance would inevitably be delayed. An armoured column had originally been entrusted with seizing and holding the bridge in question, but it soon became obvious that the panzers could not hope to achieve this objective as their approach would inevitably leave the Soviet demolition team the time needed to detonate their pre-set mines. Stealth would have to be employed, and that meant using special forces.

A Brandenburg detachment was called in from the German side of the frontier, where a company of the commandos waited in readiness. The unit set out just after dawn on 26 June, but it was not until

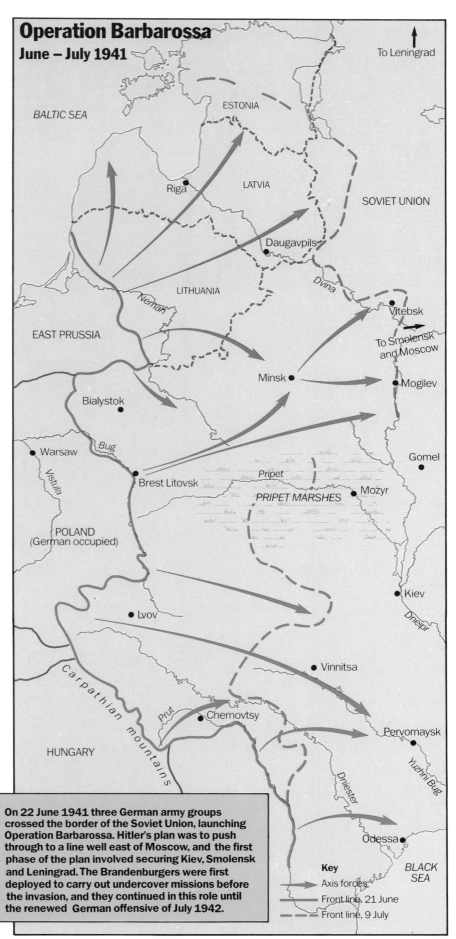

Operation Barbarossa
June – July 1941

To Leningrad

BALTIC SEA

ESTONIA

Riga

LATVIA

SOVIET UNION

Daugavpils

Dvina

LITHUANIA

Neman

Vitebsk

To Smolensk and Moscow

EAST PRUSSIA

Minsk

Mogilev

Bialystok

Bug

Warsaw

Vistula

Brest Litovsk

Pripet

PRIPET MARSHES

Gomel

Mozyr

POLAND
(German occupied)

Kiev

Dnieper

Lvov

Carpathian mountains

Vinnitsa

Prut

Chernovtsy

Pervomaysk

HUNGARY

Dniester

Yuzhni Bug

Odessa

BLACK SEA

Key
Axis forces
Front line, 21 June
Front line, 9 July

On 22 June 1941 three German army groups crossed the border of the Soviet Union, launching Operation Barbarossa. Hitler's plan was to push through to a line well east of Moscow, and the first phase of the plan involved securing Kiev, Smolensk and Leningrad. The Brandenburgers were first deployed to carry out undercover missions before the invasion, and they continued in this role until the renewed German offensive of July 1942.

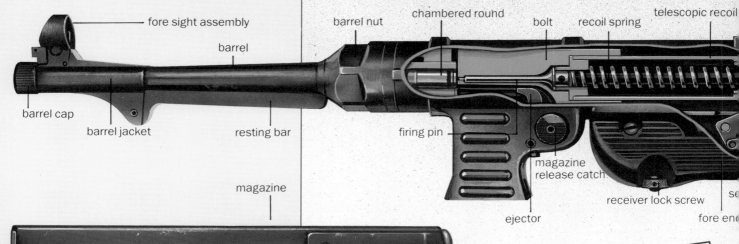

fore sight assembly
barrel
barrel cap
barrel jacket
resting bar

barrel nut
chambered round
bolt
recoil spring
telescopic recoil

firing pin

magazine
release catch

ejector

receiver lock screw

se

fore en

magazine

the early hours of the following day that they joined the panzer regiment near the target bridge, having suffered almost a day's bone-shaking travel along crowded, pot-holed roads in the back of captured Soviet trucks. The leader of the Brandenburger group was briefed by a panzer officer, and it was immediately evident that the task would not be easy.

The armour would have to lie in wait just out of sight of the Russians on the bridge, since the appearance of a German tank would be the signal for the demolition of the structure. This meant, the panzer officer calculated, that the tanks would have to be 15 minutes driving time from the bridge. So the Brandenburgers would have to seize their objective and then hold it for a quarter of an hour against the surrounding Soviet forces, until the tanks arrived.

The first problem was how to approach the bridge. A variant of the normal Brandenburg deception technique was chosen. The men, dressed in Red Army greatcoats and helmets, would drive towards the bridge in two Soviet trucks, shouting that they were closely pursued by German armour. One of the trucks would cross the bridge, but the other would apparently break down. The Brandenburgers in the first truck would try to persuade the Russians to delay blowing up the bridge until their colleagues in the second vehicle had restarted their truck and crossed the river. In the confusion, the Brandenburgers in the first truck would locate the points from which the charges were to be detonated and, as the second truck finally limped onto the bridge, they would strip off their Russian uniforms and seize their objective intact.

The operation was fixed for late evening, so that the Brandenburgers would emerge as black silhouettes against the sun as it set in the west. It was a long, hot summer's day, and around the bridge the retreating Red Army milled in confusion under the constant pressure of German infantry patrols carrying out harassing missions. Stuka dive-bomb attacks and sporadic artillery bombardment spread panic among the Soviet troops along the river embankment. This scene of chaos was ideal for the Brandenburgers' plans.

As the evening drew on, the men completed their

Right: Ukrainian troops of the Brandenburger Nightingale Group. Inset: A Brandenburg detachment, dressed in Soviet uniforms, on a clandestine mission behind Russian lines in 1941.

MP40 SMG

rear sight

rear lever

trigger

trigger guard

stock pivot/
locking catch

trigger spring

grip

Calibre 9mm
Length (stock extended) 83.3cm
Weight (loaded) 4.7kg
Magazine 32-round box
Rate of fire (cyclic) 500rpm
Muzzle velocity 381mps
Maximum effective range 200m

folding stock

Above: The MP40 sub-machine gun, sidearm of both special forces and the German regular army, was produced in vast quantities. Over one million were made between 1940 and 1944.

preparations. Carrying Soviet rifles, but with German machine-pistols concealed in the bottom of the trucks, they took up their positions in the vehicles, ready to break cover. The signal for the assault to begin was a Stuka raid, laid on to distract the defenders. As the bombers screamed in, the Brandenburgers set off towards the bridge, driving at speed. To improve the deception, the German artillery pursued the trucks with shellfire – carefully aimed to miss. When the two trucks drew near to the river embankment, the press of fleeing Russians slowed them to a crawl, and an unforeseen problem arose when desperate Soviet troops tried to clamber onto the vehicles. The first truck broke through onto the bridge, but when the second truck slowed almost to a halt as if damaged by a German shell, the Brandenburgers found themselves fighting off panic-stricken Russian soldiers with their rifle butts.

Waves of Red Army soldiers, backed by mortar and artillery fire, flung themselves against the bridge

Meanwhile, on the bridge, the leader of the commandos located the Soviet officer responsible for the demolition of the structure. While the Brandenburger engaged in a furious argument with the Soviet officer, trying to persuade him that the bridge should remain intact, other commandos surreptitiously sought out and began to dismantle the explosive charges. By the time the second truck was at last drawing near the bridge, the two officers were close to the detonation point. The leader of the Brandenburg detachment now ripped off his Soviet uniform to reveal his German identity, and the firing began. The Brandenburg officer was killed almost immediately, but an NCO succeeded in cutting the wires from the detonator. The men from the first truck were quickly in control of the east end of the bridge, while those from the second truck took up positions at the western end. They now prepared to hold the bridge for the estimated 15 minutes against a furious Soviet onslaught.

Waves of Red Army soldiers, backed by mortar and artillery fire, flung themselves against both ends of the bridge. The Brandenburgers not only held

11

FOREIGN RECRUITS

One of the most unusual foreign units to serve with the Brandenburgers in the early stages of the Russian campaign was the so-called Nightingale Group. Formed from disaffected members of the Ukrainian community, the group had a strength of three companies and was attached to the 1st Battalion of the Brandenburg Regiment for Operation Barbarossa.

As part of the plan to take vital positions in advance of the Wehrmacht's main forces, the group was ordered to secure two objectives: the town of Przemysl and a bridge across the San river. Although the operations were fraught with difficulties, both targets were seized from the Russians. Incredibly, one force was intercepted by the enemy while wearing German uniforms, but a fast-talking officer managed to convince the Soviet officers that he was on a highly secret mission for the Red Army and received an escort to Przemysl.

The fierce patriotism of the Nightingale Group ultimately decided their fate. After a successful assault on the town of Lvov on 29 June, the unit captured a radio station and then announced the creation of an independent Ukrainian state.

It was a futile gesture; the Germans would never tolerate a free country within captured territories and henceforth viewed the group with suspicion. Despite the broadcast, the Ukrainians continued to fight on the Eastern Front until the end of the year. However, they grew disillusioned with their German masters, lost heart for a cause that would never tolerate their wishes, and were finally disbanded as 'unreliable'.

them off with machine-gun fire, but continued to tear out the rest of the explosive charges on the structure. After a quarter of an hour, they were still holding firm, but there was no sign of the panzers. Another half an hour passed, night was falling, and still no tanks arrived.

The armoured column had run into very serious difficulties: the lead tank had developed mechanical problems and was blocking the only avenue of approach to the bridge. Dense stands of oak trees on either side prevented the offending vehicle from being by-passed. Pioneers were hastily brought forward to clear the way and, after felling several trees, the road was cleared. A second tank roared down the road only to be left a twisted wreck by accurate Russian artillery fire. Two others were lost. Air support was not forthcoming and a smoke screen, laid to cover the advance, was dispersed by winds.

Back at the bridge, the Brandenburgers were faced with disaster; their ammunition was almost gone and, although they had given the Russian assault troops a bloody nose, they too had suffered heavy casualties. Any further delay would see their annihilation. However, salvation was close at hand; a Stuka unit was despatched to the bridge after its original mission had been aborted. Bombs rained down on the Russian positions and the tanks were able to move on the objective under this cover.

PARTISAN WARFARE

The vast tracts of land that fell under German control during the opening months of the war on the Eastern Front were never fully pacified, and became fruitful breeding grounds for partisan groups. Although their organisation and supply were initially haphazard, these bands of lightly equipped men and women had become a serious threat to the Wehrmacht's thinly protected supply lines by early 1943. Conventional forces could protect key points on the road and rail network, but only troops trained in clandestine operations could hope to take the war to the partisan bases in the forests of Poland and the Ukraine.

The Brandenburgers seemed the obvious choice to conduct such raids: their triumphs had been gained by stealth, bluff and first-rate combat skills – essential attributes in anti-guerrilla operations – and their ranks were expanded with disaffected Soviet citizens who had intimate knowledge of the areas of partisan activity. Indeed, during the struggle, each Brandenburger battalion comprised at least one company of 'Eastern Volunteers'.

Despite the troops' undoubted qualifications, the deployment of small Brandenburg detachments in this role was a mistake. The regiment had been formed for offensive action, but in guerrilla warfare the initiative rests with the partisan and the security forces perform essentially defensive tasks. Undoubtedly, the Brandenburgers' ability to respond quickly to a threat enabled them to score some spectacular successes against the partisans, but much of their strength was dissipated in time-consuming patrols. Against a background of boredom, punctuated by bursts of bloody action, their morale crumbled. The detachments were too small to defeat decisively the partisans; at best, they could only contain their activities.

By the summer of 1944, the whole German war effort in the east was crumbling; the need for anti-partisan operations had evaporated and the Brandenburgers were deployed conventionally until the end of the war.

Left and below: One of the tasks assigned to the Brandenburgers after the early days of the invasion of the Soviet Union was the difficult and dangerous job of containing the partisan threat. In this role, the Brandenburgers were at a distinct disadvantage and had little scope for the type of offensive action for which they were raised. Much of their time was taken up with long and often fruitless patrolling and searching of civilians, but the Brandenburg hallmarks of stealth and subterfuge, combined with highly developed combat expertise, paid off, and many successes against the partisans were achieved.

Eventually, two tanks broke through to cross the bridge and take up a defensive position on the east bank. More armour arrived in support during the night and the bridge was secured. In the end, the Brandenburgers had held off the Soviet counter-offensive for a full two hours, enabling the German forces to push deeper into the Soviet Union. Few of the regular Wehrmacht troops at the bridge learnt of the Brandenburgers' desperate fight; as the position was secured, the detachment picked up its dead, and then disappeared into the night.

The regiment was increasingly involved in the bloody war against the partisans

The spectacular raids carried out by the Brandenburgers during the opening phase of Operation Barbarossa were followed by further daring strikes at the enemy's rear installations. However, by the end of 1941 the Wehrmacht had failed to deliver the decisive blow that would have ended Russian resistance. Although the Brandenburgers were used extensively in Hitler's July offensive of 1942, particularly in the Caucasus, the regiment was increasingly involved in the bloody war against partisans operating with notable success against Germany's over-extended supply lines.

By the autumn of 1942, the German offensive had stalled and the Russian steamroller was forcing the Wehrmacht onto the defensive. Under these conditions, the need for undercover missions by select groups ceased and the role of the Brandenburgers became that of a conventional front-line unit. Expanded to divisional strength in October, the commandos were practically exterminated on the Eastern Front during the next two years of war. In late 1944, the survivors were disbanded and reformed as part of a panzer grenadier division.

THE AUTHOR Jean Mabire is a military historian who has written extensively on the elite forces of the Third Reich. His most recent works include detailed studies of the Wiking, Nordland and Charlemagne Divisions of the Waffen-SS.

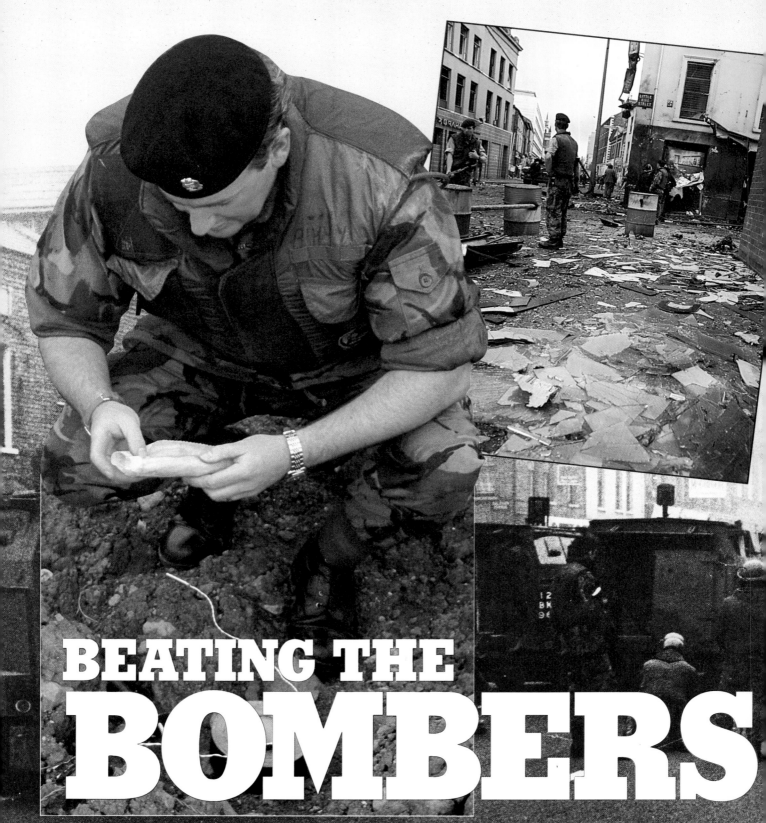

On Friday 21 July 1972 Belfast shook with the blast of a Provisional IRA bombing campaign. The men of Explosive Ordnance Disposal were immediately deployed on the task of disarming the lethal devices

Below left: An ammunition technical officer (ATO) from an Explosive Ordnance Disposal (EOD) unit sets about disrupting a PIRA charge in Northern Ireland. Below right: Troops watch EOD personnel at work in a bomb-blasted street.

IN JULY 1972, the Provisional Irish Republican Army (PIRA), put into operation a plan to mount its biggest assault yet on the city of Belfast. Targets were selected for more than 30 bombs, with the aim of causing the maximum possible terror and damage at the height of the mass week-end exodus into the country, when those who could afford it made for the hills and the seaside to escape the tension of the city.

BEATING THE BOMBERS

On Friday 21 July 1972, a sergeant and a corporal of 321 Explosive Ordnance Disposal (EOD) Unit, Royal Army Ordnance Corps (RAOC), were busy checking over their remote-controlled robot, the 'Wheelbarrow', at their base in the Albert Street Mill, situated in the heart of Belfast. Each element of this invaluable robot, its batteries, television camera and receiver, umbilical cable and hydraulic arms was individually tested. The drivers of the 'Pigs' (1-ton armoured troop carriers) and long-wheelbase Landrovers were doing their checks too, servicing their engines and testing the radios. The unit captain and three ammunition technical officers (ATOs) were playing cards. The duty NCO was at his desk, writing home to his wife and keeping one eye on the telephone. Above the EOD men, the infantry escort were lounging in readiness for the crash-out call, big boots on the camp beds, flak jackets and SLRs near at hand. It had been a very quiet morning, and it seemed too good to be true.

Out in the streets, members of the Royal Ulster Constabulary (RUC) and of the British Army were out on patrol. In 1972 Britain had 20,000 troops deployed in Ulster, drawn from a wide range of units: amongst others, the Kings Own Scottish Borderers, the Kings Own Border Regiment, the Gordon Highlanders, the Royal Regiment of Fusiliers, the Staffords and the Welsh Guards were there, together with the Royal Marine Commandos and The Parachute Regiment, and all the support services needed to keep the entire machine functioning.

EOD units represent only a tiny part of the whole British Army presence in Northern Ireland. In 1970 there had been just one EOD unit, headed by a captain with a warrant officer as his assistant. Over the years, as the PIRA bombing campaign gathered momentum, EOD units were set up in Belfast, Londonderry and Lurgan. The teams were organised in sections and attached to army brigades. The 39th Infantry Brigade covered Belfast, the 3rd controlled the southern border, and the 8th was responsible for Londonderry and the northern part of Ulster. Individual EOD teams comprised a section operator (the ATO), his assistant corporal, a driver and an armed escort. The Belfast section of four teams was to have its longest, most demanding single day on Bloody Friday, 21 July 1972.

As the population of the city carried out its everyday tasks, red-capped NCOs of the Women's Royal Army Corps systematically searched the shopping bags of women as they moved through the main arcades. The cafes and bars were full, and Irishmen, Protestant and Catholic alike, were busy repairing the damage caused by hundreds of bombs which had exploded all over the city during the previous weeks. It looked as though Belfast was going to enjoy a quiet day. But the bombers got through.

Shortly before three in the afternoon the first bombs went off, followed quickly by many more. There had been no warning. The EOD teams were immediately mobilised, and their Pigs, Saracen armoured cars and Landrovers were soon racing to the scenes of the explosions. Reports of suspicious

Although unexploded projectiles of various kinds have had to be neutralised virtually since the invention of gunpowder, bomb disposal squads as we know them today did not appear until the mass bombing of cities in World War II.

Another factor was Germany's development of the electrical time fuze, which led to a new weapon, the delayed-action bomb. Dropped on a city, this kind of bomb was not only potentially very destructive, it could also seriously disrupt the war effort by bringing whole areas to a standstill. Delayed-action bombs had already been used by Germany in the Spanish Civil War, but the British War Office was slow to respond to the new threat. However, in the spring of 1940 it authorised the formation of 25 Bomb Disposal Sections, each comprising one lieutenant, one sergeant and 14 other ranks, and during 1940 many more came into being. No specialised disarming equipment was available, however, and teams attempting to tackle bombs with hammers and chisels, block and tackle, and a few road-mending tools suffered shockingly high casualties.

Matters improved once institutions such as the Research Depot at Woolwich were able to examine the German weapons and develop means of extracting the ECR (electrical condenser resistance) fuzes from the bomb-cases. By the end of hostilities even V-weapons were being successfully defused, although the risk to operators could never be eliminated

Explosive Ordnance Disposal teams in Northern Ireland now face very different weapons to those delivered by Hitler's war machine, but the EOD task remains the same – to intervene and halt the countdown to destruction.

Below: A bomb disposal unit goes into action. Protected from the danger of blast or flying debris by a 'box' of armoured vehicles, men look on as an ATO pays out the control cable of a 'Wheelbarrow' as it approaches a suspect car in Belfast. The armoured troop carriers ('Pigs') also provide the units with safe transport in the city.

THE BOMBING CAMPAIGN

Since the outbreak of sectarian violence in Northern Ireland during 1969, the IRA bombing campaign has undergone great changes both in the scale of activity and in the sophistication of the bombs used. Only nine explosions were recorded in 1969, but in 1970 the total rose dramatically to 153 blasts, many of them from petrol bombs.

The use of explosives began in earnest in 1971, usually commercial gelignite set off by a clockwork timer. After disposal personnel successfully disrupted several examples, however, the bombs were fitted with anti-handling devices, such as a charge connected to a microswitch sensitive to the slightest movement.

In 1972 the PIRA deployed car-bombs containing explosives manufactured from readily available substances such as weedkiller. However, these mixes were highly unstable and about 50 terrorists were killed by their own bombs in that year. The technique of activating bombs remotely by wire was also introduced in 1972.

Since then, PIRA bombing has passed into the hands of experts. Electronic detonators are used, and a fuel-based explosive, still easily manufactured but far more stable, is employed. Bombs have also become smaller to prevent an unnecessary loss of life which could damage the PIRA cause.

Devices such as cassette incendiaries and large petrol cans attached to explosives were introduced in the late 1970s. Relying on fire rather than blast for their effect, such bombs were also activated by radio signal, eliminating the need for unreliable timing devices. Lastly, developments in electronics have been put to deadly effect in a bewildering array of booby-trap bombs and photo-electric cells have been built into sophisticated trigger mechanisms. In one particularly neat set-up, a bomber stuck a pro-IRA poster over a light-sensitive cell. The soldier who tore it down narrowly escaped death in the explosion which followed.

packages were flowing in to the EOD headquarters. Areas were fast being cordoned off by the infantry as, screeching to a halt, the EOD teams worked feverishly to unload their robots and set them to work. Guided by the information supplied to them by the Wheelbarrows' cameras, ATOs were able to detonate a number of bombs with small controlled explosions, scattering the components harmlessly in readiness for subsequent forensic examination. But in some cases there was nothing for it but physically to confront the ugly, ticking beast. One NCO tackled a bomb that had been set on the girders of a railway bridge, precariously balancing himself on the scanty footholds and aware, should the package be equipped with a tilt-switch, that one abrupt move could be his last. Although more bomb-disposal teams were rushed in by helicopter as the scale of the offensive became evident, there were just too many bombs to be defused in time.

Three bus stations were hit, a railway station, an hotel, a foot-bridge and several offices. Most horrifying was the explosion at Queen Street bus station. Would-be passengers caught in the blast lay mangled everywhere, with severed limbs, hands and feet strewn grotesquely in the carnage. Someone's intestines lay draped over a wall. Throughout the city the bombs claimed 11 lives, including two Welsh Guardsmen, and 130 people were injured; a few were soldiers but many victims were Roman Catholics. By evening, as a dreadful pall of smoke hung over the city, 96 people lay in hospital, many of whom are crippled to this day. Seeking to locate any piece of evidence which could lead to the arrest of the perpetrators, the EOD teams had their work cut out for them. Crunching over broken glass and splashes of blood, they compiled reports on every explosion, clinically recording the cause, the weight of explosive used, and the casualties and damage inflicted.

Seen in the context of British bomb-disposal history, Bloody Friday was remarkable only in the sheer scale of the attack. Since World War II, technicians of the Royal Army Ordnance Corps have carried out their dangerous work all over the world. The pioneers of bomb disposal had to make do with a pair of pliers, expertise born of experience, and more than a dash of hope. Modern bomb-disposal techniques make much greater use of custom-developed technology. The greatest benefit is that the necessity of physically encountering the bomb is much reduced, and many explosive devices are now neutralised using such equipment as the Wheelbarrow. It is when there is no possibility of employing remote-controlled equipment that the act of bomb disposal presents the hard, personal danger of bygone years.

The harrowing task of disarming a fuzed bomb takes a special kind of nerve. In normal circumstances the combat soldier is brought face to face with his enemy, but the bomb disposal officer is distanced from the conflict. The enemy has withdrawn, leaving a mechanism which has the power to obliterate both he who seeks to neutralise it and the target it was positioned to destroy. A bomb cannot be ignored and, frequently, it cannot be broken apart in situ without the risk of enormous damage being done to property. No option remains but for a highly trained

Top right: One method of dealing with a car bomb is to plant a small explosive charge using 'Wheelbarrow'. The bomb is then detonated from a safe distance (left). Far left, from top: This cunning booby-trap bomb is triggered when the book is opened, separating the metal strips at the top of the page; a bomb activated by a clockwork timer; a cassette incendiary device.

operator to approach the bomb and, by using all the technology and expertise at his command, render it harmless.

Since the outbreak of renewed Irish Republican Army (IRA) terrorist activity in 1969, the province of Northern Ireland has presented the bomb disposal men of the British Army with a host of deadly and increasingly sophisticated challenges. Explosives planted with timing mechanisms, bombs activated by wire remote-control and by radio, booby-trap devices and sophisticated mortar bombs have all been used against the Security Forces. Whenever a bomb fails to detonate, either because it is faulty or because its timer has a period yet to run, an opportunity arises to prevent one more addition to the terrorists' toll of destruction.

In 1972 the Provisional IRA (PIRA), whose bombing campaign was quite separate from that of the official IRA, had no shortage of explosives, and the control of the sale of detonators had not been sufficiently tightened to ensure that few, if any, got into terrorist hands. When the campaign began, explosives and detonators had been stolen from quarries and road-works. When these sources dried up, the terrorists had little difficulty in smuggling large quantities across the border from the Republic of Ireland. At least 150 'unofficial' crossing points could be used, and there were countless places where people could just walk over. The government of the Republic was pledged against the terrorists, but had little power to prevent their activities. Explosives and weapons were also being smuggled ashore from international cargo ships or through airport controls, mostly donated by sympathisers based in the US.

Contrary to popular belief, the men of Britain's bomb-disposal squads are not all volunteers in the usual sense of the word. EOD teams consist of ammunition technical officers and ammunition technicians, who are NCOs, (the term ATO is now generally applied to both categories of men). Officers and NCOs are trained to maintain, repair and dispose of all Land Service ammunition at the Army School of Ammunition, but the officers also receive more detailed instruction in physics, metallurgy, ballistics and the chemistry of explosives at the Royal Military College of Science. Both are trained to the same standard in bomb disposal.

Personnel selected from the Royal Army Ordnance Corps for bomb-disposal training first undergo a psychometric test designed to uncover any latent mental unsuitability for the nerve-racking task. The qualities sought are: 'judgement, foresight, the ability to learn quickly from previous actions, a logical mind, the ability to be decisive and, at the same time, flexible, self-confidence and prudence.'

There are inevitably instances when no amount of formal training can act as a substitute for field experience. This observation applies not only to the operators themselves, but also to the army unit commanders with whom they have to deal. On one occasion, a company commander of a county battalion insisted that an abandoned van should be cleared away on the following day. Normally such an operation, in the context of the Northern Ireland bombing campaign, would involve an elaborate

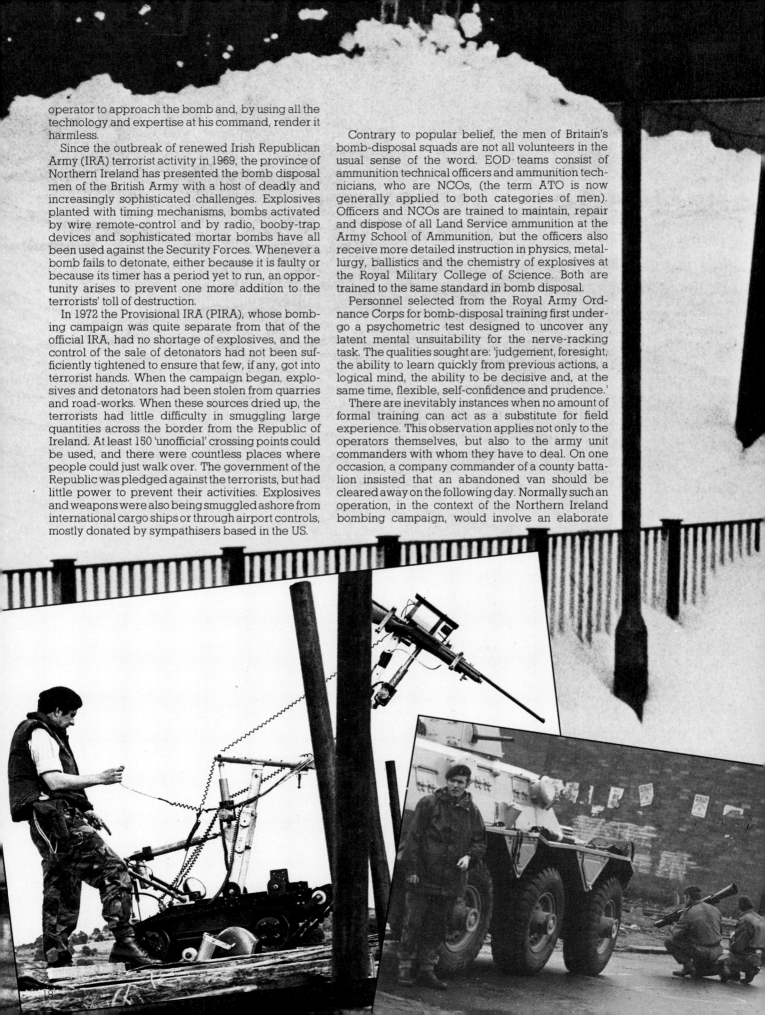

The brainchild of a retired lieutenant-colonel working in a government research centre, 'Wheelbarrow' was introduced in 1972 as a means of dealing with unexploded bombs without endangering bomb-disposal personnel. The earliest type of Wheelbarrow was three-wheeled, but rubber-tracked versions soon proved more versatile. The robot was driven by battery-powered motors and guided via a cable connected to a control box. The cable limited its range, however, and the radio-controlled Wheelbarrow appeared in 1977.

Once Wheelbarrow is in position, the operator is able to examine the problem on a TV monitor linked to a small camera on the robot. He then deploys one of a number of accessories which are attached to an adjustable boom fixed above the chassis. A five-round automatic shotgun attachment can be used to destroy a package or to open a car boot, or a bomb can be disrupted with a mechanical grab. Explosive charges can also be disintegrated with high-speed 'bullets' of water shot from a type of gun known as the 'pig-stick'. Wheelbarrow even has a device to shoot a nail into the ground to prevent a door closing on it. Should a charge be in a high position, an Eager Beaver fork-lift truck can be used to lift Wheelbarrow to the correct height.

A number of Wheelbarrows have been blown up on operations, only to be reconstructed within 24 hours. Their value has been demonstrated time and time again, and there is no doubt that their use has saved several EOD operators from death.

Above: Officers of an Explosive Ordnance Disposal unit and their equipment. The man on the left is wearing full body armour, which affords good protection from flames and high-velocity fragments. The helmet has built-in headphones. The second ATO holds the control box of the 'Wheelbarrow'. One advantage of Wheelbarrow is that operators can confer while viewing the problem on the TV monitor, minimising the possibility of an error in diagnosis. In later models of Wheelbarrow the boom can be telescoped to offer a much better range of angles of approach (far left). The L14A1 Carl Gustav shoulder-fired recoilless gun (above, foregound, and left) is used to fire an inert warhead, a solid lump of metal, at a target when more conventional methods of bomb disarmament are impracticable. Background: Aqueous foam is used to muffle the blast of explosives. The pressure exerted by the blast is absorbed by the bursting of millions of tiny bubbles.

Background: Helpers move in after a 100lb bomb shatters a car in County Tyrone, injuring six people.
Right: This security forces' Landrover was flung aside by a 100lb bomb laid in ambush in County Fermanagh.
Bottom: Firemen tackle a blaze caused by a tanker explosion triggered by explosives in Londonderry.

series of checks. A dog team would be deployed to sniff out explosives, there would be an air reconnaissance and aerial photographs would be produced, and the Royal Engineers would conduct an area search. As it was, the young ATO flew over the van at first light, noticed nothing amiss, and then took his teams to the spot. The doors and windows were blown open with controlled explosions and the van was checked over. Nothing suspicious was found and it was determined that, with a policeman at the wheel, soldiers would be detailed to push the van away.

The vehicle would not budge, however, and a Landrover was brought in to tow it. No sooner had it begun to roll than a massive explosion engulfed the van, killing the driver and reducing the vehicle to a twisted wreck. In the subsequent search it was established that 200lb of explosive had been buried at the side of the road and had been triggered by an anti-movement device placed under the nearside rear wheel. It was particularly galling for the investigators also to discover a white flex running up an adjoining slope, to a manual ignition point on the crest, evidently an alternative method of detonating the charge which had been installed when the explosives were buried. Had the usual checks been carried out, death could have been averted.

For the EOD operator in Northern Ireland, the key to survival is a highly developed suspicious nature which is not easily allayed. As the terrorists' devices become ever more cunning, the EOD operator has only his intelligence and his sixth sense of 'something not quite right' to guard him from the explosion that may cost him his life. He must be prepared against jumping to the obvious conclusion and thus missing the latest twist in the bombers' thinking.

In December 1976 a wrecked car was discovered near a border crossing point. On the road at the rear of the vehicle, which had been deliberately blown up, were two milk churns, one standing and one lying on its side. The ATO who was called to the scene immediately suspected a trap. The car was in ideal ambush country, and if the churns contained explosives, a radio-controlled detonator could easily have

LETTER FROM IRELAND

Brigadier Peter Macdonald served in Northern Ireland as a bomb disposal officer and kept up a regular correspondence with his sister regarding his work. One letter, written in late 1972, recounts the sad death of a colleague:

'Two evenings ago there were some explosions out in the country near the border. There were six craters in a rough circle, but with a gap as if there had been a place for a seventh bomb but it hadn't gone off. Bill and an officer found a wire running towards the craters and began to follow it very carefully, keeping a look out for any traps.

'The officer said he would follow it, so he waded into the pond while Bill went round and began to follow the wire again where it came out on the other side. It went through a drystone

wall, so Bill walked down the wall to the gate, checked it out, went through it down to the grass verge on the other side.

'Bill saw that there was a bit of turf cut out of the grass and that the wire disappeared into the ground. The turf that had been cut out was replaced, but was dying off and a different colour. I'm told he called out something like, "This must be one of the new remote-controlled ones." Anyway, he bent down to take a closer look – it went off and he just vanished. Incredible!

'An infantry chap nearby wasn't even hurt, but he got a face full of Bill. He rushed off back towards the officer who was running up. The officer called out, "Is the ATO all right?" "You must be joking," says the sergeant, then pukes all over the ground. The biggest bit of Bill they found was as big as the palm of your hand. They put what there was in a plastic bag.'

been set up with its aerial concealed by one of the nearby telegraph poles.

After the standard checks had been carried out, establishing that no radio-controlled device was present, the ATO moved in and, by using hook and line, shook out the contents of the upright churn – explosives. When the same procedure was carried out with the horizontal churn, explosives fell out, but something remained at the bottom. Not prepared to put his hand inside to identify it, the ATO and his WO2 used lines to slam the churns together. The last object was shaken out and the men were able to examine the complete bomb.

The upright churn had been filled with explosives and had a length of Cordtex fuze running through the middle of it. Apart from that it was empty, and was harmless unless a detonator was introduced. The horizontal churn also had Cordtex leading through the explosive, but in this case it was connected to a timing and power unit. An unsuspecting or over-confident operator, working against the clock because of the short day, could easily have been led into thinking that the second churn would be identical to the first. But had the cord in the second churn been pulled, it would have fired the detonator of the timing and power unit which was fixed firmly to the bottom by a wooden slat. Following the infinitely cautious procedure that becomes second nature to the good ATO, the bomb had been safely neutralised.

For their work, the men of the RAOC have been awarded three George Crosses, 49 George Medals, 40 Queen's Gallantry Awards, 12 MBEs for gallantry, 17 BEMs for gallantry and 73 Mentions in Despatches. Just how many lives, and how many thousands of pounds' worth of property, have been saved by the calm, cool-headed and deliberate men of Explosive Ordnance Disposal can only be speculated.

THE AUTHOR Brigadier Peter Macdonald served with the Royal Army Ordnance Corps, specialising in bomb disposal, in Cyprus, Aden and Northern Ireland. He has published several books including *Wide Horizons* and *Stopping the Clock.*

SOE NORWAY

The British government sent Sir Charles Hambro (above) to Stockholm in October 1940. He set up an SOE 'office' there, which was of great value in establishing contact with operatives in Norway and acting as a lifeline for those agents who were forced to make their way across the border when pursued by German forces.

Although the Norwegian government-in-exile was firmly committed to the defeat of the Germans, it found relations with the British government very difficult to begin with, and this in turn had important consequences for SOE operations in Norway. The main problem was that the Norwegians were unhappy with British schemes that they felt could only bring reprisals upon the Norwegian people, and they resented British attempts to assert control over the Norwegian resistance movement *Milorg.*

There was, indeed, a very difficult period soon after the founding of *Milorg*: the Norwegian government-in-exile refused to recognise the new organisation at first and this caused severe embarrassment in Sweden, where the SOE office had been enthusiastically encouraging the formation of resistance groups among exiled Norwegians.

By the end of 1941, however, relations had much improved. The British recognised that they had to consider the views of the Norwegian authorities as being of prime importance; and under Colonel J.S. Wilson, SOE relationships with *Milorg* also improved greatly. By 1942, the 'Shetland Bus' was taking large quantities of arms over to Norway, and in 1945 it was the 45,000 men of *Milorg* who came into the open and disarmed the 400,000-strong German occupying forces.

SABOTAGE!

Often at the centre of bitter controversy, the SOE fought a dangerous, undercover campaign against the German war machine

9 JUNE 1944, three days after D-day. Captain Birger Sjorberg, together with two other SOE agents, was hiding out in a hut in Stavassdalen in Norway, waiting for another opportunity to strike at the critical sources of raw materials that the Germans needed for their war effort. Suddenly, shots rang out. The Germans had discovered their hideout.

Sjoberg and his two comrades returned the fire, killing a Gestapo officer. But the hostile fire intensified. Sjoberg was wounded and the hut was almost surrounded. He detonated a charge and set off the explosives he had stockpiled for their sabotage operations. In the resulting confusion one of his fellow agents escaped – the other was badly injured and captured, later to be tortured until his death. Sjoberg himself died moments after he had set off the charge – another victim in a vicious undercover war played out in occupied Norway.

The Special Operations Executive (SOE) was set up in July 1940, during the dark days in the aftermath of the fall of France. It was designed, in Churchill's words, to 'set Europe ablaze' – in other words, to underpin resistance to the German forces occupying large parts of Europe. The operations of SOE are, to a certain extent, still shrouded in mystery; and they are certainly still bathed in controversy. In the wartime armed services, many individuals were hostile to the very idea of the existence of this new secret force, while the difficulties of operating within occupied nations, when governments-in-exile in London were demanding some control over SOE activities, caused difficulties, and often furious debate.

A further bone of contention lay in the methods that the SOE agents used: assassins, saboteurs, poisoners – blackmail and terror were their stock-in-trade. In the ruthless and highly dangerous business of undercover warfare they could not afford to fight with kid gloves on. SOE personnel had to be extremely courageous, totally determined and convinced of the rightness of their cause.

Not all the victims of SOE operations were German troops – if you blow up a troop train you may kill the soldiers on it but you will almost certainly kill the engine driver, who has probably been forced to carry out his task unwillingly; similarly, an explosive charge that destroys a vital machine in a French factory may well kill or cripple the innocent machine operator. The same arguments can be used, of course, in relation to area bombing, but where sabotage is concerned, the agent is much more closely involved with his victims, and has to be tough enough to get on with his job.

The question of ends and means, the potential importance of small sabotage teams, and the courage needed to carry out such operations are nowhere more clearly shown than in SOE operations in Norway. A neutral at the outbreak of the war, Norway had been invaded by the Germans in April 1940. Its economic and strategic importance was recognised

by all the combatants, and even as the Germans invaded, British vessels were violating Norwegian territorial waters to lay minefields intended to interfere with the movement of Norwegian iron ore.

Apart from the iron ore, there were two key products that the Germans required from Norway: heavy water, essential for the production of atomic energy, and pyrites, necessary for the manufacturing of material used in radar and wireless telegraphy.

Soon after the fall of Norway, the Scandinavian section of SOE was set up, operating under Sir Charles Hambro, and the decision was taken to use Norwegian nationals in clandestine operations – to the exclusion of British agents. There were plenty of Norwegians thirsting to take the war back to the Germans, and under Martin Linge, a former actor in the Oslo National Theatre, they were formed into a unit under SOE control and given the training they would need for the dangerous work to come.

The Norwegian coast, indented by fjords and bays and girt with islands, is about 2000km long as the

Far left: Colonel Jack Wilson, head of the SOE Norwegian section. Left: An SOE agent is trained for the hazardous task of parachuting into German-occupied territory. Below: Members of the Norwegian resistance organisation *Milorg*, kitted out in winter camouflage, lie in wait for an approaching German patrol.

Far left: SOE agents, in training, seize a 'German' motorcycle courier. The gathering of vital intelligence was an everyday part of SOE behind-the-lines work. Left centre: Agents go through the rigours of parachute drill. Left: To protect SOE agents during operations in German-occupied territory, operatives were often provided with elaborate cover stories and false identity papers.

crow flies, but there are at least 16,000km of land along this line for an occupying power to watch. Into the fjords, small boats could creep and hide up, taking off fugitives or landing agents. This was a risky business, but the German patrols could not be everywhere. The 'Shetland Bus', a clandestine fleet of small vessels, soon became a regular transport in and out of German-occupied territory.

British commando raids on Norwegian territory, on the Lofoten islands and on Vaagso and Maloy late in 1941, strained relations between SOE and the Norwegian government-in-exile. These raids,

Norway 1941-1943

NORWEGIAN SEA

Tromso

LOFOTEN IS

Narvik

NORWAY

Trondheim
Thamshen

Orkla

SWEDEN

FINLAND

Bremanger

Bergen

Helsinki

Rjukan   Oslo

Stockholm

SOVIET UNION

BALTIC

The German invasion of Norway began on 9 April 1940, and by the end of May German forces were in control of most of the country. Norway was highly important strategically as a source of iron ore and other raw materials, and within a short time the British Special Operations Executive had established a section to carry out clandestine raids on key installations.

which achieved little in the way of lasting results, were met with savage German reprisals and the Norwegians felt that they were having to pay an undue price for actions that were little more than propaganda victories.

In 1942, however, things began to look up. The Norwegian resistance organisation *Milorg*, which had previously been hostile to SOE, started to co-operate more fully, and the skills of SOE could be employed in striking at economic targets without attracting too many reprisals against the civilian population. It was during this period that Captain Sjoberg led teams that destroyed installations and disrupted communications. The main targets, however, were the pyrites mines and the heavy water plant.

Pyrites was extracted in great quantities at the Orkla mines in northern Norway, and the first operation against these installations took place in April 1942. Codenamed Redshank, it involved three agents: Peter Deinboll, son of the chief engineer of the Orkla company, Per Getz and Thorlief Cory.

On 17 April the three men left the UK, and after an uneventful 24 hours at sea transferred to a fishing vessel on the Halken fishing banks. They were dropped in a lonely inlet, and then made their way unobtrusively towards the mines. Their cover story during their journey was that they were distributing illegal newspapers – at this stage, SOE was very concerned about the penetration of *Milorg* by Quislings, Norwegians sympathetic to Hitler.

The team arrived without mishap at their target, the transformers and generators at Bardshang. These were a vital part of the Lokken power grid that supplied both the mine and the electric railway that took the ore to Thamshen for shipment. The solitary guard was overpowered and tied up safely out of harm's way and the charges were laid. Getz and Cory left immediately for Sweden.

Deinboll stayed behind, however, to see the effect of the explosives. In the event, they were very successful. The power supply was totally wrecked, and as a result the Orkla Metal Company had to close down for several weeks, and the electric railway also shut down while it transferred to steam locomotives. Still keeping to their cover story, the three agents reached Sweden and made contact with the local SOE base. Eventually they were sent back to the UK. The operation was a great achievement: supply had been interrupted without the loss of innocent lives and the SOE had chalked up a considerable propaganda coup.

In October 1943, Deinboll parachuted back into Norway, as part of Operation Feather 1. Together with six other agents, his target was again the Orkla mines. As before, direct sabotage of the mines was

SOE DIRECTIVE
The final orders for the attack on the heavy water plant, drawn up by Joachim Ronnenberg: 'All men to wear uniform. Positions to be taken at midnight, 500m from the fence. Attack at 0030 hours, after guards are changed. If alarm is sounded, covering party to attack guards immediately, while demolition party is to proceed. Demolition party to destroy high-concentration plant in the cellar of electrolysis factory. Entrance by forcing cellar door; failing this by using ground floor door; failing this through the cable tunnel. Each man carrying out demolition to be covered by one man with .45 pistol. Sentry with Tommy gun to guard entrance. If fighting starts before demolition party reaches target, men of covering party to take over placing explosives. If anything happens to the leaders of the party, everybody is to act on his own initiative to ensure success of the operation. If any man is about to be taken prisoner, he undertakes to end his own life.'

The communication by sea with Norway was nicknamed the 'Shetland Bus'. Set up in 1940, it was under the control of Major L.H. Mitchel, a British Intelligence officer, and initially based in Lerwick. Mitchel soon recruited some Norwegian fishermen to his operation. These men were under the command of Leif Larsen, a sailor since boyhood, and an epic warrior – he ended the war as the most highly decorated man in any of the Allied forces.

The first journey from Scotland to Norway was on Christmas Eve, 1940, and the whole establishment of the 'Bus Company' was just four fishing boats. These boats were totally defenceless against German air attack, and had to rely on stealth and the cover of darkness. Later, they were replaced by more up-to-date warships – British MTBs and finally American-built submarine chasers. Up to the spring of 1942, the 'Bus' maintained a steady service across the North Sea, making over 40 trips during this time. But then activities began to increase, and during the winter of 1943/44 over 80 crossings took place.

There was always danger in crossing to Norway, and the sailors who took part (never more than 100 at any time, 40 on duty and the others resting or on leave) had to be prepared for any sacrifice. Jan Baalsrud, the sole survivor of one vessel that was sunk, was forced to travel secretly across Lappland. He lay wounded six days and nights in the snow in his sleeping bag, losing all the toes of his right foot and four of his left from frostbite – and reported for duty as soon as he was repatriated by the Swedish Red Cross. Such was the spirit of the men who kept open the lifeline to the agents in Norway.

Victims of the Norwegian SOE. Right: The ferry boat laden with heavy water that was sunk by Knut Haukelid. Right above: The shattered remains of the electrolysis cells at the Norsk Hydro plant.

impossible, but the resourceful Norwegian carried out a series of small-scale operations against transport, and succeeded in slowing down the movement of ore. Then, in April 1944, he was joined by more SOE saboteurs for Operation Feather 2. In a series of attacks during May and June, the mines were finally put out of action.

The other main objective, an attack on the heavy water plant at Rjukan, to the west of Oslo, went into operation in late 1942. Before launching the raid, an SOE agent, Captain Odd Starheim, managed to bring Einar Skinnarland, an engineer who had worked on the construction of the plant, back to Britain. Skinnarland was keen to help, and was at once sent back to Norway, explaining away his three-week absence from work with the story that he had been ill.

That October, four other agents were sent in to join Skinnarland and made their way towards the plant. But rather than wait for the saboteurs to do their work, the British decided to launch a glider-borne assault with specially trained Royal Engineers and commandos. The attack was a disaster. Both the gliders crash-landed miles from their objective, and the Germans killed all those who survived the crashes.

A further six agents were then sent out to join the four men camped out in the exposed countryside near the plant. The new men had brought in sufficient explosives to blow up the entire works and the attack was set for the night of 27/28 February 1943.

As the SOE men moved down from the hills towards the plant, they had to be extremely careful not to let any local inhabitants know that they were carrying quantities of explosive – any news that something untoward was happening might reach the Germans. The night of the attack was clear and moonless – but freezing cold. The 10 men slipped towards the perimeter fence and cut the chain of an unguarded gate. Four men carrying explosives moved into the compound, splitting into two groups of two, and immediately found a problem: the Germans had mounted sentries by a cellar door that the raiders had hoped to use to get in. Searching for a new way into the heart of the plant, the men became separated, but two agents found a cable intake into

their objective, the cellar under the electrolysis factory.

A startled night-watchman was awoken with a pistol in his ribs, and the SOE men began methodically laying their charges, assisted by the other group which had eventually found the same cable intake. They warned the night-watchman that he had only 20 seconds to leave the building once the fuzes were set, and then slipped out into the cold night.

The explosion that followed was not very noticeable – in fact, the German on duty did not even realise that there had been any sabotage. The SOE men themselves were disappointed at what they thought was a meagre result for their months of waiting.

But the explosives had done their work. The plant was put out of operation for six months, and never again worked at full capacity.

One of the operatives on that raid, Knut Haukelid, remained in Norway. When the plant eventually began to produce heavy water again, he led another daring raid – this time on a ferry carrying 15,000 litres of heavy water en route to Germany. With two more agents, he disguised himself as a greaser and placed charges on the ferry. The timing was perfect, and the boat sank in the deepest part of the lake it was crossing. Once again, Nazi Germany had been denied the material for creating an atomic bomb.

SOE had, of necessity, to fight a dirty war. Its methods were not those that everyone would have chosen; and there can be no doubt that in attracting retaliation on innocent civilians, it had to choose its targets carefully, balancing the possible gains against the German response. But in such actions as the sabotage of the Orkla mines and the heavy water plant, it proved itself a vital part of the war against Hitler, showing that small groups of well-trained agents could achieve results decisive to the final outcome.

THE AUTHOR Nigel Foster was a member of the British Intelligence Corps. Following training at Lympstone, he was attached to 3 Commando Brigade.

Cut off by communist forces in the Central Highlands of Vietnam, Australian Warrant Officer Keith Payne earned the Victoria Cross

ON 24 MAY 1969, deep in the jungle highlands of South Vietnam, a Mike (mobile strike) Force battalion of Montagnards was surrounded and attacked by a regiment of the North Vietnamese Army (NVA). The battalion withdrew in disarray, leaving a number of wounded men to their fate in enemy territory. This is the story of the single-handed rescue of those men, whom the battalion had given up for lost. For his sustained courage, skill and leadership in performing this feat under the most extraordinary circumstances, Warrant Officer Keith Payne was awarded the Victoria Cross.

Keith Payne was a member of the Australian Army Training Team, Vietnam (AATTV), a unit which had first been committed to the war zone in 1962. The Australian government had been quick to respond to US requests for a con-

HEROISM AT BEN HET

tribution to the Vietnam war effort. It suited their strategy of 'forward defence' against communism in Southeast Asia, and it was calculated that if Australia demonstrated support of the US in Vietnam, America would be more likely to react positively to any Australian requests for support. Initially the role of the Team was to train the indigenous South Vietnamese forces in jungle techniques, but by 1964 it had expanded to include advising field units of both the Army of the Republic of South Vietnam (ARVN) and para-military forces; in this role the Australian advisers worked alongside the US Army Special Forces.

When Payne, a veteran of the campaigns in Malaya and Borneo, joined the AATTV in 1969, he was sent to the Australian detachment serving with the Special Forces in II Corps, based in Pleiku Province. He was given command of the 212th Company in the 1st Mike Force Battalion of recruited Montagnards. His unit was deployed northwest of Pleiku, in the tri-border area of Laos, Cambodia and Vietnam.

In April and early May 1969 increased NVA activity was observed in the tri-border area. Any attempts to dislodge the communist forces were ferociously repelled, and the Special Forces were convinced that the NVA was building up to a major operation. Finally, in late May, the North Vietnamese laid siege to the village of Ben Het. Only 14km from Laos, Ben Het was a Special Forces' outpost astride Route 512, which led to the heart of South Vietnam. The capture of Ben Het would give the enemy control of the entry point of an important infiltration line. The siege began with the arrival of the 24th NVA Regiment north of Ben Het and of the 27th NVA Regiment to the east. In addition, the Special Forces' commander believed that the 66th NVA Regiment was infiltrating from Laos down the Ho Chi Minh Trail to reinforce the siege troops. The mission of Payne's battalion was to locate the infiltration route, find and engage the 66th Regiment, and to hold the route until reinforcements arrived.

With the absence on leave of the regular commander of the 1st Battalion, the executive officer, a US lieutenant, took over as acting commander. The three companies of the battalion, the 211th, 212th and 213th, were commanded in turn by Warrant Officer Tolley of the AATTV, Payne, and Sergeant 'Monty' Montez of the US Special Forces. With only 52 men in his company, yet needing a minimum of 75 for the operation, Payne obtained 37 volunteers who had completed a bare 12 days' training with the Special Forces. Payne's company was divided into three platoons, commanded by Warrant Officer Latham of the AATTV, and Sergeants Clement and Dellwo, both of the US Special Forces. These leaders and their under-trained, under-strength and undisciplined band of Vietnamese Montagnards were to be flung against the best that the NVA had to offer.

The two battalions had unknowingly established themselves very close to the men they were seeking

On 18 May, the 1st Battalion flew to the Special Forces' camp at Dak To on the route to Ben Het and began advancing towards the outpost. During this phase the Montagnards came under occasional shelling and mortar fire but the enemy was not seen. The battalion was then lifted by helicopter to a ridge line 9km southwest of Ben Het. Four days later the 5th Mike Force Battalion was landed by helicopter on a ridge 4km to the south and Payne's battalion joined it the same afternoon. The two battalions established defensive positions on the ridge line and on the crest of an adjoining hill. The vegetation was primary jungle, a dense tangle of ferns, bamboo and vines that thinned out on the ridges to allow relatively easy movement. Occasional clearings were to be found on the tops of hills. The sides of the ridge slipped steeply down into the surrounding valleys.

During the night, the two battalions received orders by radio to carry out company clearing patrols in order to locate the 66th NVA Regiment. After a series of air strikes by Phantom jets the next morning, Tolley's company was the first to leave the defensive position. It ran straight into the enemy, and with several casualties was forced to withdraw. Montez' company was the next to try. The men succeeded in pushing only 25m beyond where Tolley had been ambushed before they too came under heavy fire and withdrew. It was apparent that the two battalions had unknowingly established themselves very close to the men they were seeking.

Fresh orders that night from Pleiku required the 1st Battalion, with the 5th Battalion in support, to

Page 27: Captain Shilston of the AATTV questions mountain villagers suspected of harbouring the Viet Cong. Inset: The AATTV badge incorporating a Montagnard crossbow. Below: Captain Peter Reid instructs a radio operator and two Montagnards armed with Armalite M16A1s at a Mike Force forward base in Quang Tri province.

commence clearing the enemy from the ridge. In the morning of 24 May a concentrated air strike was ordered on the suspected enemy positions, and at 1430 hours the 1st Battalion began moving southwards along the narrow crest of the ridge line. To the fore were the companies led by Payne and Montez, with Tolley's company delaying in the rear to pick up the weapons lost in the previous day's fighting and to place the bodies of the dead in zippered plastic bags for evacuation by helicopter. The enemy position, a hilltop some 300m by 120m in area and scarred by trenches and mortar pits, was found to be empty.

A rocket-propelled grenade exploded close by, decapitating the radio operator and whipping Payne's Armalite out of his hands

Suddenly the enemy opened fire from the jungle perimeter. The North Vietnamese had pulled back to escape the air strikes, and were now moving forward to trap the battalion in the clearing. Withering fire from four machine guns, rockets and highly accurate mortars scythed into the position. Given no time to take cover, the Montagnards suffered heavy casualties. An NVA company then wedged itself between the two forward companies and Tolley's and began firing on Tolley while the machine guns continued to engage Payne and Montez. Unable to join the rest of the battalion, Tolley drew his company into an all-round defensive position and returned the fire. Supported by Montez, Payne then tried the technique of 'fire and move' to manoeuvre two platoons closer to the enemy machine guns, but the enemy force was too strong.

The NVA was now attacking from three sides and pressing closer to the beleaguered troops. Shouting words of encouragement to his inexperienced men, Payne ran from point to point along his perimeter, positioning his soldiers and blazing away at the enemy with his Armalite. Seizing grenades from his men he hurled them into the teeth of the enemy guns. Suddenly a rocket-propelled grenade exploded close by, decapitating the radio operator and whipping Payne's Armalite out of his hands. He grabbed a GPMG M60 machine gun and continued his storm of fire, now bleeding profusely from a head wound.

Faced by Payne's determined action the enemy faltered, then again pressed forward. The half-trained Montagnards began to run in panic, streaming off the ridge down the steep slopes, but Payne cut across the exposed ground and managed to stem the disordered retreat. Still under enemy fire, and himself now wounded again by mortar and rocket splinters in the hands and arms, Payne organised the companies into a temporary defensive line in the valley, approximately 350m from the ridge. The toll had been heavy. Payne, Montez, Latham, Lieutenant Forbes (the US artillery co-ordinator), and Lieutenant James (the acting battalion commander) had been wounded, Montez seriously. Several Montagnard soldiers had been killed or wounded and many more were not accounted for. Tolley began to move back to the previous night's defensive position as helicopter gunships arrived to hose down the enemy with fire, but many lost or wounded men were cut off from the battalion, lying or wandering behind enemy lines.

At dusk Payne approached the battalion commander and stated his intention of infiltrating the enemy territory and collecting as many of the lost and wounded as he could find. He knew that he would

THE MONTAGNARDS

The question of how to control the wild Central Highlands of South Vietnam, an area crossed by an ever-changing system of infiltration routes into the south from Cambodia, Laos and North Vietnam, was perhaps the greatest strategic problem facing the ARVN and its US and Australian advisers. It became increasingly apparent that there could be no solution without the co-operation of the nomadic aboriginal people of the region, collectively known as the 'Montagnards'.

The task of enlisting the support of the Montagnards was fraught with difficulties. A deep racial animosity existed between the tribesmen and the Vietnamese, and the South Vietnamese government had failed to develop French initiatives designed to ensure their autonomy. Instead, the tribal lands had been partitioned off for settlement by Vietnamese.

However, when the Americans formed the CIDG (Civilian Irregular Defense Groups) many Montagnards joined up in order to obtain the weapons and considerable economic benefits that were being offered. At first, they acted as garrisons of fortified CIDG camps built to defend their villages from Viet Cong infiltrators. The first of many Mike (mobile strike) Forces was then formed in October 1964, evolved from aggressive patrols mounted by the CIDG camps. Acting either independently or in conjunction with other CIDG or conventional units, the Montagnard Mike Force became an essential tool of the South Vietnamese intelligence-gathering and counter-insurgency programme.

The Montagnards suffered heavily from their involvement in the Vietnam War. Their traditional way of life was irreversibly altered, and many were wiped out in their camps by the Viet Cong. And when the Americans withdrew from Vietnam, all hope of Montagnard independence went with them.

Ben Het
1st Mike Force Battalion, May 1969

During April and May 1969 the North Vietnamese Army built up its forces in the South Vietnamese province of Kontum close to the Laotian and Cambodian borders. The 24th and 27th NVA Regiments laid siege to the village of Ben Het, guarding what was potentially a major infiltration route into the Vietnamese central highlands. With the suspected arrival of the 66th NVA Regiment in the area, the 1st Mike Force Battalion (MFB) was deployed with orders to find and engage the enemy.

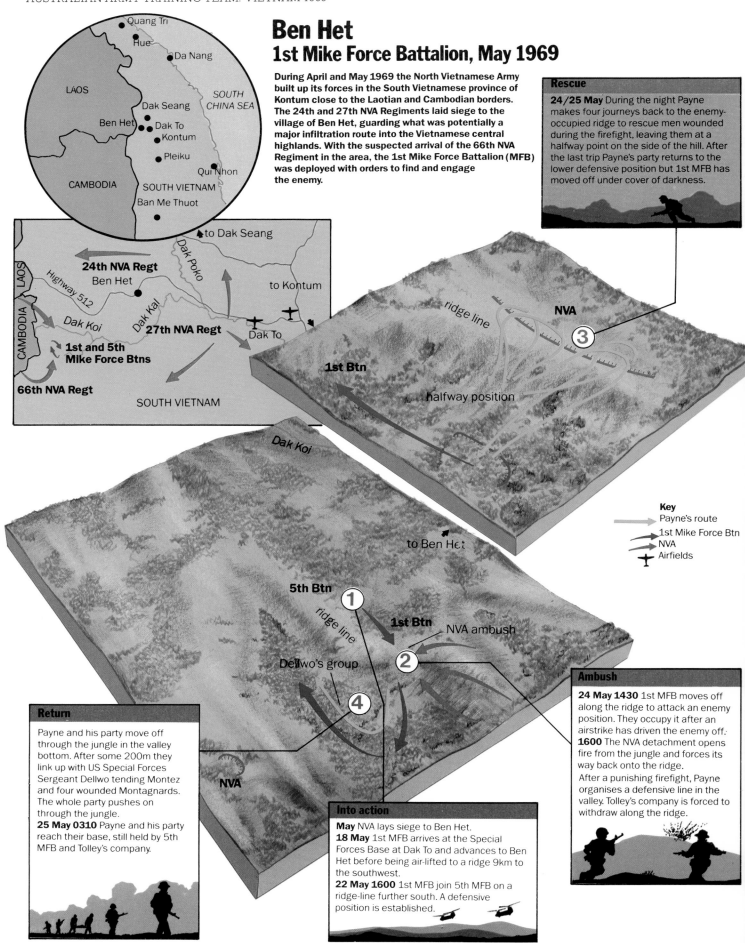

Rescue

24/25 May During the night Payne makes four journeys back to the enemy-occupied ridge to rescue men wounded during the firefight, leaving them at a halfway point on the side of the hill. After the last trip Payne's party returns to the lower defensive position but 1st MFB has moved off under cover of darkness.

Key
Payne's route
1st Mike Force Btn
NVA
Airfields

Ambush

24 May 1430 1st MFB moves off along the ridge to attack an enemy position. They occupy it after an airstrike has driven the enemy off.
1600 The NVA detachment opens fire from the jungle and forces its way back onto the ridge.
After a punishing firefight, Payne organises a defensive line in the valley. Tolley's company is forced to withdraw along the ridge.

Return

Payne and his party move off through the jungle in the valley bottom. After some 200m they link up with US Special Forces Sergeant Dellwo tending Montez and four wounded Montagnards. The whole party pushes on through the jungle.
25 May 0310 Payne and his party reach their base, still held by 5th MFB and Tolley's company.

Into action

May NVA lays siege to Ben Het.
18 May 1st MFB arrives at the Special Forces Base at Dak To and advances to Ben Het before being air-lifted to a ridge 9km to the southwest.
22 May 1600 1st MFB join 5th MFB on a ridge-line further south. A defensive position is established.

have the best chance alone: the presence of another adviser would have helped, but Dellwo was the only one not wounded and he was needed for medical duties and supervision of the defences. It was no use taking any Montagnards, Payne felt, as he could not speak their language and they would only make a noise and increase his chance of being detected. Thus, equipped with a radio and an Armalite rifle, he moved out alone into the darkness; many of the battalion expected never to see him again.

Payne made four separate trips through the enemy lines and onto the hill where the action had been fought. He was helped by the moonlight and the way the jungle thinned on the crest of the ridge. On his first trip he recovered the badly wounded Montez and a handful of Montagnards. Returning to the hill, he could hear the enemy soldiers moving around and firing single shots; they were killing the wounded. Payne added to his steadily growing band of stragglers each trip, leaving them at a half-way point before going back for more. Weakened by loss of blood and the strain of the last few hours, Payne was now reaching a state of physical and mental exhaustion. With pinpricks of light from rifle shots and

sparks from discharging mortars not far distant, he sank down beside a fallen tree. In his cupped hands, and with the light of the striking match muffled by his jacket, he lit a cigarette. It was a mad thing to do, he knew, but he needed time to think and steady himself, and it helped.

The cigarette finished, and himself partly recovered, Payne continued on his mission. The search lasted three hours. Once he was fired upon by a group with two machine guns and two Russian AK-47

Above: Warrant Officers Ray Simpson, VC (left) and Keith Payne, VC. Below: Captain Peter Shilston radios his company commanders.

HEROES OF THE AATTV

The heroism and sacrifice of the AATTV in Vietnam was recognised by many awards, and no fewer than four men won the Victoria Cross.

The first was Warrant Officer 2 (WO2) K.A. 'Dasher' Wheatley. On 13 November 1965 he was on patrol east of Tra Bong outpost. The patrol was split into three groups and Wheatley's came under fire. The Montagnards fled and Wheatley's fellow officer, WO2 Swanton, attempted to save a wounded Vietnamese before he was himself hit. Wheatley kept up covering fire, then dragged Swanton away from the Viet Cong position. He remained with Swanton until they were overrun by a Viet Cong assault group that killed them both. His posthumous VC was the first awarded to an Australian since World War II.

A second posthumous VC was won in 1967 by Major Peter Badcoe. An enigma to his friends, Badcoe became legendary as an inspiring and fearless leader, frequently turning the tide of battle by the sheer force of his personality. He was appointed operations adviser of Thua Thien province in December 1966 and it was there that the acts that earned him the VC were performed. On each occasion he rallied his men to beat back the Viet Cong. He met his death making a lone assault on a machine-gun post.

In 1969 the VC was won by two AATTV members, WO2 Keith Payne and WO2 Ray Simpson. A veteran of World War II, Korea and Malaya, Simpson was on his third tour of Vietnam. Operating west of Ben Het, his experiences with the Montagnards were typical of the war. In the face of heavy fire the tribesmen deserted, and on two occasions only a solitary stand by Simpson prevented the killing of wounded AATTV members by the Viet Cong.

Above: After being informed of his award of the Victoria Cross in Saigon, Keith Payne, centre, celebrates. To Payne's left is Ray Simpson, whose own Victoria Cross was won in the same battle zone only two weeks previously.

Soldier, AATTV, Vietnam, 1970

While regular Australian troops wore the standard uniforms of the Australian Army, members of specialist units such as the 'Team' tended to wear more exotic dress. This soldier is wearing Vietnamese-manufactured Tiger Stripe fatigues which were worn by Special Forces troops in both the US and South Vietnamese armies. Tiger Stripe camouflage became associated with elite forces in Vietnam, to the extent that ordinary Vietnamese troops and even civilians had their own patterns privately run-up in emulation of units such as the Green Berets and the Team. Other items of US origin include M56 web equipment and M8 smoke grenades. Over his left shoulder is a satchel for holding demolition charges, while locally-made ammunition pouches are arranged round his waist belt. Footgear consists of black leather boots of the Australian army – made from kangaroo hide. Instead of the AR-15 (M16) assault rifle, which was the more usual firearm for Team troops, this soldier carries a 7.62mm Self Loading Rifle, this example having a short barrel. While the AR-15 was light and had a full automatic capability, some troops preferred the larger-calibre bullet fired by the SLR.

assault rifles, but they missed. When he finally returned with the last band of stragglers he found that the advisers and the battalion had gone.

Seeing a phosphorous trail from leaf-mould overturned by recent passers-by, he decided to take a chance and follow it. Payne had gone 200m when he stumbled across Dellwo and a US medical sergeant. They had hidden themselves off the track and were tending Montez and four Montagnards with serious wounds. The battalion commander had set out with the remaining advisers and Montagnards to reach the 5th Battalion base and summon assistance. The most seriously wounded had been left in the care of the two gallant sergeants. Until Payne's arrival the party had almost given up hope.

Carrying the wounded made the operation noisy and slow

Knowing that if he could follow the phosphorous trail, then the enemy could too, and doubting that anyone would be back before the enemy found them, Payne decided to try to get the whole party back to safety. They had well over 1000m to traverse through the jungle at night, and carrying the wounded made the operation noisy and slow. Forced to travel off the ridges to keep out of sight, the going was hard over steep and slippery ground. Payne and the two sergeants took shifts carrying Montez, who was a big and heavy man. Payne radioed continually for an evacuation helicopter, but none were available. The medics then reported that Montez would not last if he was not evacuated soon. When at last a helicopter arrived it was too late – Montez was dead.

Pressing on, Payne reduced the danger of discovery by arranging for a propeller-driven aircraft to fly over them, drowning out their noise. Then, seeing the sparks flying from one of Tolley's mortars in action near the 5th Battalion, Payne realised that the ordeal would soon be over. The party staggered into the base: it was 0310 hours on 25 May. The rescue had been little short of a miracle.

The citation for Payne's Victoria Cross stated that his sustained and heroic personal efforts were outstanding and undoubtedly saved the lives of many Montagnards and several of his fellow advisers. But many did not return. Of Payne's 89 men only 31 survived. Montez' company experienced similar losses, and between 20 and 30 of Tolley's men died.

After the mauling it had received, the 1st Mike Force Battalion was withdrawn for a rest, re-equipping and re-training. Under an Australian commander it returned to Ben Het but by that time the NVA, who had themselves suffered heavily from constant ground and air action, had withdrawn.

The Training Team, on average only 100 hand-picked professional soldiers, finished the war in Vietnam with four Victoria Crosses and numerous Imperial, American and Vietnamese awards, including the Vietnamese Cross of Gallantry with Palm and American Meritorious Unit citations. For its size it was probably the most highly decorated unit ever to be formed in the Australian Army. The Team achieved far more than was expected of it, and the sheer range of its fighting experience stands virtually alone in Australian military history.

THE AUTHOR Ian McNeill served as an infantry officer in Vietnam with the Australian Army Training Team in 1965-66. He is author of *The Team: Australian Army Advisers in Vietnam 1962-1972.*

WAR IN THE HILLS

Organising Montagnard tribesmen into defensive formations against the communist forces, the Special Forces added a valuable component to the US war effort in Vietnam.

ONE URGENT priority of the US Army Special Forces in Vietnam was the eradication of Viet Cong (VC) influence among the Montagnard tribesmen of the Central Highlands. Communist control of this area would, in effect, cut South Vietnam in two, and the VC were taking the opportunity to 'swim freely among the people', in the words of Chairman Mao, recruiting supporters for their cause. Since the Montagnards had little reason to trust the South Vietnamese government, there was a strong

Above: A South Vietnamese 'cidgee', festooned with M60 machine-gun rounds, prepares for an anti-Viet Cong operation. Left: A Special Forces Weapons NCO checks over a 106mm recoilless rifle.

33

M14 Rifle

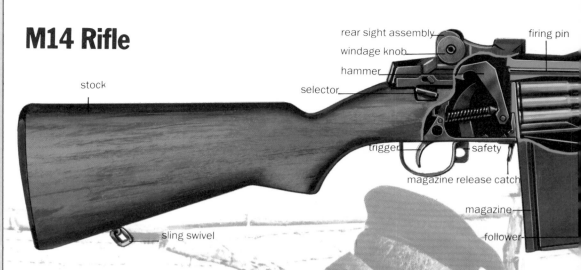

rear sight assembly
windage knob
hammer
selector
firing pin
stock
trigger
safety
magazine release catch
magazine
sling swivel
follower

US SPECIAL FORCES IN VIETNAM

The involvement of the US Army Special Forces with the tribesmen of Vietnam's Central Highlands began in December 1961 with the establishment of the pilot Village Defense Program at Buon Enao village in Darlac Province. Seven men were detailed, along with a South Vietnamese contingent, to develop a programme of civic action in the area.
In early 1962 a 12-man A-team from the 1st Special Forces Group (Airborne) – 1st SFG (Abn) – joined the men at Buon Enao to train the tribesmen in military skills. Early success led to rapid expansion, and by August 1962 five A-teams were deployed in the CIDG Program, and over 200 villages were under protection.
Further development led to the formation of Headquarters US Army Special Forces (Provisional) Vietnam, to which personnel from the 1st, 5th and 7th SFGs were assigned for six-monthly temporary duty (TDY) tours. In July 1964, 18 A-teams were controlling 11,250 troopers in CIDG camps on the Cambodian and Laotian borders alone.
So great did the Special Forces' commitment become that, in October 1964, the entire 5th SFG (Abn) arrived to take control of all Special Forces activity in the war. At the time, the 5th SFG comprised just 951 men, but by July 1966 it had grown to 2627 with a huge indigenous force under command.
Above: A CIDG unit shoulder flash.

possibility that they could be persuaded to side with the North. For many years the South Vietnamese people and successive governments had discriminated against the fiercely independent hill people, treating them as little more than unsophisticated savages. The US Special Forces, on the other hand, were determined that the Montagnards should become the 'fishermen' who would help them 'net' the communists. To this end, considerable resources of arms, money, medical aid and other material benefits were showered upon the Montagnards to gain their loyalty. The tribesmen, although unused to Western affluence, were quick to accept the incentives.

Once a pioneering group had set civic action programmes in motion in an area, detachments from the US Special Forces and the Vietnamese Special Forces (the Luc Luong Dac Biet, or LLDB) would begin military training. Defensive positions such as stockades and trenches would be built around the village, and the men would receive instruction in the use of the M1 carbine and the M3 'grease gun' sub-machine gun. Basic tactics and radio operation were also taught, enabling village defenders to call in reserve strike forces of trained and heavily armed troops that had been organised to garrison the area and carry out patrols.

By the end of 1963, the US Special Forces, with the aid of the LLDB, had trained 18,000 strike force

troops and more than 43,000 hamlet militiamen. The Civilian Irregular Defense Group (CIDG) Program as the campaign among the Montagnards came to be known, had, meanwhile, become the responsibility of Military Assistance Command Vietnam (MACV) as part of Operation Switchback, and Montagnard training periods had been standardised, with strike force personnel receiving six weeks and hamlet militiamen receiving two weeks.

Early in 1963, the 'cidgees' began to patrol more aggressively, rather than passively responding to attack

Early in 1963 there was a subtle shift in the thrust of the CIDG Program, as 'cidgees' began to patrol more aggressively, searching out or setting ambushes for the VC rather than passively waiting to respond to attack. In October the Border Surveillance Program (originally known as the 'Trail Watcher Program') came under the CIDGs, and Special Forces-trained irregulars were deployed in patrolling key infiltration routes along the borders of South Vietnam. Thus a force originally conceived to protect its own villages was quickly evolving new roles, and the control of large areas from military encampments together with intelligence-gathering operations soon took precedence over village-based guard duties.

e — chambered round   gas port   barrel   fore sight assembly

bayonet lug   flash suppressor

sling swivel   gas piston

operating rod

Calibre 7.62mm
Length 111.7cm
Weight 3.88kg
Feed 20-round box magazine
System of operation Gas
Rate of fire (cyclic) 750rpm
Muzzle velocity 853mps

Above: The M14 rifle which was used extensively in Vietnam prior to the introduction of the M16 assault rifle. Below and below left: Green Beret SFC Willie C. Smith, of the 1st Special Forces Group, trains Vietnamese volunteers in the finer points of hand-grenade usage at the Nui Ba Den Special Forces outpost in 1964. Below right: Further grenade training. Special Forces advisers instruct 'cidgees' in the use of the M79 grenade launcher.

The majority of the indigenous CIDG personnel came from the populous Rhada tribe of Montagnards, but as the programme expanded it became necessary to establish strongpoints in areas dominated by other minorities. Men were recruited from the ethnic Cambodians within South Vietnam, from such religious sects as the Hoa Hao and the Cao Dai, and from the Nung tribe. The ethnic Chinese Nungs, in particular, proved themselves adept soldiers and were often selected for special missions or vital security duties.

However, the involvement of new minorities in the CIDG brought its own problems, for traditional animosities existed between the tribes. Moreover, perhaps the strongest hostility lay between the mountain people and the South Vietnamese as a whole, a hostility which led to the 1964 rebellion of Montagnard troops. Although the US Special Forces managed to defuse the uprising in most camps by appealing to Montagnard loyalty to America, some members of the LLDB were killed or injured before peace was restored.

In addition to the conflicts between the LLDB and the Montagnards, the LLDB often came into conflict with the US Special Forces. One cause was the lack of aggressiveness often displayed by the LLDB, earning them the sarcastic title of the 'Look Long Duck Backs'. The LLDB also had a reputation for avoiding night ambushes and patrols, and for disliking operat-

MIKE FORCE

As the CIDG Program expanded, cutting into Viet Cong communications and negating communist influence in the Highlands, the CIDG camps came under increasingly concentrated attack. In response, the formation of Mobile Strike Forces (Mike Forces) was authorised in October 1964, and operations began in mid-1965. Originally totalling 600 men, the forces were organised into units of three companies and a headquarters.

Trained for airborne or airmobile warfare, Mike Forces comprised the elite, quick-reaction element of the CIDG camps. Unlike other parts of the CIDG organisation, they were exclusively controlled by the US Army Special Forces. Among the early Mike Force recruits were many members of the ethnic Chinese Nung tribe.

So successful was the Mike Force concept that by July 1968 11,000 men were involved, with 34 companies distributed between five Mobile Strike Force Commands (MSFCs). Of these commands, 5th MSFC came directly under the 5th Special Forces Group (Airborne), while the 1st to the 4th MSFCs were attached to I, II, III and IV Corps of the US Army. Each MSFC had its own fixed number of battalions, depending on operational necessity, plus a reconnaissance company and a headquarters. The 4th MSFC also maintained an assault boat company. By the autumn of 1968 5th Special Forces Group was employing 3500 men, supervising 7000 Mike Force personnel and 27,000 CIDG.

The 1st Mobile Strike Force Command was based at Da Nang, 2nd at Pleiku, 3rd at Long Hai and 4th at Can Tho: based at Nha Trang, the 5th MSFC was deployed all over Vietnam.

ing in small units. Consequently, although the LLDB were theoretically in command, with the US Special Forces as observers and advisers, the 'advisers' often ended up in combat command. A 'green beret' sergeant was frequently seen carrying responsibilities which, in normal circumstances, would fall to an officer of at least the rank of captain.

The build-up of conventional US troops in Vietnam during 1965 and 1966 had much to do with the shift by CIDG units towards more offensive operations. Special Forces-trained irregulars often acted as scouts for US Army units and, in the case of airmobile units such as the 1st Air Cavalry and the 173rd Airborne Brigade, the cidgees acted as stalking horses, patrolling in enemy territory until they came under attack; they would then attempt to hold the enemy down until the heavily armed airmobile infantry flew in. The cidgees proved very effective when they were operating under a commander who understood them and how to use them. Unfortunately, most of the US commanders failed to trust the cidgee force and did not employ them correctly, and, under such men, the Montagnards enjoyed only very limited success. The most astute of the commanders real-

ised that the greatest value of the CIDG units lay in intelligence gathering, and Montagnards participating in such specialised operations as Projects Delta, Omega, Sigma and Gamma made valuable contributions to their success.

The Apache Force trained US ground troops for battle, and warned them against booby traps and other weapons employed by the VC

The Mobile Strike (Mike) Forces which evolved out of the CIDG Program were widely used in the Greek letter projects and in 'Blackjack' operations. During the latter, mobile guerrilla forces were inserted into 'Indian country' – communist-occupied positions – to make a reconnaissance; they would then be reinforced by Mike Force battalions which would exploit the recce's findings to make a strike of the maximum effectiveness. Other Blackjack operations involved raids and sabotage in areas believed safe by the enemy. The reconnaissance platoons used in these raids were the elite of the Mike Forces, trained at the MACV Recondo School.

Below: War in the Delta. Special Forces and 'cidgees' aboard an airboat set out on patrol in the Mekong Delta. Right: A member of Special Forces deploys a purple smoke grenade to mark a landing zone for incoming helicopters. Far right: Captain Roger Donlon at the Nam Dang Special Forces Camp which was attacked by a battalion-sized enemy force July 1964. Bottom: A CIDG artillery team prepares to fire a 105mm howitzer. CIDG personnel were trained in the use of artillery by Special Forces heavy-weapons advisers.

Special Forces Vietnam

CHINA
NORTH VIETNAM
LAOS
THAILAND
SOUTH CHINA SEA
CAMBODIA
SOUTH VIETNAM

Demilitarized Zone
Lang Vei
Khe Sanh
Quang Tri
Hue
SOUTH CHINA SEA
Da Nang
Kontum
Pleiku
Qui Nhon
Central highlands
SOUTH VIETNAM
Buon Enao
Ban Me Thuot
HQ Nha Trang
II
Da Lat
WAR ZONE C
WAR ZONE D
Bien Hoa
III
HQ Saigon
Plain of Reeds
Don Phuc
Chau Doc
IV
Cao Lanh
Mekong delta
Can Tho

Key
● Special Forces A detachments, October 1964
○ Special Forces B detachments, October 1964
Special Forces HQ
— Corps Tactical Zones
▨ Area inhabited by Montagnards

As US military involvement in the Vietnam conflict increased, Special Forces deployment reached higher levels. Under the CIDG program, begun at Buon Enao late in 1961, large numbers of the indigenous population were trained by Special Forces detachments and used in counter-insurgency operations.

One unit whose role fell between the special operations carried out by indigenous personnel and the CIDG Program was the 'Apache Force'. This interesting unit was made up of Montagnard CIDG troops and Special Forces advisers who specialised in orienting newly arrived US ground troops for operations in Vietnam. After it had prepared the men for battle and warned them against the booby traps and other weapons employed by the VC, the Apache Force would usually accompany them on operations for their first few days in the combat zone. Later, the Apache Force evolved into the combat reconnaissance platoons which played such an important part in the Mike Force attacks that characterised the later aggressive CIDG strategy.

By 1967, the CIDG camps were being constructed as 'fighting camps' designed to withstand heavy enemy attack through deep pre-planned defences, and machine guns and mortars in interlocking fields of fire. The CIDGs were also intensifying their night operations during this period and there was a marked rise in VC casualties. By 1967 the LLDB was also showing some improvement, partly as a result of US Special Forces Detachment B-51 at Dong Ba Thin. This improvement in the LLDB began to make it feasible for the US Special Forces to hand over control of a number of CIDG camps to the South Vietnamese, an expedient which had not been implemented since the 1964 Montagnard revolt.

Though lightly equipped, the Mike Forces could bring devastating firepower to bear by calling down air strikes or artillery support

Forward planning for the CIDGs in 1967 and 1968 saw overall emphasis remaining on the construction of CIDG border surveillance camps to interdict VC infiltration routes. In the Mekong Delta, where Special Forces-trained irregulars had played a large part in clearing the VC from the Plain of Reeds, Special Forces bases were built as floating camps. Landing pads, barracks and store-rooms were built on platforms that rose with the river waters, thus allowing the camps to remain in operation even when the delta was flooded. The Mike Force attached to IV Corps, which operated in the delta, was equipped with air boats and hydrofoils.

Early in 1967, CIDG units began operations from camps opened in War Zone C, for years a notorious VC stronghold. Other hard-contested areas also

DEFENCE OF NAM DONG

In July 1964 the remote CIDG camp of Nam Dong, 15 miles from the Laotian border and surrounded by 2000ft mountains, was scheduled to be handed over to the Vietnamese Civil Guard.

The camp's Special Forces A-team, A-726, was led by Captain Roger H.C. Donlon (above), and on 5 July he was already worried by shooting that had broken out between Vietnamese and Nung elements in the base. Then, at 0230 hours on the 6th, Viet Cong white phosphorus shells and grenades began to rain down onto the buildings – about 900 Viet Cong guerrillas had massed to destroy the camp.

Before long the entire camp was ablaze, with men running desperately to collect guns and ammunition from the burning huts. Following an urgent call for help, the radio shack was destroyed. After 15 minutes the Viet Cong appeared at the perimeter to finish off the garrison. Wounded in the stomach, Donlon personally killed a 3-man demolition team at the gate, all the time directing his men's fire and attempting to help casualties. At 0404 hours a flare-ship from Da Nang arrived to bathe the scene in an eerie light. Calls from the Viet Cong for surrender were answered with a hail of fire and eventually the Viet Cong, aware that reinforcements were imminent, began to withdraw. In the camp, 55 men lay dead, and another 65 were wounded.

For his courageous leadership in the defence of Nam Dong, Captain Donlon received the Medal of Honor.

Above: An adviser from 5th Special Forces Group (Airborne) accompanies a CIDG unit in a counter-insurgency sweep against the Viet Cong near the border with Cambodia. Special Forces personnel were involved at every level of the CIDG training programme – from the basics of smallarms use, to the arts of troop deployment and tactical planning.

Captain, Camp Strike Force, 5th Special Forces Group, Vietnam 1965

This officer, working on the Montagnard CIDG Program, is dressed in green jungle fatigues with black leather and nylon boots. Rank is denoted by the silver bars on the beret badge and the white lapel bars. The breast wings indicate that this Green Beret is para-trained and he also wears the artillery badge, crossed guns and missile. Armament consists of an M2 carbine and a .45 calibre Colt M1911A1 pistol attached to M56 webbing.

came under CIDG control as strategic military bases were established. These camps came under constant attack by the Viet Cong and by the North Vietnamese Army (NVA), and were successfully defended only by deployment of Mike Forces in conjunction with US gunships such as the AC-47 (known as 'Puff the Magic Dragon'). During this period the Mike Forces were organised into companies of three rifle platoons and a weapons platoon, a total of 185 men. Though lightly equipped, the Mike Forces could bring devastating firepower to bear by calling down air strikes or artillery support.

The CIDG Program benefitted greatly from its logistical organisation, one which effectively circumvented both the corrupt South Vietnamese system and the cumbersome arrangements of the US Army. The CIDG Program and other Special Forces operations were supplied from forward bases in each of the four Corps Tactical Zones. Fighting camps could be re-supplied very quickly, using aerial re-supply if necessary. Any special items, such as long-range patrol rations specifically designed for the diets of indigenous troops, were acquired through the US Army Counter-Insurgency Support Office at Okinawa. The Special Forces supply network also provided special equipment such as foreign weapons for clandestine operations.

When the Tet Offensive descended on the populated areas of South Vietnam in January 1968, the cidgees gained a great deal of respect as urban fighters. Indeed, they inflicted a severe blow to VC morale after some attackers launched their sector of the offensive prematurely against cities garrisoned by Mike Forces, such as Ban Me Thuot and Nha Trang. Not only were the US units alerted to the offensive by these ill-coordinated attacks, but the raiders were also driven back by the Special Forces-trained Montagnards.

As VC and NVA elements massed around Khe Sanh, Special Forces camps, such as Lang Vei, came under heavy fire

During the build-up for the Tet Offensive, and in the course of the offensive itself, most of the CIDG camps other than those of I Corps were left alone as VC strength concentrated near the cities. However, as VC and NVA elements massed around Khe Sanh and the northern cities such as Hue, Special Forces camps, such as Lang Vei, under I Corps' Special Forces Detachment A-101, came under heavy fire. Lang Vei had been attacked frequently since its establishment in December 1966, and on 4 May 1967 it had been virtually destroyed in an assault which included VC infiltrators within the ranks of the camp's own Montagnards. Lang Vei was finally overrun during the Tet offensive on 7 February 1968 by a tank-supported NVA force.

After distinguishing themselves in the Tet Offensive the cidgees enjoyed a greater respect within the framework of the anti-communist forces. They were subsequently deployed in the defence of II, III, and IV Corps, while conventional units of the Army of the Republic of Vietnam (ARVN) were moved into I Corps to win back areas newly occupied by the North Vietnamese. CIDG units were also given priority in weapons re-supply, and they received issue of M16 rifles and M60 GPMGs in April 1968.

Beginning early in 1968, the process of turning over CIDG camps to Vietnamese control was speeded up. As the mission of countering infiltration assumed even more importance in the aftermath of the Tet Offensive, CIDG personnel were used primarily along the western border of South Vietnam to interdict infiltration routes. More and more responsibility for the CIDG Program, however, was being turned over to the LLDB to prepare them for the complete absorption of the programme. Special Forces civic action and psychological operations (psy ops) were also turned over to the Vietnamese as rapidly as possible under the Nixon administration's policy of 'Vietnamization'.

CIDG companies assaulted a VC training area and uncovered large caches of crew-served weapons and other equipment

Even though the directing of strategic border surveillance and interdiction camps was being turned over to the LLDB during 1969, Special Forces strength in Vietnam peaked in that year at over 4000 men, though some were assigned to special operations units and were thus only under 5th SFG (Airborne) control in theory. By early 1970, it had been decided to end the CIDG Program and absorb the CIDG units into the Army of the Republic of Vietnam. A few camps were closed down during the autumn of 1970, but 37 were converted to ARVN Ranger camps with their CIDG complement becoming ARVN Ranger battalions, primarily 'Border Rangers' who retained the mission of countering infiltration along the borders. However, what evidence there is suggests that the cidgees' effectiveness declined sharply under ARVN control.

During 1970, CIDG units participated in operations in Cambodia along with some Special Forces members. CIDG companies from Doc Hue and Tra Cu played an especially important role when they assaulted a VC training area and uncovered large

Below left: the CIDG forces saw plenty of action during the Vietnam War. Here two 'cidgees' lend support to a wounded comrade after a brush with the Viet Cong. Below right: Two Special Forces personnel relax prior to an operation in War Zone C, northwest of Saigon. Heavily armed, they carry CAR-15 Colt Commandos (one fitted with a grenade launcher beneath the barrel) a LAW rocket launcher, an array of grenades and a silenced M3A1 sub-machine gun.

caches of crew-served weapons and other equipment.

On 31 December 1970 the participation of the 5th SFG (Airborne) in the CIDG Program officially ended and on 3 March 1971 it officially departed for Fort Bragg, though some Special Forces troopers assigned to advisory missions or special operations were to remain in Vietnam much longer.

Overall, the CIDG Program was successful, the Mike Forces ranking among the best indigenous Vietnamese troops of the war. The CIDG Program, along with the heavy blow landed on the Viet Cong during the Tet Offensive, made a real contribution to curbing communist insurgency in Vietnam. If there was one problem with the CIDG Program it was that the Special Forces performed the 'hearts and minds' aspect of their mission too well. The Nungs, Montagnards and other ethnic minorities readily gave their loyalty to the Special Forces, and, by association, to America, but this never became a loyalty shared by the government of South Vietnam.

THE AUTHOR Leroy Thompson served in Vietnam as a commissioned officer in the USAF Combat Security Police. He has written several books on the US Special Forces and is the author of *Uniforms of the Elite Forces.*

When the British moved into the Dodecanese islands in 1943, the German Special Forces, the Brandenburgers, were sent in to flush out the invading forces

Below: Spearhead of invasion. Men of the Brandenburg Para Company complete their final preparations before the flight to the island of Leros on 12 November 1943. Bottom left: The target seen from the cockpit of a Ju 88.

IN LATE 1943, an able and energetic German officer, Lieutenant-General Müller, was ordered to capture the Greek island of Leros from the British. Although the operation, code-named Leopard, was to take place in one of the war's backwaters, Müller's assault force, gathering on the Greek mainland, included elements of the Brandenburgers. The battle for the tiny island was to prove the sternest test faced by Hitler's commandos in the eastern Mediterranean.

Müller's proposed battle plan had four phases. After the island's defences had been neutralised by bombing during phase one, assaults would go in at a number of places along the coast. Once ashore, the individual groups would then join forces and enter the fourth and final phase: the defeat of the garrison.

When the Luftwaffe's assault ended, the German aircraft had made more than 1000 attacks on Leros, but the island's guns had not been knocked out. By 11 November dive-bombers from Stukageschwader 87, operating from nearby Rhodes, and He 111s flying from more distant airfields on the Greek mainland, had softened up the enemy. Operation Leopard was launched. Convoys of ships carrying German assault troops were already at sea; the airborne troops were ordered into action.

However, the confidence of the German paras must have ebbed a little during the early morning of 12 November, D-day for the operation. The men in the first assault wave were drawn from the 1st Battalion of the 2nd Parachute Regiment and from the Brandenburger's Para Company. They paraded in the bright moonlight, and at dawn on the 12th emplaned at Tatai airfield near Athens. The 40 machines carrying the paras took off and flew at almost wave-top height, heading for Gurna Bay on

STRIKE ON LEROS

the west coast of Leros. The aircraft were less than three minutes flying time from the drop zone when a signal was flashed recalling them to Athens. The seaborne group of Captain Aschoff's Western Task Force, also heading for Gurna Bay, had been driven back by gunfire from the island's coastal batteries. Until the progress of von Saldern's Eastern Task Force had been determined, no landings were to be made on the western side of the island.

In fact, the assault by the Eastern Task Force had been successful and two beach-heads had been established. At 1000 hours the paras emplaned again. Three hours later, they were approaching Gurna Bay, one of two huge indentations – the bay of Alinda on the eastern side is the other – which all but bisect the island of Leros.

As the troop-carrying aircraft drew nearer to the island, they changed formation from shallow 'vics' to files of 12 machines in line astern, and then climbed to an altitude of 400ft. Even at this height, they were flying below the anti-aircraft guns sited on the mountain peaks and were quickly enveloped in a devastating barrage of flak. The crashing explosions of anti-aircraft shells rocked the slow-flying Ju 52s, and streams of machine-gun tracer struck their wings and fuselages. But the aircraft held their rigid formation; a straight and level course was essential to the success of the drop. Smoke poured from some aircraft but they continued on the correct heading. It was only seconds from the jump-off time.

The landing zone chosen by Captain Kuhne, the commander of the airborne assault group, was a small strip of ground between the Gurna and Alinda Bays which offered, tactically, the best chance of splitting the island's defenders. However, it was little more than half-a-mile wide, and Kuhne did not know that the area was defended by the 2nd Battalion, the Royal Irish Fusiliers – one of the three battalions of British infantry forming the island's garrison.

The paratroopers dropped from an altitude of 450ft: sufficient height for the parachute canopies to open safely, but a height that kept the descent time to a minimum. The sudden billowing of hundreds of parachutes over the British positions brought the infantry into action. But, before their fire could have any effect, the Germans were on the ground and taking cover on the rocky, scrub-covered lower slopes of Mount Germano. The paras did not stop to dig in; mobility and firepower were the keys to success. Along the drop line between Mount Germano and the Rachi Ridge, whistles and flares were used to gather the scattered groups. Before long, a potent fighting force had been gathered. Kuhne ordered No.1 Company to extend its front northwards and No.5 Company to cover the bay of Alinda and the small town of Leros. These two thin screens of paras would have to withstand any British assaults while Nos. 2 and 4 Company, together with the Brandenburger company, attacked Rachi Ridge and secured it as a base for future operations.

The Eastern Task Force had had a bad day. The convoy carrying the Brandenburgers' Küstenjäger (coastal raiders) detachments made one attempt to land on the coast but was forced to turn back by fire from the island's gun batteries. The convoy then cruised offshore, out of range of the coastal guns, as Stukas went in to neutralise the opposition. While the air raid was in progress, German destroyers steamed in to lay smoke around the attacking craft. Under cover of this screen, the Küstenjägers' fast

Below: German anti-aircraft gunners watch torpedo boats lay down a smokescreen to cover the first assault wave. Although one landing craft laden with troops was blown out of the water by a well-aimed shell, the rest reached the beaches and quickly unloaded their vital cargoes (below left).

DESTRUCTION

The final demise of the Brandenburgers was brought about by a combination of political intrigue within the upper echelons of the Nazi hierarchy, and the unit's poor deployment during the campaign on the Eastern Front after 1942.
The rift between Admiral Canaris, the founder of the Brandenburgers, and Hitler stemmed from the Abwehr's failure to gather useful intelligence, and Canaris' association with elements of the armed forces whose political allegiance to the Nazi cause was open to question. In early 1944 Canaris was under suspicion of conspiracy, and after investigation by the Gestapo was executed.
As Canaris fell from grace, the Brandenburgers were regarded with suspicion. In particular, Himmler was intensely jealous of a 'private' army that rivalled his own Waffen-SS.
During late 1942 the changing strategic situation on the Eastern Front saw the Brandenburgers, by this stage a divisional-sized unit, deployed in a conventional role. Heavy losses and news of political manoeuvrings in Germany, destroyed the unit's cohesion, and in 1943 many Brandenburgers joined a Waffen-SS commando force being formed by Otto Skorzeny. Following the dismissal of Canaris, the Brandenburg Division was dismantled and then reformed as part of the Grossdeutschland Division in the spring of 1944. Few men survived the bitter combat of the war's final stages. Above: The insignia worn by Brandenburger units attached to the Grossdeutschland Division.

Following the Italian exit from the war in 1943, the Allies attempted to seize the Dodecanese islands in the eastern Mediterranean in order to preserve Turkish neutrality and prevent the Germans from establishing a stronger presence in the area.

The Allies' ability to mount such an operation, however, was compromised by the need to maintain the momentum of the Italian campaign and only the 234th Brigade, backed by limited air and naval support, was earmarked for the capture and defence of the islands. Commanded by Lieutenant-General R.A.G. Tilney, the Leros garrison initially comprised the 4th Battalion, the Royal East Kent Regiment and C Company, of the King's Own Royal Regiment in the north of the island; the 2nd Battalion, the Royal Irish Fusiliers and B Company of the Royal West Kent Regiment in the centre; with the 1st Battalion, the King's Own Royal Regiment holding the southern sector.

Artillery support was provided by the 3rd Light Anti-Aircraft Battery and a troop of 25-pounders. The garrison also included roving groups from the SBS and LRDG.

Tilney could also draw on the reluctant services of the island's 5500-strong Italian garrison. Although these troops manned 24 batteries, most were either poorly trained reservists or administrative personnel and unlikely to put up much resistance to an invasion force.

During the fight for the island, a further two companies of the Royal West Kents were brought over from Samos. However, the reinforced garrison was unable to offset the enemy's air superiority, and some 4000 men were forced to capitulate when the island fell.

assault vessels raced at top speed towards the sheer cliffs on the north side of Pandeli Bay and another part of the convoy set course for Alinda Bay.

The vessels carrying the Küstenjägers suddenly appeared out of the smoke screen: two fast motor boats and two landing craft crammed with men. The boats drove towards a narrow strip of sand at the base of the cliffs, but before they reached the beach a 15cm shell struck and sank one of the two landing craft. However, most of the men it was carrying reached the shore, arriving as the first beach-landing groups were fastening climbing ropes to the cliff face. Moments later, the assault troops began to scale the vertical wall of rock above which lay Mount Appetici, the Küstenjäger detachments' objective.

Only 130 men completed the ascent. Exhausted by the climb, they scattered among the cliff-top boulders and prepared for the next phase of their assault: a move across flat and open ground, extending towards the mountain. Machine-gun and mortar fire were already raking the Jägers' positions.

Above the Jäger groups, a liaison aircraft circled slowly – the air link. A succession of flares requesting dive-bomber support went up. Within minutes, the air link had directed the Stukas to the target. However, the aircrafts' pilots mistook the target, and unleashed their bombs on the men in the rocks. Red flares rose into the sky; urgent and demanding, they cancelled the next assault. Air link established the correct target and then redirected the Stukas. Bombs crashed down with deafening explosions, marching forward in a moving barrage. The Jägers rose up out of the rocks and advanced behind the bomb line; a small group of men marching towards a very large mountain.

Skilfully and swiftly, they made their way forward and then charged the emplacements

That first assault was unsuccessful. The Küstenjägers were unable to take the objective as they were pinned down by fire from the fusiliers' machine-gun and mortar positions. The Jägers lay under the British fire. It was a punishing and destructive fire which raked them. All the Brandenburger officers were killed or wounded. In an effort to revitalise the attack the Stukas were recalled, but again they mistook the target and their missiles hit the German troops.

Shattered by this costly error, the Küstenjäger detachments pulled back under fire and then regrouped. At a battlefield conference it was agreed that the mountain was too big an objective for the small number of men available. But, if they could not capture the mountain, they could contain the British troops on it by setting up a chain of machine-gun posts. The main Jäger body, meanwhile, would take out the Italian battery on Castle Hill, a small mountain to the southeast of Leros town. Moving at a trot, the Jägers passed through the fire of British machine guns, mortars and artillery, and shook out into their assault formations. Skilfully and swiftly, they made their way forward and then charged the emplacements. They raced across trenches; hand grenades burst inside Italian pill-boxes, and in a swift, cutting operation the Küstenjägers took out the coast guns.

During the night of 12/13 November, British artillery maintained a harassing fire against them and enemy patrols were out, visible in the bright moonlight. The Küstenjägers were held in the recently captured positions for three days, without support or reinforcement. They could advance no farther.

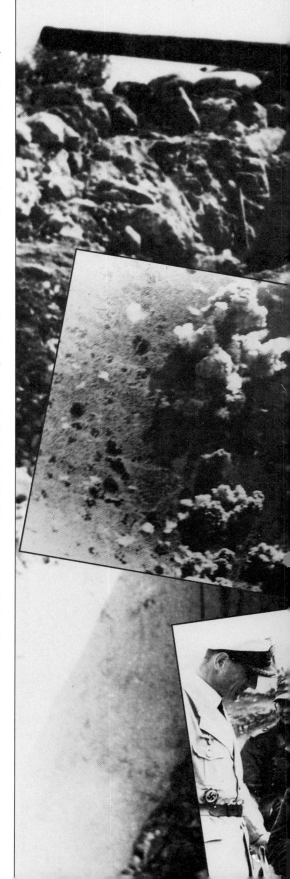

Below: A lone German officer inspects the shattered remains of a coastal battery after the fall of Leros. Massive air strikes by the Luftwaffe (below centre) pulverised the island's defences. Lack of Allied fighter cover, and limited anti-aircraft protection allowed the Stukas to strike at will. Bottom: The German command General Müller (centre), plots his next move.

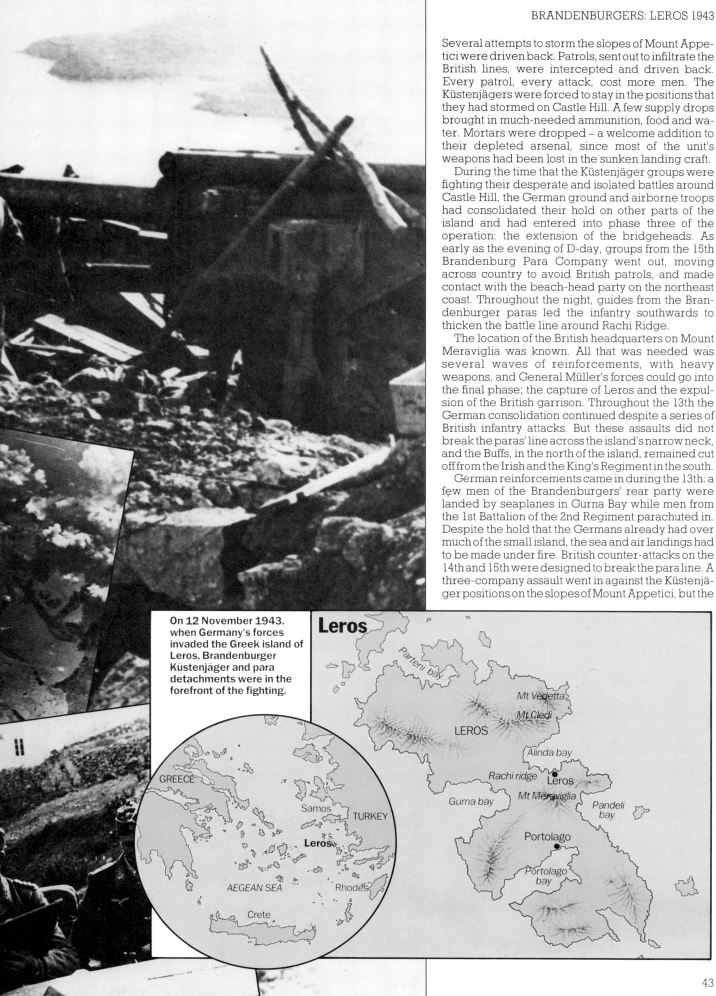

Several attempts to storm the slopes of Mount Appetici were driven back. Patrols, sent out to infiltrate the British lines, were intercepted and driven back. Every patrol, every attack, cost more men. The Küstenjägers were forced to stay in the positions that they had stormed on Castle Hill. A few supply drops brought in much-needed ammunition, food and water. Mortars were dropped – a welcome addition to their depleted arsenal, since most of the unit's weapons had been lost in the sunken landing craft.

During the time that the Küstenjäger groups were fighting their desperate and isolated battles around Castle Hill, the German ground and airborne troops had consolidated their hold on other parts of the island and had entered into phase three of the operation: the extension of the bridgeheads. As early as the evening of D-day, groups from the 15th Brandenburg Para Company went out, moving across country to avoid British patrols, and made contact with the beach-head party on the northeast coast. Throughout the night, guides from the Brandenburger paras led the infantry southwards to thicken the battle line around Rachi Ridge.

The location of the British headquarters on Mount Meraviglia was known. All that was needed was several waves of reinforcements, with heavy weapons, and General Müller's forces could go into the final phase; the capture of Leros and the expulsion of the British garrison. Throughout the 13th the German consolidation continued despite a series of British infantry attacks. But these assaults did not break the paras' line across the island's narrow neck, and the Buffs, in the north of the island, remained cut off from the Irish and the King's Regiment in the south.

German reinforcements came in during the 13th: a few men of the Brandenburgers' rear party were landed by seaplanes in Gurna Bay while men from the 1st Battalion of the 2nd Regiment parachuted in. Despite the hold that the Germans already had over much of the small island, the sea and air landings had to be made under fire. British counter-attacks on the 14th and 15th were designed to break the para line. A three-company assault went in against the Küstenjäger positions on the slopes of Mount Appetici, but the

On 12 November 1943, when Germany's forces invaded the Greek island of Leros, Brandenburger Küstenjäger and para detachments were in the forefront of the fighting.

Leros

Jägers skilful use of the new MG42 and an almost continuous barrage of shells from their 81mm mortars, smashed the British attack.

The main British effort then switched to Rachi Ridge and Mount Germano, but the assaults were dogged by bad luck. The German para reinforcements, landed on the previous day, were fresh; the Buffs and the West Kents (who had arrived from Samos) were men exhausted by Stuka attacks and the strain of battle. During one attack, the approach march by the West Kents passed across the front held by 15th Para Company whose machine-gun and mortar fire struck the assault troops as they formed up. However, the West Kents fought their way through the Brandenburgers' defensive fire and retook Germano. Then they linked up with the Buffs. For a brief time, it seemed as if the German hold on the central sector of Leros might be weakening, and the combined British infantry force was ordered to capture St Nicola. If the town fell, the German forces around Leros would be bottled up.

The battle for the little stone houses of St Nicola was the fiercest action fought during the assault on the island: bloody hand-to-hand combat in the small, dark, scantily furnished rooms. However, the paras withdrew men from other sectors to support the fighting in the village, and the strength of numbers told. The Kents were forced out of the tiny village and into the low hills on its western side.

During 15 November, the German ground commanders became aware that Operation Leopard was losing momentum – bad weather on the 14th had prevented reinforcements coming in with heavy weapons. The service of 145 Luftwaffe aircraft more than compensated for the lack of field guns, but, nevertheless, reinforcements were needed most urgently, and the 3rd Battalion of the Brandenbur-

gers' 1st Regiment was ordered to Leros.

At 0200 hours on the 16th, the battalion landed under fire in the bay of Leros town and went straight into action. During the last hours of the night, they captured the heights to the south of the town, and were then ordered to change front and attack a new objective. In the growing light of a new day, the men of the 1st Battalion saw their next target – Mount Meraviglia and the British headquarters. As the assault went in, the last British shells and the fire from several machine guns caused the Brandenburgers terrible losses. Although they struggled up bare slopes, the advance was irresistible. The companies drove forward, overrunning anti-aircraft positions and field defences, and machine pistolling the stubborn defenders. By 1500 the mountain had been taken. Losses had been very heavy and included the 3rd Battalion's commanding officer, Captain Fröböse, who was severely wounded.

Later, a patrol from the battalion gained touch with the Küstenjägers on Castle Hill and the two groups formed up for the final attack on the British HQ. It was to a party of Jägers that Brigadier Tilney, the commander of the 234th Brigade on Leros, surrendered.

The bloody battle for Leros had been a trial of endurance for both sides. The Brandenburgers, deployed in the unfamiliar role of conventional shock troops, were unable to use subterfuge to take the island and had to rely on their combat skills. Although lacking heavy equipment, they carried the battle to the enemy and, by a combination of tenacity and courage, broke the back of British resistance.

THE AUTHOR James Lucas served with the Queen's Own Royal West Kent Regiment during World War II and is currently Deputy Head of the Department of Photography at the Imperial War Museum, London.

Below: The victor and the vanquished meet after the capitulation of the Leros garrison on 17 November. The British commander, Brigadier Tilney (right), ordered his men to surrender after a small detachment of Brandenburgers stormed his headquarters on Mount Meraviglia. Although the British troops had fought with great resolution and many were willing to continue the fight, German air and ground superiority made any further resistance futile.

OBSERVATIONS FROM RACHI RIDGE

Rachi Ridge, a great mountainous spine running down the centre of Leros, saw some of the fiercest action of the whole invasion. Jeffrey Holland was involved in the defence of the ridge with elements of the British 234th Brigade: 'The German assault troops were a tough and very tenacious enemy. They would move quickly from position to position but would never retreat – they seemed willing to accept a very high casualty rate. Their officers and NCOs frequently exposed themselves to our fire when directing an attack, and their orders were always followed to the letter. In defence, the German infantry seemed almost indifferent to our mortar fire. …there seems to be little doubt that the Germans on Leros were better organised than the British.'

V FORCE

Following in the finest traditions of the RAF, the revolutionary V-Force was created, responsible for countering the threat of a Soviet pre-emptive strike

WITH THE ADVENT of atomic weapons in 1945, the strategic bomber force of the Royal Air Force underwent a phase of vigorous and ambitious development in the immediate postwar years. In 1947 the Air Ministry defined the basic requirements for the new generation of bombers: they were to be powered by four jet engines and capable of carrying atomic weapons. In 1952, Britain became an atomic power, and during the next three years the RAF formed a force of highly trained aircrew and ground technicians whose task it would be to operate the United Kingdom's nuclear deterrent – the V-Force. Its name derived from the decision of Sir John Slessor, Chief of the Air Staff and Marshal of the RAF, to designate the new strategic bombers as the V-Class after their unfamiliar wing shapes. Eventually, there were to be three such aircraft: the swept-wing Vickers Valiant, the delta-wing Avro Vulcan and the crescent-wing Handley Page Victor.

From the outset, the standards exacted from the V-Force crews were extremely high

The first to enter service was the Valiant, the development of which had been rushed in order to provide a stop-gap strategic bomber, pending the design and development of the more complex Vulcan and Victor. In the event, the Valiant was to prove a successful design, making a significant contribution to the tactics and techniques required for the revolutionary form of warfare that had entered the world stage.

The RAF's first Valiant was delivered to No. 232 Operational Conversion Unit (OCU) at Gaydon, Warwickshire, in January 1955, and this unit set about the job of training crews for the first front-line V-bomber squadron. The crews from the first two courses were to comprise No. 138 Squadron, which was formed under the command of Wing Commander R.G.W. Oakley on 8 February 1955. From the outset, the standards exacted from the V-Force crews were extremely high but, as experience grew, they were somewhat relaxed. Nevertheless, only the RAF's most proficient and reliable aircrews were eligible for training on Valiants and it was a duty for which they were picked, rather than themselves volunteering. An aircraft captain needed a minimum of 1750 hours' flying as a first pilot on another (usually four-engined) aircraft, and his assessment as a pilot had to be 'above the average'. Second pilots were required to have flown for at least 700 hours as first pilots on a previous operational tour, and to have experience of the Canberra twin-jet

bomber. No pilots straight out of training, however able they had proved themselves to be, were considered eligible for the V-Force during its early period. As an experiment, however, in 1957 four pilots were assigned from advanced flying training to No. 232 OCU as prospective Valiant co-pilots. They all qualified without difficulty and, thereafter, increasing numbers of V-bomber co-pilots were 'first tourists' straight from training. It was a wise change in policy, since the V-Force was threatening to absorb virtually all the most skilled and experienced pilots from within the RAF.

In addition to the pilot and co-pilot, three other crew members manned the V-bombers. They comprised two navigators and an air signaller, seated side-by-side and facing rearwards in the bomber's fuselage, behind the pilots. All of the V-bombers had relatively small pressure cabins to house their five-man crews, and in addition to the problems of cramped accommodation on long flights, which affected all of them, the rear crew members' positions were extremely claustrophobic – 'like facing backwards in a broom cupboard at midnight', was one V-Force man's description. Unlike the pilots, the three rear crew members were not provided with ejection seats. Consequently, if an emergency occurred at low level, they stood little chance of successfully abandoning their aircraft. This shortcoming was tragically illustrated in October 1956, when one of the early Vulcans, approaching Heathrow Airport in poor visibility, crashed at the end of an overseas goodwill tour. The two pilots (one of whom was Bomber Command's Air Officer Commander-in-Chief, Sir Harry Broadhurst) ejected safely, but the three men in the rear were killed. Under these circumstances, the aircraft's captain had been presented with the agonising choice of saving himself, or staying with the bomber

in an attempt to help his crew to escape. However, it was the official view that it was his duty to use his ejection seat, as a last resort, even if this meant abandoning his comrades to their fate.

The duties of the two navigators were divided between pure navigation, which was handled by the Nav Plotters, and managing the complex Navigation

Right: On arrival back at Luqa airfield, Valiant bomber crews undergo a mission debrief. Left: Wing Commander Rupert Oakley of No. 138 Squadron descending the steps of the first Valiant to arrive at RAF Wittering. Main picture (left to right): the Vulcan, Valiant and Victor – Britain's V-Force trio. Page 1701: The Avro Vulcan, and the ultimate weapon it was designed to carry.

While the RAF's bombing missions over Suez did not succeed in completely knocking out the enemy airfields, three nights of operations were sufficient to eliminate the Egyptian air force from the calculations of the Anglo-French commanders.

OPERATION MUSKETEER

The Suez Campaign of October/November 1956 provided the RAF's Valiant bombers with their debut in battle. In many ways it was an unfair test of the aircraft's operational capabilities, since the Suez attacks required conventional rather than nuclear bombing – and the techniques of the two missions were quite different. Furthermore, the Valiants had been in service for less than two years and their navigation and bombing radars were not fully tested. Consequently, the bombing missions had to be carried out visually, using makeshift bomb-sights transferred from other aircraft. It was decided to operate at night, in order to make the task of the Egyptian air force in intercepting the bombers as difficult as possible. It was known that Egypt had received over 100 MiG-15 jet fighters from the Soviet Union.

When hostilities opened between Israel and Egypt on the afternoon of 29 October, four Valiant squadrons, on detachment from their UK bases, were operating from Luqa airfield on Malta. They comprised No. 148, 207 and 214

Squadrons from Marham, and No. 138 Squadron from RAF Wittering. The Valiants were despatched on the night of 31 October to attack four of the seven main Egyptian airfields. Their mission was to coincide with a similar attack by Canberras operating from both Malta and Cyprus. The four airfields were to be bombed visually, relying on target markers dropped by Valiant and Canberra pathfinder aircraft. Bombing from high level, the Valiants were led by Wing Commander Rupert Oakley, the commanding officer of No. 138 Squadron, but it was a Valiant of No. 148 Squadron (badge shown left) that dropped the first bombs.

Attacks on the Egyptian airfields continued during the next two nights, four of the targets being in the Delta area and a further eight in the Canal Zone. Photographic reconnaissance by the Canberras of No. 13 Squadron showed that the high-level bombing attacks on 31 October had not been particularly effective against aircraft on the ground, and subsequent attacks were made from a lower level. Although many of the Egyptian air force's aircraft were evacuated by their pilots to the safety of Syria, approximately 50 were destroyed by air attack.

AVRO VULCAN

The prototype of the Vulcan, the Avro Type 698, made its first public appearance in September 1952 at the Farnborough air show. The first production model appeared in 1955, and in 1956 the Vulcan entered service with the RAF as the B. Mk 1.

Early service experience showed the need for an improvement of the aircraft's aerodynamics, and this led to the development of the Phase 2 Wing. A number of modifications were incorporated on the B. Mk 2, including new flight control systems. The restructuring of the wing offered greater performance when diving and pulling out at high speed.

To allay doubts as to the Vulcan's safety, rapid-inflation seat cushions were fitted to the rear compartment, to push the occupants out of a stricken aircraft against high-gravity forces.

The Vulcan B. Mk 2A was fitted with four Bristol Olympus engines, providing a maximum speed of 645mph and a service ceiling of 60,000ft. The range of the aircraft was 4600 miles. Terrain-following radar was fitted in the nose, in addition to passive radar warning systems located at the front of the Vulcan, and at the top of the fin.

Conventional armament comprised 21 'iron bombs' of 1000lb each, and a few of the bombers were fitted with self-defence Sidewinder pylons in May 1982. Other variants of the Vulcan included the SR. Mk 2A, for maritime reconnaissance, and the K. Mk 2 — an air-refuelling tanker conversion.

Right: Painted in anti-flash white, with blue insignia and serial, XL321 was one of the first Vulcan B.Mk 2s to enter service with the rocket-propelled Blue Steel stand-off missile. This aircraft belongs to No. 617 Squadron, the famed 'Dambusters'. Below: Inflight refuelling – from the crew's perspective.

The US Strategic Air Command holds an annual bombing competition, awarding the Mathis Trophy to the crews most adept in precision bombing and navigation. In 1974 a Vulcan force was accorded this honour – a tribute to the high standards of the V-Force crews. Below right: The delta-wing Vulcan in full flight.

ttom (left to right): The
ctor-equipped No. 100
uadron, pictured here after
ing presented with the
not Trophy, one of the
F's premier bombing and
vigation awards; Vulcans
station during a Quick-
action Alert; the
wildering array of
uipment that an Air
ectronics Officer has at his
posal.

and Bombing System (NBS) radar, which was the responsibility of the Nav Radars. The former were recruited from experienced navigators, assessed as 'above the average', who had previously served at least one operational tour on Canberras. The Nav Radars were trained at Bomber Command's Bombing School at Lindholme, Yorkshire, and were expected not only to achieve a high standard in operating their radar equipment, but also to possess an expert knowledge of its workings so that, if necessary, they could carry out maintenance work in flight. However, it soon became apparent that much of the bombers' electronic equipment was not accessible in flight, and the need for Radar Navs to master the intricacies of electronic engineering gradually disappeared. As the duties of the Nav Radar became somewhat easier, so those of the air signallers increased in complexity. Originally, their duties were primarily to act as radio operators, but when the complex nature of the new electronic systems was realised, their specialisation was changed to that of Air Electronics Officer (AEO). The early AEOs were given degree-level courses in electronics to enable them to cope with the bewildering array of new equipment. However, as operational experience increased, the academic standards were relaxed. Eventually, the AEOs came to specialise in the arcane skills of electronic warfare, which the V-Force would require if it was to penetrate the enemy's radar screen and deflect his radar-guided air-defence weapons.

No.138 Squadron, as the first front-line V-bomber unit, was required to carry out an enormous amount of development work before the Valiant could be considered operationally effective. In July 1955 the squadron moved from Gaydon to RAF Wittering, Northamptonshire, where it carried out extensive flying trials alongside the Bomber Command Development Unit. These included Operation Too Right, the first overseas deployment by two Valiants, carrying the flag of Britain's V-bomber force to Singapore, Australia and New Zealand. But it fell to No.49 Squadron to carry out nuclear weapons tests. The first of these was over Maralinga, South Australia, on 11 October 1956, and was accomplished by a Valiant captained by Squadron Leader Ted Flavell. In the following year, on 15 May 1957, No.49 Squadron's commanding officer, Wing Commander K.G. Hubbard, dropped Britain's first thermonuclear bomb over Christmas Island in the Pacific. Because of the much-increased destructive power of this weapon over the earlier A-bombs, Hubbard's Valiant had to perform an intricate evasive manoeuvre immediately after weapons' release if his aircraft was to escape unscathed. This involved the execution of a maximum-rate turn through 180 degrees, followed by the application of full power. If the Valiant was to reach the safe 10-mile distance from the bomb when it detonated, the entire manoeuvre had to be completed within 50 seconds, with no margin for error. Wing Commander Hubbard carried out the evolution faultlessly and was awarded the Air Force Cross for his pioneering work.

Between the two epoch-making nuclear tests, came the Valiant's blooding in action during Operation Musketeer, the ill-fated Suez campaign. The first Valiant to drop high explosive bombs in earnest, on

'BLACK BUCK'

The RAF Vulcan attacks on the Falkland Islands, mounted from the British base on Ascension, involved a round trip of 8000 miles.

The first mission, codenamed 'Black Buck 1', was flown on 1 May 1982 against Port Stanley airfield. Due to the distances involved, 10 Victor tankers were required to support the lone Vulcan that took part in the raid. Captained by Flight Lieutenant Martin Withers from No. 50 Squadron, the Vulcan dropped its stick of 21, 1000lb bombs diagonally across the runway, using radar bombing techniques. The target was cratered and effectively closed to Argentinian high-performance jets. A second attack was carried out by Squadron Leader John Reeve's Vulcan three days later.

After a third mission had been called off due to adverse winds, the Vulcans concentrated their attacks on the Argentinian air-defence radars, using Shrike AGM-45 radiation-homing missiles. Although the first such mission was abandoned when a tanker aircraft suffered a technical failure, Black Buck 5, flown on 31 May, was more successful and two Shrikes were fired. During a follow-up attack on 3 June, a further two Shrikes were fired by a Vulcan's Air Electronics Officer, destroying a Skyguard radar station linked to anti-aircraft guns. The final Black Buck mission was flown on 12 June by Flight Lieutenant Withers. Troop positions and buildings were attacked with radar air-burst bombs. Two days later the Argentinian forces on the Falklands surrendered. In all, six missions were flown.

31 October 1956, came from No. 148 Squadron, which was based at Marham, Norfolk, but operated from Luqa, in Malta, during the Suez crisis. Eventually, a total of 10 units operated the Valiant, including the OCU, and in addition to its bombing role the aircraft was adapted for strategic reconnaissance, electronic warfare and in-flight refuelling.

The second V-bomber in service, the Vulcan, reached No. 230 OCU at Waddington, Lincolnshire, in late 1956, and the first two operational units to form on the type were Nos. 83 and 101 Squadrons. The V-bomber trio was completed by the Victor, which entered service with No. 232 OCU in November 1957. The unit's A Squadron was responsible for training crews for the new bombers, while B Squadron continued operational conversion on the Valiant. No. 10 Squadron formed at Cottesmore, in Rutland, as the first front-line Victor unit in April 1958. Improved versions of both the Vulcan and the Victor, designated Vulcan B. Mk 2 and Victor B. Mk 2 respectively, came into service during the early 1960s, and the V-Force's capabilities were further enhanced by the introduction of the Blue Steel stand-off missile. By 1962 the V-Force had reached the peak of its efficiency, with some 140 bombers in service, grouped in 17 units. More than 100 of these were capable of fulfilling their war mission at a moment's notice.

During periods of political tension, the bombers would be dispersed in groups of four

In order to maintain its effectiveness as a deterrent, the V-Force had constantly to keep ahead of a fast-growing threat from the Soviet air-defence forces. During the early years of its existence, the V-Force was able to rely on the high operating altitude of its bombers to evade enemy interceptors and missile defences. Flying at 50,000ft and above, the V-bombers were beyond the reach of most Soviet aircraft and missiles of the late 1950s. When improved Soviet systems began to enter service in the early 1960s, the V-crews sought to evade them by avoiding heavily defended areas, by using Blue Steel air-to-surface missiles to avoid overflying their targets' defences and, as a last resort, by jamming the radar and communications on which the enemy depended to control his forces. It was in this latter

capacity that the V-crews' AEOs came into their own.

However, it was not only in the air that the V-bombers were vulnerable to attack. As the threat to their bases from Soviet pre-emptive attack increased, measures were implemented to ensure that the V-bombers could not be destroyed on the ground. During periods of political tension, the bombers would be dispersed in groups of four to over 20 airfields scattered throughout the United Kingdom. There they would be maintained on Quick-Reaction Alert (QRA), awaiting the call to scramble. It was estimated that the RAF would receive only four minutes' warning of an Intermediate-range Ballistic Missile (IRBM) attack from the Soviet Union. Yet, within half this time, the V bombers could be airborne and en route to their targets.

Traditionally, bomber operations had been planned well in advance of take-off, with many hours given over to pre-flight briefing before the crews climbed into their aircraft. Clearly, the V-Force was unable to operate in this manner and Bomber Command's commander-in-chief in the late 1950s Air Chief Marshal Sir Harry Broadhurst, was determined to imbue his crews with some of the elan and quick reactions of the fighter pilot. To accomplish this, Broadhurst decided to 'put a jerk into Bomber Command by bringing in a few fighter people like myself.' One of these officers was Air Vice-Marshal Kenneth Cross, who in 1959 succeeded Broadhurst as commander-in-chief. He soon acquired a fearsome reputation as an officer whom only the highest standards would satisfy, and in this respect was somewhat similar to the US Strategic Air Command's legendary General Curtis LeMay. Another fighter pilot to join Bomber Command during this period was Group Captain J.E. 'Johnnie' Johnson, the leading British fighter ace of World War II. He became Station Commander at Cottesmore, and later moved to Headquarters No. 3 Group as Senior Air Staff Officer. This infusion of new blood soon had its effect in Broadhurst's own words, 'It didn't take long for the new philosophy to penetrate.'

By late 1963, the Soviet air-defence forces had been improved and strengthened to such an extent that the V-Force was forced to alter its tactics radically, in order to be confident of reaching its targets in the event of a conflict. This involved descending to low level once the bomber

reached the outer limits of Soviet radar coverage, after which the mission was carried out at a height of a few hundred feet, where radar was blinded by the earth's curvature and the clutter of ground returns. Although such tactics could evade the Soviet air defences of the 1960s, which were designed to operate at high level, it imposed additional strains on the V-bomber crews and their aircraft. In contrast to the smooth air of the stratosphere, low-level flying subjected the aircraft to gusting winds, which not only imposed an unforeseen strain on the bombers' airframes, but also increased crew fatigue and so lowered efficiency. The Valiant, the first of the V-bombers, had to be withdrawn prematurely from service in late 1964 because of airframe fatigue problems, exacerbated by operations at low level. At that time it was providing NATO with a tactical nuclear strike force, in addition to carrying out the strategic reconnaissance and in-flight tanker roles. The first role was taken over by Vulcans, while Victors assumed the latter two.

They had to remain within reach of their aircraft, ready to scramble at a moment's notice

During the mid-1960s, morale in the V-Force was not as high as it had been during the early years. The United Kingdom's nuclear deterrent was due to pass to the Royal Navy's Polaris submarines in 1969, and thereafter the Vulcans were to continue in the tactical nuclear strike role, assigned to NATO. It seemed to the V-Force crews that they had become a forgotten organisation, with none of the press and publicity which had heralded their earlier exploits. Yet the requirements of QRA at this time still demanded great personal sacrifices of the crews. For periods of 24 hours and longer, they had to remain within reach of their aircraft, ready to scramble at a moment's notice, day or night. It was at once a tedious and an exacting duty. Moreover, at a time when the RAF still maintained numerous overseas stations, a V-Force crew might spend its entire career within a 100-mile radius of Lincoln. Despite these tribulations, the crews maintained a high level of efficiency. Nor were their efforts

entirely unappreciated. Julian Amery, Secretary of State for Air 1960-62, paid them the following tribute:

'They are to this country just about what the fighter pilots were to the British people in 1940. They form the elite in the nation. They are trained as an elite. It takes at least five years to produce the captain of a V-bomber and costs about £100,000.'

Once the Polaris submarines had entered Royal Navy service, the Vulcan B. Mk 2s took on the role of a tactical nuclear strike force in support of the NATO and CENTO (Central Treaty Organisation) alliances. Two squadrons were stationed at Akrotiri, Cyprus, to meet the latter commitment, while five remained in the United Kingdom. The surviving Victors were assigned to the in-flight refuelling role. By the spring of 1982 it seemed that the Vulcans would fade quietly into oblivion, with their role being taken over by the RAF's new Tornados. Yet the Falklands conflict in 1982 required the V-bombers to make one last appearance on the world stage. The carefully honed skills of the Vulcan crews, ably supported by Victor tanker aircraft, were admirably demonstrated in the bombing of Port Stanley airfield. They were the longest-range bombing missions ever carried out in the history of warfare.

THE AUTHOR Anthony Robinson was formerly on the staff of the RAF Museum, Hendon, and is now a freelance military aviation writer. His books include *American Air Power* and *Aerial Warfare*.

Following the seizure of the Falklands by Argentina, Vulcan pilots began specialised training for in-flight refuelling and received detailed briefings in preparation for the 'Black Buck' missions. The operations were flown from Wideawake airfield on Ascension, nearly 4000 miles from Port Stanley. Below left: A Vulcan B. Mk 2 taxies past a Wideawake dispersal point. Below: An aerial view of Port Stanley shows the results of bombs dropped by the first Black Buck Vulcan. One of the 21-bomb stick scored a direct hit, landing on the runway centreline.

NILE RAIDERS

In 1942, a detachment of the German Special Forces, the Brandenburgers, set out on Operation Salaam. This was a 2000-mile trek across the wastes of the Sahara, to plant secret agents into Cairo, the nerve-centre of British-held Egypt

THE BRITISH Middle East Command, which included the eastern Mediterranean, was the only area in which ground operations were being carried out against the Axis forces late in 1940 and early in 1941. Operations were mounted against the Italians in 1940, and in the spring of 1941 Mussolini's armies had been reinforced by a German Afrika Korps, commanded by General Erwin Rommel. Within Rommel's arsenal of men and machines poised to engage the British were his invaluable and highly specialised 'Brandenburg' commando teams.

From the middle of 1940 the Axis and British armies had struggled to win total victory, but without success. By the spring of 1942, Rommel was preparing an offensive which he would unleash that summer. But before he could undertake the operation he needed accurate intelligence on the strength and intentions of his enemy – the British Eighth Army. To date, the information which had come to him had proved to be not only inadequate but unreliable. Although there were a great many Egyptians who were prepared to work for German Intelligence, and although British security was often astonishingly lax, the material received by the Afrika Korps was not of a calibre upon which the German commander could confidently base his plan for a drive to the Nile.

Since local and native sources had never produced reliable details, it was decided to infiltrate German agents into British-held Egypt, and so, out of the Afrika Korps' need for accurate information, was born Operation Salaam, which produced the only planting of German spies in Cairo during the desert war. Chief among the problems of infiltrating the two-man team was how the men were to reach the Egyptian capital. British command of the sea and the air ruled out a parachute landing or a ship-borne operation. There remained only the overland route across the desert.

The man who was chosen to guide the team which would 'drop' the agents was Captain Count Almasy. He considered how British Intelligence would anticipate a German insertion operation. The Eighth Army knew that the Germans had no units like the British Long Range Desert Group which could make wide-ranging sweeps. Therefore, any German infiltration would have to be a direct thrust so as to

In April 1942 a column of Brandenburgers guided by Captain Count Almasy left their base in Axis-occupied Libya bound for Assiut in the Nile Valley. Their mission: to insert two German agents into Cairo – well behind British lines. Avoiding Allied patrols took them on a thousand-mile detour through the desert, crossing the barren Great Sand Sea and the thousand-foot high Gilf Kebir plateau. Despite the hostile desert, pushing on regardless of setbacks, the column reached its objective near Assiut. The two agents made their way by rail to Cairo – and Operation Salaam was over.

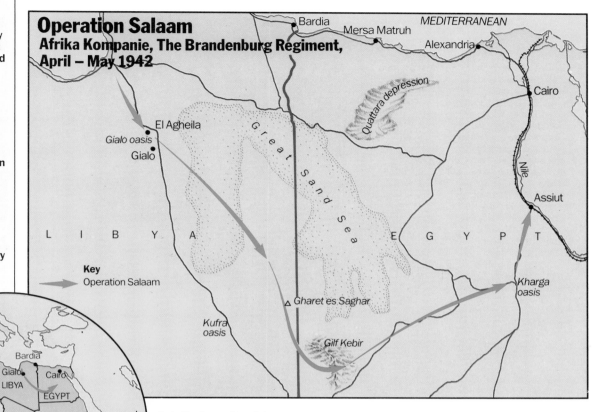

Operation Salaam
Afrika Kompanie, The Brandenburg Regiment, April – May 1942

Key
→ Operation Salaam

Left: Having suffered three casualties in their first attempt, the five remaining members of the Brandenburg team reconnoitre outside Gialo. They are (from left to right) Woermann, Count Almasy, Munz, and the two agents, Sandstetter and Eppler.

cover the shortest and safest route. Thus, Almasy concluded that the British would expect a German infiltration through the battle front which at the time, in the spring of 1942, was fixed and static.

Having made his appreciation, Almasy decided to do the complete opposite. He would take his group on a wide-sweeping, trans-desert route to outflank the British line and to drop the agents near a railway station some 400 miles south of Cairo. His party would undertake a round trip of more than 2000 miles through a waterless desert that was so little explored, so poorly surveyed or mapped and so dangerous that even the Eighth Army's highly experienced desert patrols ventured there only rarely, and then with extreme caution.

Basic items of equipment were often unavailable. Sand channels and sand mats had to be obtained from faraway Berlin

Almasy had impeccable qualifications to lead such an enterprise. In pre-war years he had gained a reputation for daring desert explorations and had, indeed, covered a major part of the route that his group would follow. He and the other seven men of the group were all members of *Abwehr*, the German counter-intelligence organisation, and each had

been selected for his particular specialist skill. They shared, in addition, a common knowledge of desert conditions. Each of them had been individually 'hardened' in the training centre run by the Brandenburg commando formation.

It might have been supposed, given the importance of the mission, that the Salaam detachment would be given the very highest priority in the matter of supplies, but this was not so. Salaam had no transport until lorries were confiscated from a German paratroop battalion that was reluctant to part with them. Basic items of equipment were often unavailable. Sand channels and sand mats had to be obtained from faraway Berlin, together with special radio sets. But if the requisition and supply situation was lamentable, Almasy's route planning was both thorough and totally professional.

At the Salaam base camp near the Mediterranean coast, Almasy explained the plan to his group of eager, well-trained men. There would have to be two journeys: an outward one to 'drop' the agents at the Yapsa pass, and the 'home' run from Yapsa to the Mediterranean. Each journey would be made in two bounds. The Italian-held oasis at Gialo would be the objective of the first bound, and would provide the halfway house where the group could rest and re-provision on the outward and on the home runs. Almasy explained that the five trucks in which the group would travel, British Bedfords and Fords, had been chosen for camouflage as British patrols were active and numerous in the desert below Gialo. The German group would also dress like British soldiers, in khaki drill. Each truck would have painted on it the German straight-sided cross, but this identifying mark would be hidden under sand and mud. If there was a danger of capture, a vigorous brushing would remove the sand to reveal the cross, thus indicating that the group had not been sailing under false colours – a capital offence.

One of the lorries would also carry a white iden-

BRANDENBURG IN AFRICA

The head of the Abwehr, Admiral Wilhelm Canaris, formed the Brandenburg 'Afrika Kompanie' in the spring of 1941. Commanded by Oberleutnant (Lieutenant) von Koenen, a man with wide experience of Africa, it consisted of 60 volunteers selected for their personal resilience, insight into the North African environment and their linguistic capabilities. It was originally intended that the Afrika Kompanie should make short reconnaissance penetrations on behalf of Rommel's Afrika Korps to evaluate the dispositions of the British Eighth Army. With the British on the retreat by June 1942, however, it was planned that they should be infiltrated behind the British lines to seize key bridges over the Nile and the Suez Canal in anticipation of final German victory. Events went strongly against Germany, however, and the Brandenburgs were not deployed. By December 1942 Rommel was beaten back to Tunisia, where Allied troops were waiting to entrap him.

The task of disrupting the British supply lines to their First Army in the Tunisian mountains was entrusted to Brandenburg. Two glider-borne detachments landed to destroy two vital bridges, but they met with disaster and the bridges survived.

Towards the end of the African campaign, Brandenburg units were sent to locate an unoccupied route for withdrawal west into Algeria. Although one patrol succeeded, communications were poor and no advantage was taken. By 6 May Germany was ordering her specialised units out of Africa, but many of the men recruited by Canaris were stranded by lack of transport and taken prisoner.

tifying shield. This was an Eighth Army device to warn sentries or picquets that the vehicle had priority and was not to be delayed. Almásy stressed that fighting was to be avoided at all costs. Only personal weapons would be carried and there would be no room for extra ammunition. All available space in the trucks would be filled with water, fuel, spares and food. In all, five lorries were to be used, a 'fail safe' precaution against vehicle breakdowns or losses.

During the middle of April the group set out from their base on the coast and soon reached Gialo. Final checks were made, compasses tested and then, in the bright, cold dawn of 29 April, the small convoy set out. Within two days it was back in the oasis again. The medical officer had succumbed to desert fever, and Almásy's military commander in the group had suffered a heart attack while digging a truck out of the sand. To complete the toll of disasters, one of the drivers had gone down with dysentery. The Brandenburg team left the three casualties to make their way back to the coast, and set out again on 15 May. Now reduced to five in number, the burden of work on each man would be much increased, but not one doubted that the mission could be accomplished. Almásy had had to amend his original route because the Kufra oasis, where the group had intended to rest, had been captured by Free French forces. The only remaining route was across the wastes of the Great Sand Sea, which stretches eastwards from Gialo almost to the Nile.

It was a journey that few desert-experienced travellers would have undertaken at any time, but to

Top right: The Brandenburg team commandeered five trucks captured from the British. This one is occupied by Afrika Korps infantrymen. Centre right: Agents Hans Gerd Sandstetter (left) and John Eppler before the raid. Bottom right: The Gharet es Saghar.

attempt it in the heat of early summer was an act of madness, excusable only by Rommel's urgent need. The average temperature in the desert in that season of the year rises to well over 115 degrees. The region consisted of great dunes of soft, yielding, clinging sand, which rise to 100ft or more. In the valleys between the dunes there would be patches of firm going, perhaps even a few miles of it, but eventually the firm going would end quite abruptly and the leading lorry would be trapped in the sand. It would first have to be unloaded in order to lighten the vehicle weight. Then the wheels would have to be dug free and metal channels put under them. The driver would ease forward, and the other four men of the group would strain and push the reluctant vehicle, alternately digging and pushing until firm going was reached again. Then the unloaded supplies, spares, food and water would be portered to the truck and reloaded. This was not the end of the exhausting procedure. Each of the trucks had to be moved in the same way. Small wonder then that the total distance covered by the Salaam group on that first day was less than 35 miles – and there were a thousand or more to cover.

Day after back-breaking day the struggle lasted. On the early morning of the third day the group

climbed a large dune and their spirits, already low, were further depressed. For as far as the eye could see, and there was perfect visibility in the cool morning, there was only wave upon wave of sand. There was no tree to break the monotony, no animal life to distract them; only here and there the bones of small birds which had fallen out of the sky, struck dead by the terrible heat. There was no sign of a way through the sea of sand. Yet there was a route, and Almasy was determined to find it. The trucks reconnoitred but found neither a route through nor any firm going. The laborious routine was continued; unload, push, reload. There was no shade except that provided by the scorching lorries. No cool breeze. Bodies, already lean, lost what fat remained. There was a very real danger of dehydration, yet the water had to be conserved: the truck radiators needed constant refilling and every gallon put into the lorries meant less for the team to drink. The monotony, the back-breaking, heart-breaking task of moving the vehicles; the terrible thirst that could not be fully slaked and, finally, the fear – the fear of being lost in this terrible wilderness – would have driven weaker men over the edge and into madness. But the psychological tests carried out before recruitment into Brandenburg proved themselves and the Salaam group remained intact, resolute and sane.

The men had to clear a path by rolling away the smaller boulders, and then slowly ease the trucks around the other unmoveable rocks

For five days the agony continued until Almasy found the hard going he sought. Gradually the dunes became lower and the lorries could get up speed, seeking to make good the time lost in the Great Sand Sea. The ground under the wheels became more firm, firmer still and then became rock. The rock had been scoured by the desert sand until the surface had been cut into low corrugations, and the effect on the vehicle springs can well be imagined. That corrugated causeway led to the Gharet es Saghar. This was a wilderness of boulders so close together that they formed an intricate obstacle course through which vehicles had to be negotiated slowly and carefully. The men had to clear a path by rolling away the smaller boulders, and then slowly ease the trucks around the other unmoveable rocks. All day the convoy picked its way through the Gharet and, at last light, the trucks broke out of this devil's garden.

During the next day Salaam reached the point where the direction had to be changed northeastwards. Ahead lay the Gilf Kebir, a plateau of rock with a huge escarpment rising to well over 1000ft, more than 170 miles long and over 60 miles across. The Gilf had to be crossed. There was no way round it other than to make a long diversion for which Salaam had neither the time nor the fuel.

Almasy had explored the Gilf during a pioneering expedition in 1937, and was soon able to locate not only the El Akwaba pass to the summit, but, more importantly, a cache of water that he had buried during his early exploration. The path to the top of the Gilf was tortuous, at times so narrow that the vehicle wheels were hanging over the edge of the precipice. One of the trucks was lost during the passage. Then came the tiring, deadly task of unloading its freight and distributing it among the other trucks. But now the team worked with new spirit. Almasy had assured them they were nearing the end of the outward journey. Another truck, this one fully laden,

was left at the foot of the Gilf and one, also loaded with fuel and water, had been left in the Gharet. By gradually reducing the number of vehicles not only was fuel saved, but, more importantly, there would be bases in miniature waiting to be used during the equally gruelling 'home' run.

The crossing of the Gilf Kebir was accomplished and ahead lay the next obstacle; the Kharga oasis. The going was good now and the danger came less from the terrain than from British patrols. It was anticipated that they would hold the oasis in strength, to check on those who were crossing the desert. But no, there were no Eighth Army units, only a Sudanese sentry manning his post on the road. Almasy spoke fluent Arabic and had the features and colouring of a native. Allaying the man's suspicions, he was able to explain the significance of the white 'priority' shield and bluff the sentry into allowing them to pass through the checkpoint with minimal delay. The truck drove up the asphalt road which connects the oasis at Kharga with the region of the Nile, and towards the final obstacle – the Yapsa pass. From its summit the Brandenburg men could see, shimmering in the distance, the lush green of the Nile valley. On the summit of the pass the two agents – Eppler and Sandstetter – changed into civilian clothes and headed for the railway station at Assiut to catch the Cairo express. Operation Salaam was over.

Now the difficulties of the return journey faced the three men, and the trip was not without its own incidents. The abandoned lorries were found and their contents reloaded. The vehicles were then burned. In the last remaining truck the three men drove towards Gialo. Eventually each of them sensed that something was wrong. They soon disco-

In 1960 John Eppler was reunited with the man who tracked him down in Cairo, Major A.W. Sansom of Field Security (right). The occasion was the release, in London, of *Foxhole in Cairo,* a film based on their exploits in 1942.

Although a German national, John Eppler was the adopted son of one of Cairo's most aristocratic families. Approached by the Abwehr as a potentially valuable recruit, he undertook numerous important assignments. He organised a network of agents throughout the Middle East, and when the Grand Mufti of Jerusalem (who claimed to be the spokesman of the Palestinian Arabs) was negotiating with Hitler, it was he who acted as interpreter.

vered that magnetic forces in the sand and rocks had caused compass error and they were seriously off course. That night, by astro-navigation, Almasy calculated their position and planned a new route. The wandering away from the correct course had used both fuel and water. The situation was critical but Almasy was confident that something would turn up, and it did. In a valley between two dunes they found a group of lorries; a British ration and water point for the LRDG patrols. The Salaam group helped themselves. Refreshed and refuelled they pressed on, reached Gialo, rested there, then left to arrive only days later at their home base.

The journey had been a success – but the drop had been made in vain. British Intelligence had known that Almasy was in the desert and that he was active. Through top secret intercepts the British had full details of the operation, including the day on which it had begun. Had the German group not been held up at Gialo with its sick members but had left on time as planned, then the whole team would have been caught by British and French desert patrols. The Allies had mounted their own operation, Clap Trap, to intercept and to 'lift' the Salaam group. The whole operation had been 'blown' even before it began. The two agents in Cairo were soon tracked down and arrested. All the strain, the effort, the privation and the misery undergone by the Brandenburg team had been for nothing.

THE AUTHOR James Lucas served with the Queen's Own Royal West Kent Regiment during the North African Campaign and is currently Deputy Head of the Department of Photographs at the Imperial War Museum London.

Head of the German Secret Service, the Abwehr, Admiral Canaris set up a crack special forces unit, the Brandenburg Regiment, in 1939

FROM THE very first days of World War II, the German High Command showed a clear grasp of the importance of special forces to its Blitzkrieg strategy. If the armour and motorised infantry were to advance with lightning speed into enemy territory, they needed control of vital rail junctions, crossroads, tunnels and, above all, bridges. Not even paratroopers could be guaranteed to seize all such objectives before a retreating enemy had time to detonate demolition charges and thus hold up the advance. The only solution was to use guile and subterfuge to infiltrate enemy lines, employing small groups of highly-trained commandos to take and hold key points until the vanguard of the German armour arrived.

By 1939, a force capable of fulfilling this role had been established by the German intelligence and counter-intelligence organisation, the Abwehr. Since January 1935, the Abwehr organisation had expanded rapidly under the decisive leadership of Admiral Wilhelm Canaris, an intelligent, refined officer with a gift for foreign languages and an experience of intelligence operations dating from World War I. Canaris had succeeded in promoting the role of the Abwehr despite competition from the rival SS security service, the SD, led by the notorious Reinhard Heydrich. By 1939, the Abwehr comprised three sections: Abwehr I dealing with espionage and intelligence, Abwehr II covering sabotage and special units, and Abwehr III concerned with counter-intelligence. The special forces that were to become famous as the Brandenburgers naturally came under Abwehr II.

The first commander of these special forces was Captain von Hippel, who had also played a major role in developing the concept. Hippel had observed the value of the commando tactics used by von Lettow Vorbeck in Germany's African colonies during World War I and had also studied the writings of T. E. Lawrence (Lawrence of Arabia). Under Canaris,

Feldwebel, Brandenburg Regiment, Gennap bridge May 1940

This senior NCO has just completed the operation to seize one of the vital crossings over the Maas river. He is carrying a Belgian Army greatcoat and is wearing an enemy field cap. Apart from these items, he is dressed in the standard Wehrmacht uniform of the period. His shoulder straps, piped in black, indicate that he is a member of the engineers. His personal weapons consist of a 9mm MP 38 machine pistol and a single stick grenade, tucked inside his waist belt.

LEHR REGIMENT BRANDENBURG zbV 800

The Brandenburgers originated in a single group of roughly company strength raised by the German Abwehr intelligence organisation in the first half of 1939. The original recruits were drawn from Germans in the Sudentenland area – once part of Czechoslovakia – and the Silesian region of Poland.

Used successfully for special force operations during the invasion of Poland in September 1939, the unit was given formal company status on 25 October as Baulehr Kompanie zbV 800. A rapid expansion followed. By early 1940, three companies were assembled at Brandenburg-am-Havel, west of Berlin, for intensive training in commando and parachute techniques. It was from the name of this town that the title 'Brandenburgers' was taken. After operations in Norway and Denmark during April 1940, the Brandenburgers played a key role in the Low Countries offensive in May.

Left: A Brandenburger poses with some of the paratroopers who stormed the Belgian fortress of Eben Emael.

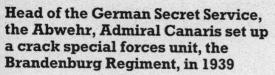

CANARIS'S COMMANDOS

Second Lieutenant Gräbert, infiltrated into Poland. They were disguised as Polish railway workers, and were consequently able to move freely along the Polish rail network without attracting the attention of Polish troops. Arriving at Katowice shortly after the start of the invasion, they rapidly uncovered their concealed weapons and opened fire on the astonished Poles. The deception was so complete that some of the men, speaking perfect Polish, persuaded a body of troops who were fighting their colleagues to board a train which they then drove off into a distant siding. The seizure of the junction was a total success. When General von Rundstedt's troops arrived at Katowice, the railway and its rolling stock fell into their hands in perfect working order.

Not all the operations accompanying the invasion of Poland went this smoothly, however. Other units failed to prevent the Poles destroying the bridges over the Vistula at Dirschau and Graudenz, and their colleagues sent to hold the Jablunka tunnel had an even worse time. Their commander, Second Lieutenant Herzner, never received an order delaying the operation and opened fire hours before the main invasion began. Isolated, the group was forced to retreat across country pursued by Polish troops. Since war had not yet been declared and the Germans still wanted to maintain some diplomatic respectability, Hitler's government issued a statement claiming the men involved were Slovak irregulars.

These failures were soon forgotten, however, when the special forces carried off the apparently impossible task of preventing the destruction of the

Left: Brandenburgers, dressed as civilians, were used to capture key points in enemy territory during the Polish campaign. Far right: Canaris, the founder of Hitler's commandos.

Hippel had set about recruiting and organising a force to be composed almost entirely of Germans who had either lived abroad (in Africa or South America) or came from the German communities around the country's borders – in the Sudetenland area of Czechoslovakia, for example, or the Silesian region of Poland. The reasoning behind this was simple: such men were perfectly versed in the language and customs of another country, and would even be able to pass themselves off as, say, Poles or Czechs. In terms of personal qualities, the main requirements were individualism and self-reliance, imagination and a readiness to use unorthodox methods as and when required. Only volunteers were recruited, to guarantee the level of commitment needed from men who would often be called upon to go into action disguised in foreign uniform or civilian dress, and thus face almost certain execution if captured.

The Brandenburgers uncovered their concealed weapons and opened fire on the astonished Poles

Canaris and von Hippel were both German officers of the old school – conservative, nationalist, but essentially unimpressed by Nazi-style ideological enthusiasm. They stamped their own brand of patriotism upon the organisation, which was to lead them eventually into direct conflict with the Nazi establishment. Yet in the early years of the war, few units were to contribute more to the realisation of Hitler's dreams of conquest.

In 1939, Hippel's men formed a single unit known as the 'German' Company, most of whom were fluent Polish speakers, recruited among the German population on both sides of the frontier with Poland. They were immediately, and spectacularly, put to use on the very first day of World War II – 1 September 1939.

The German forces invading Poland wanted the railway junction at Katowice captured intact. To this end, even before the invasion began, 80 men, led by

The Polish campaign
September 1939

At dawn on 1 September 1939 the invasion of Poland was launched. Nine of Hitler's armoured divisions crossed the border, sweeping through the Polish defences and driving deep into the enemy's rear. Von Bock's Army Group North swept across the Polish Corridor while von Rundstedt's Army Group South pushed east and north to Warsaw. But at Katowice the way had already been prepared by an advance guard of Polish-speaking commandos.

Demblin railway bridge, indispensable to the continuing advance of the German forces after a week of victorious combat. With all-out war now raging, the conditions for clandestine operations had changed. The first requirement was to slip through the front line. All the men selected for the Demblin raid were from Upper Silesia, if anything more fluent in Polish than in German, and they were all scrupulously kitted out in Polish uniforms. Moving through the combat zone, they mingled with a column of soldiers and civilians fleeing in the face of the German advance. There was no attempt at concealment – quite the reverse. Marching in parade ground order and occasionally breaking into a Polish Army marching song, these almost unbelievably impeccable infantrymen must have attracted plenty of attention, contrasting startlingly with the chaos all around them.

Headed by an NCO called Kodon, the force reached the bridge on 10 September. Struggling forward through the crowds of panic-stricken refugees, Kodon located the commander of the Polish pioneers entrusted with the task of blowing up the bridge. Somewhat surprised by the arrival of this fresh unit, the pioneer commander tried to 'phone his headquarters, but the Germans had cut the lines.

At this point, a Stuka raid on the area around the bridge gave Kodon a chance to suggest to his 'colleagues' that they should hand over control of the bridge. The offer was gratefully accepted and Kodon's men found themselves in sole command of the bridge, across which soldiers and civilians were still fleeing in large numbers.

For five long hours, Kodon and his men waited, until at last the first panzers appeared. Immediately, Kodon provoked a panic reaction in the crowd to

clear the bridge – and it was all over. The commandos had nothing more to do than change back into German uniform and prepare for their next mission.

Impressed by these achievements on the Polish front, the German High Command decided to expand and develop the special forces. At the end of 1939, the various commandos, which until then had operated in very loose association with one another, were brought together for training at Brandenburg-am-Havel. From this time forward, they were to be known as the Brandenburgers. Now expanded to battalion strength – and soon to rise to regimental status – the Brandenburgers were put through the

ADMIRAL CANARIS

Leader of the Abwehr, Germany's intelligence and counter-intelligence organisation, from 1935 to 1944, Admiral Wilhelm Canaris was a paradoxical figure, an anti-Nazi who contributed greatly to Hitler's early victories in Europe, and a German patriot who allowed his organisation to become a virtual ally of his country's enemies at war. Born in 1887, Canaris served as a U-boat commander in World War I.

When Hitler came to power in 1933, Canaris was in command of the battleship *Schlesian*. Appointed head of the Abwehr two years later, he rapidly expanded its organisation, but he was opposed to Hitler's plans for war, which he believed would bring disaster to Germany. His relations with the SS intelligence organisation, the SD, deteriorated, although Canaris cultivated a personal friendship with its leader, the notorious Reinhard Heydrich.

As the course of the war turned against Germany, Canaris was increasingly alienated from the Nazi regime. The intelligence performance of the Abwehr fell below any reasonable standard, and some of its failures were very close to treason. By 1944, Canaris was in contact with the conspirators plotting to overthrow Hitler and had allowed them to use the Abwehr's network for their purposes.

On 18 February 1944 all the German intelligence services were unified under SS control, and Canaris was removed from his post. After the unsuccessful attempt to kill Hitler the following July, in which some of Canaris's direct associates were implicated, he was arrested and, on 9 April 1945, he was executed in Flossenburg concentration camp.

'guards' presented themselves to the guardpost on the bridge ten minutes before the planned German attack. At a signal from Walther, the 'prisoners' attacked the guardpost and firing broke out. Three of the Brandenburgers were wounded, but they still needed to take out the second guardpost at the other end of the bridge.

Walther had only two Brandenburgers and the two Dutch accomplices at his disposal, but in the confusion of the moment their subterfuge continued to work. The remaining guards could not decide how to react, seeing that there were men in their own uniform among the group advancing towards them and, while they hesitated, Walther tossed a grenade in their direction and swiftly took control of the detonator set up to ensure the destruction of the bridge.

At this point, the first panzers arrived and began to roll across the bridge. Walther ran towards them, but the tankmen, unaware of the Brandenburgers' mission, took him to be a Dutch soldier and mowed him down with a burst of machine-gun fire. Walther was seriously wounded, but survived to receive the Iron Cross for his part in the mission.

The Brandenburgers' work did not end, of course, when the main invasion started. There was plenty for

most rigorous training. From semi-amateurs, they were turned into highly skilled professionals. With the benefit of the organisation and training, the Brandenburgers were ready for their next major campaign – the invasion of the Low Countries: The Netherlands, Belgium and Luxembourg.

The Netherlands presented an especially acute challenge to the commandos. With its numberless bridges over canals and rivers, the country would be unsuitable for Blitzkrieg tactics unless the Brandenburgers could do their work. Once more, they were in action from the very start. The German offensive was timed for dawn on 10 May 1940, and during the night of 9/10 May the Brandenburgers went in.

Second Lieutenant Walther had instructions to seize the major railway bridge at Gennap, on the Meuse, between the German province of Westphalia and the Dutch province of Brabant. Although The Netherlands was a neutral country, it stood in daily expectation of a German attack. A subtle ruse was needed if the bridge was to be taken and held until the main force arrived.

This time, the Brandenburgers decided to wear German uniforms – but only as part of a more complex deception. Their plan was to pass themselves off as German prisoners. With their weapons carefully hidden, they advanced towards the bridge flanked by accomplices in the uniform of the Royal Dutch gendarmerie – in fact, Dutch Nazis who had volunteered to aid the Germans against their own country. The group of seven 'prisoners' and two

Right: Using a makeshift bridge of duck-boards and rubber boats, German infantry wait their turn to cross the Maas river in Holland on 11 May 1940. The seizure of a number of crossings in the Low Countries was a key part of Hitler's strategy for the Blitzkrieg in the West. The Brandenburgers' training and temperament made them the ideal choice for the assignment. With a mixture of bluff and ferocious aggression, small groups grabbed bridges at Gennap, Roermond and Stavelot. Far right: Waterborne units preparing for Operation Sea Lion – the invasion of Britain. After its cancellation, the Brandenburgers began to train for the attack on Russia.

them to do as the offensive continued across the Low Countries. Second Lieutenant Gräbert soon got chance to make up for his failure on the invasion night when, on 27 May, he was given the task of preventing the opening of the sluice gates at Nieuport. This was an objective of major importance, for the opening the gates would flood a large area of the Yser plain, blocking the German advance – a tactic the Belgians had used very effectively in World War I. The cruc

The campaign in the Low Countries
May 1940

NORTH SEA

NETHERLANDS

Groningen

Amsterdam

The Hague

Utrecht

Deventer

Rotterdam

Arnhem

Waal

Nijmegen

Breda

Gennap

BRABANT

WESTPHALIA

Ostend

Antwerp

Maas

Dunkirk

Nieuport

Ghent

Albert canal

Roermond

Louvain

Rhine

Brussels

Fort
Eben Emael

Maastricht

Aachen

Namur

Liège

Arras

Mons

Sambre

Stavelot

BELGIUM

GERMANY

FRANCE

LUX

Sedan

Ardennes

Only hours before the German offensive in the Low Countries was due to begin, on the night of 9/10 May 1940, German special forces were deployed to secure the invasion routes by seizing bridges and holding them until the arrival of the main invading army. They took the key bridges at Stavelot, Roermond and Gennap; and as the German armoured divisions drove on to the North Sea the clandestine work of the Brandenburgers continued.

pump houses were located on the south bank of the Yser River, alongside the Ostend-Nieuport road bridge.

On 27 May, German forces were close to Ostend and the Belgians were on the brink of surrender. Disguised in Belgian infantry uniforms, Gräbert and a dozen men infiltrated the chaotic mass of fleeing civilians and soldiers around Ostend, driving a captured Belgian Army bus. With considerable difficulty, they finally approached the bridge towards sunset. The south bank was being held by a detachment of British troops, and the bridge had been mined with demolition charges. As the bus drew near to the bridge, the British opened fire. Gräbert's men dismounted, took cover, and changed into German uniform.

When darkness fell, Gräbert and an NCO crawled across the bridge with machine-gun fire slicing the air just above their heads. Inching forwards, they felt for the leads to the demolition charges and cut them as they went. As soon as they reached the other side, the two men opened fire – the signal for the other Brandenburgers to race across into the attack. Using sub-machine guns and hand grenades, the Germans soon cleared the small groups of defenders from their positions. The pump houses and the bridge fell into their hands intact.

With the German victory in the West in the summer of 1940, the first phase of Brandenburger operations came to a close. Their training programmes were set to prepare them for a part in the invasion of England, but this, of course, never materialised. Their next active deployment was in spring 1941, during the German takeover in Yugoslavia and Greece; but in the summer of 1941 they were to face their stiffest test – during Operation Barbarossa, the German invasion of the Soviet Union.

THE AUTHOR Jean Mabire is a military historian who has written extensively on the elite forces of the Third Reich. His most recent works include detailed studies of Wiking, Norland and Charlemagne Divisions of the Waffen-SS.

Left: An American-trained guerrilla army. Anti-Sandinista 'Contra' troops parade at one of their camps on the southern border of Nicaragua. Right: El Salvadorean soldiers are instructed in the use of a 57mm M18 recoilless rifle. Below: With the help of Special Forces personnel, elements of the Honduran Army have been extensively trained in counter-insurgency techniques. Below right: A member of a Mobile Training Team in Panama pinpoints the target during practice on the rifle range.

WAR IN THE BACKYARD

As a result of the communist victories in Southeast Asia during the mid-1970s, the Central American isthmus has become the main stage upon which the East-West Cold War tensions are played out.

US interest in the area began in the 19th century with the building of lucrative coffee and fruit empires, and interest increased after 1914 with the building of the Panama Canal. American military presence throughout the Caribbean was thus steadily built up to consolidate US interests. However, following Fidel Castro's Revolution of 1959 and the Cuban Missile Crisis of 1962, it became increasingly obvious that both the Soviet Union and Cuba saw Central America as an ideal breeding ground for communist insurrection.

The US had already intervened in Guatemala in 1952, when a CIA-organised force had overthrown the reformist government of President Guzman. Military assistance continued and, between 1966 and 1968, US Special Forces aided the Guatemalan regime in a counter-insurgency campaign against rebel guerrillas. US paratroopers and marines were also deployed to the Dominican Republic in 1965, when a civil war between the right-wing junta and rebel forces threatened the security of American residents. Towards the end of the 1970s, the US became increasingly concerned that the instability gripping Central America might spread towards her southern borders. In 1979 a People's Revolutionary Party took control over Grenada, and in the same year President Somoza of Nicaragua was toppled by the Sandinistas.

With El Salvador in the throes of a vicious civil war, the US was determined to confront the perceived communist threat. In the 1980s, this has taken the form of military and economic aid to Honduras and El Salvador, the invasion of Grenada in October 1983, and the training of Contra rebels actively engaged against the Nicaraguan regime.

Whether used as military training teams or as combat units, the Green Berets form the cutting edge of US overseas deployments

'ANYTHING, ANYTIME, ANYHOW, ANYWHERE', the bold motto of the US Special Forces, is as true a description of the work of the Green Berets today as it was of the work of their predecessors, the 1st Special Service Force of World War II. In a precarious nuclear age, this unique breed of soldier has become earmarked for what the Pentagon refers to as 'low intensity conflicts', or in layman's terms – the 'dirty' jobs. By their very nature, the peacetime activities of the Green Berets tend to be conducted under a veil of secrecy. They thus frequently pass unobserved, and even when they are noticed, accurate identification of the specific units involved varies from the difficult to the impossible. Nevertheless, it is known that elements of the Special Forces have been active continuously in various parts of Latin America since the early 1960s, either in direct military operations, usually of a counter-insurgency type, or in training local forces for this role.

The United States Army Special Forces were formed at Fort Bragg, North Carolina, in 1952 by Colonel Aaron Bank, in response to Soviet support of so-called 'liberation movements' in the Third World. The US required a force capable of fighting communist-backed guerrillas on their own terms, and the Green Berets were tasked to fulfil this role.

With the success of Fidel Castro's Cuban Revolution in 1959, the US began to concentrate its efforts in Latin America, and in April 1960 the 8th Special Forces Group (Airborne) was activated at Fort Gulick in Panama, tasked to train Latin American military personnel at the United States Army School of the Americas. In addition, numerous other military missions were set up, beginning in Colombia and expanding into Chile, Venezuela, Bolivia and Guatemala. In the latter two countries, ad hoc teams from the 8th Special Forces Group (SFG) were directly active in counter-insurgency operations. In 1972, when the 8th SFG was deactivated, its functions were taken over by the 3rd Battalion of the 7th SFG.

During the Vietnam War the Green Berets performed an active combat role, and their Civilian Irregular Defense Group programme was used to instruct villagers on how to defend themselves against guerrilla activities. Known variously as 'Sneaky Petes' and 'snake eaters', the Green Berets experienced considerable friction with the regular army establishment, and, in the backlash that followed the war, the defence budget of the Special Forces was cut back disproportionately – despite it being the most highly decorated unit of its size. As one former Green Beret recalled, 'it was just like the phone stopped ringing one day.' The covert association between the Central Intelligence Agency (CIA) and the Special Forces was resented by the the the top army brass, and of 11 groups (13,000 men) in 1969, only seven remained active in 1974. These had been reduced to three (3000 men) by 1980. With America at peace, it seemed as though the 'snake eaters' were no longer needed.

During the 1970s the Green Berets kept a low profile, until the rise in international terrorism forced America to turn once again to the special forces community. In 1977 the 1st Special Forces Operational Detachment D, better known as Delta Force, was drawn from the ranks of the Special Forces Groups and tasked with meeting the new threat.

With the accession of Ronald Reagan to the US Presidency in 1981, the priority given to elite strike forces was dramatically increased. Pointing to the

alarming level of Soviet and Cuban support to guerrilla movements in the Third World, President Reagan and the Pentagon set about creating a military instrument capable of bolstering pro-US forces, and possibly undermining pro-Soviet regimes. Crucial to this was the expansion of the Green Berets. As a 1983 report commissioned by the US Army stated: 'We have come to realise that we cannot slug it out with nuclear weapons and we must prepare for an era when low intensity conflict is the norm.'

There are increasing rumours of SFG units becoming actively involved in a limited combat role

In 1982, the army set up the 1st Special Operations Command (SOCOM) at Fort Bragg, the home of the Green Berets. SOCOM is now responsible for the preparation and deployment of all US Special Operations Forces (SOF) – elite units from the army, navy and air force. In 1985 SOF comprised four Special Force Groups, three Ranger battalions, the 96th Civil Affairs Battalion, one Psyop group, Delta Force and the 160th Task Force of the 101st Army Air Assault Division.

Under Reagan the SOF has experienced a 30 per cent increase in active manpower to the current level of 14,900. By 1990, this level is expected to reach 30,000, with a corresponding increase in specialist technical equipment. In areas where the large-scale deployment of regular troops is politically impossible, the SOF seems certain to become the main combat unit of the future. Within this scenario it is the task of the Green Berets to be ready for rapid deployment anywhere in the world, either as a shock force or as part of a military mission. In the words of Colonel Todd of the 3rd Battalion, 1st SFG, 'anything

In the post-Vietnam era, US military analysts have added an ominous new phrase to the lexicon of war – the 'low intensity conflict' – which has resulted in a renaissance of the role of the Green Berets and other US Special Operations Forces. Although critics argue that this merely increases the risk of being dragged into another Vietnam-style conflict, America's anti-guerrilla army continues to enjoy an unprecedented build up in Central America. Below: US military personnel man a listening post in Honduras, monitoring enemy radio traffic.

we do is directed towards reducing the likelihood of sending US troops into combat.'

At present there are four 776-man SFGs, each with three battalions. The 5th and 7th are based at Fort Bragg, and the 10th at Fort Devens, Massachusetts. The fourth, the 1st SFG, was activated in 1984 at Fort Lewis, Washington, in response to President Reagan's call for an expansion of the anti-guerrilla forces. The current overseas deployment of the Special Forces is as follows: the 3rd Battalion of the 7th SFG is on permanent station in Panama; the 1st Battalion of the 10th SFG is at Bad Tolz in West Germany; and the 1st Battalion of the 1st SFG is located on Okinawa, southwest of Japan. There are also Special Forces detachments in El Salvador, Honduras, South Korea and Berlin. Although the composition of both the South Korea and Berlin detachments is a closely guarded secret, it is known that the latter would go underground and disrupt enemy movements in the event of an invasion by Warsaw Pact forces. Indicating the importance attached to the role of the Green Berets, a further SFG will enter service in 1990.

According to the US Army, the peacetime role of the Green Berets is one of tuition, a task they have performed since early 1959 when units were responsible for the training of South Vietnamese troops. However, there are increasing rumours of SFG units becoming actively engaged in a limited combat role – not surprisingly the US Army is highly sensitive about these 'strike operations' and information on them is scarce. Nevertheless, when a Special Forces unit is employed with an unconventional movement, for example the 'Contras' in the Nicaraguan situation, the formidable fighting skills of the Green Berets will enable them to engage in any type of combat, including guerrilla activities, subversion, sabotage and escape and evasion. Working closely

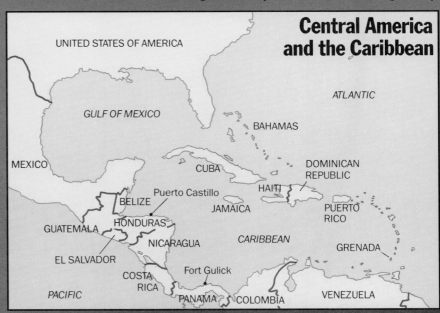

Central America and the Caribbean

UNITED STATES OF AMERICA

GULF OF MEXICO

ATLANTIC

BAHAMAS

MEXICO

CUBA

DOMINICAN REPUBLIC

HAITI

PUERTO RICO

JAMAICA

BELIZE

Puerto Castillo

GUATEMALA

HONDURAS

CARIBBEAN

EL SALVADOR

NICARAGUA

GRENADA

COSTA RICA

Fort Gulick

PACIFIC

PANAMA

COLOMBIA

VENEZUELA

DELTA FORCE

Special Forces Operational Detachment D, better known as Delta Force, was the brainchild of US Army Colonel Charles Beckwith. In 1962-63, while on an exchange programme with the British Special Air Service (SAS), Beckwith became convinced of the need for an American equivalent of the British elite unit.

After years of canvassing support for this project, Beckwith finally succeeded and the Delta Force became operational on 19 November 1977. The crucial factor that had swayed the Pentagon in Beckwith's favour was the alarming growth in international terrorism during the 1970s, tragically illustrated by the outcome of the hostage crisis at the 1972 Munich Olympic Games. Following the basic pattern of the British SAS, Delta is divided into squadrons, which in turn are subdivided into 16-man troops. Selection courses have the accent on individual qualities, and standards are extremely high. For example, snipers must achieve 100 per cent accuracy at 600yds and 90 per cent at 1000yds. Training courses also make extensive use of the 'shooting house', to enable Delta Force to deal with terrorists in a variety of environments without causing injury to hostages or civilians.

After various unit tasks were successfully undertaken, Delta Force was deployed to the Middle East and participated in the ill-fated mission to rescue hostages from the American embassy in Tehran in April 1980. The ultimate failure of the operation was attributed to mechanical difficulties rather than any deficiencies on behalf of Delta Force. Despite the Tehran mission, Delta Force remains the US's most effective weapon against terrorism.

Above: A Green Beret, wearing the badge of the 1st Special Forces Group on his right shoulder, listens attentively as his pupils discuss counter-insurgency strategy. Left: Stalking the target and using camouflage to blend into the terrain. Below left: Two members of a Mobile Training Team on station in Honduras. Below: Salvadorean troops receive weapons training to prepare them for a combat role.

with guerrilla leaders, the Green Berets would be in a position to direct the movement's tactics in a manner that best adhered to the overall strategy dictated by SOCOM.

The task of teaching military techniques to Latin American troops is carried out by Mobile Training Teams (MTTs) of the Green Berets. In El Salvador there are 55 Special Forces military advisers/trainers, with MTTs rotating in and out and providing instruction in weapons usage, tactical intelligence, planning and communication. In short, the instructors can teach anything from firing a rifle to flying a helicopter.

In its 35-year history the School of the Americas had taught over 44,000 military personnel

Green Berets have trained several counter-insurgency battalions that are now considered to be the elite of the Salvadorean Army, an army that has undergone sweeping changes in size, weaponry and professionalism with the help of the US Special Forces. Although the Special Forces Groups are prohibited from entering combat, this policy has only been loosely enforced and instructors have participated in operations with the Salvadorean Army from the outset. This was consistently denied by Washington until 1984, when it was simultaneously announced that the size of the military mission in El Salvador was being doubled. The reports of US forces providing combat support are still increasing, and in October 1984 the *Washington Post* reported that senior US advisers had spent the night at a field command post, deep in the heart of rebel territory, on the first night of a Salvadorean Army offensive.

In 1984 Fort Gulick reverted to Panamanian control under the terms of the Panama Canal Treaty – in its 35-year history the School of the Americas had taught over 44,000 military personnel the techniques of counter-insurgency warfare. In addition, the Panamanian National Guard possessed a US-trained special forces unit that was nominally a company but approached battalion strength. With the winding down of the Panama Canal Zone as the main US military base in Central America, Honduras seems to be have been selected as an alternative. Two hundred members of the 3rd Battalion of the 7th SFG arrived in Honduras in May 1983, to supplement the existing 1400 conventional US troops. They started work immediately, seeking to improve the counter-insurgency capability of the Honduran Army. The Green Berets expanded the existing paratroop/special forces unit from squadron to battalion strength and they continue to engage directly in operations near the Salvadorean frontier. These are known as 'Emergency Readiness Deployment Exercises', and, on one occasion, Green Berets carried out a parachute jump north of the capital, Tegucigalpa, only 20 miles from the Nicaraguan border – in order to demonstrate their rapid deployment capability. The six-month long Operation Big Pine II was another illustration of the close co-operation between the US Special Forces and Central American military personnel, and involved Green Berets from the 7th SFG, stationed at Fort Bragg and Fort Gulick. The next major exercise, codenamed Cabanas, was carried out in June 1986 and was reported to involve US, Honduran and Contra troops.

By mid-1986, the Regional Military Training Center at Puerto Castillo, on the Caribbean coast of Honduras, which had been established in 1983, had

Left: Supervised by Special Forces personnel, troops pour out of a C-130 Hercules transport during a rapid deployment exercise in Honduras. Below: Getting to grips with para techniques.

In addition to their formidable combat skills, the Green Berets are expected to acquire a comprehensive working knowledge of their equipment, an inventory that amounts to over 80 types of weapon. Below left: A military adviser explains the intricacies of the M16 rifle to Honduran soldiers at the Regional Military Training Center. Below: A Salvadorean trooper receives instruction on the use of the M79 grenade launcher.

trained over 10,000 Salvadorean and Honduran troops. Mobile Training Teams have also been sent to Costa Rica, Belize and Guatemala, and Special Forces personnel are known to have engaged in several covert counter-insurgency operations in close collaboration with the CIA. Secrecy remains paramount in most of the Special Forces activities; for example, during Operation Quail (an exercise conducted at the Honduran Army's Special Forces Command at La Venta), the Green Berets arrived in civilian clothes under orders to stay away from any other US military personnel stationed in the area.

With regard to Nicaragua, the role of the Special Forces looks certain to expand during the next decade. Since the triumph of the left-wing Sandinista Revolution in 1979, the US has increasingly seen Central America as the battleground between democracy and communism. American aid to the Nicaraguan rebels – the Contras – began in 1981, comprising weapons, funds and training. It was essentially a CIA operation, but there were suspicions that Special Forces personnel were lending covert assistance. Indeed, while the CIA is subject to American legislative control, the activities of the Special Operations Forces are not accountable directly to Congress – a factor that adds to the secrecy surrounding SOF operations. Due to Congressional pressure, aid was terminated in 1984, only to be resumed in June 1986 in the form of a military package worth 100 million US dollars. Now that further assistance seems likely, President Reagan has stressed that the strength of the Green Berets should be increased in order to train greater numbers of the Contras at bases in Honduras, El Salvador

or even in the United States itself. Both Reagan and the Pentagon see this as the only way of counterbalancing the training afforded to Sandinista troops by Cuban military advisers.

The unorthodox conflicts in which the Green Berets operate require a special type of soldier: bold, resourceful and highly trained. Despite changes in command structure on the higher level and the gathering together of America's elite forces under the umbrella of a joint agency (SOCOM), the traditional role of the Green Berets as counter-insurgency and counter-revolutionary warfare combatants remains at the heart of the Special Forces concept – as their activities in Central America clearly demonstrate. The Green Berets are engaged in the protection of 'America's backyard', in addition to maintaining combat readiness for deployment to any corner of the globe. In the light of this, the training of Special Forces personnel remains as tough as ever.

The Green Berets remain an integral and increasingly active element in the US order of battle

All potential recruits must be airborne qualified, and acceptance into the unit is dependent upon the completion of a gruelling 16-week course at the Special Forces School in Fort Bragg. Following a 31-day examination of the candidate's basic military skills, he must demonstrate his SERE (Survival, Evasion, Resistance and Escape) capability during a three-day manhunt. The course then continues with each man specialising in two of five skills: weaponry, engineering, communications, medicine and intelligence. This cross-training ensures that valuable skills will not be lost in the event of one of the team being killed during contact with the enemy. In the final five weeks of the course, the recruits are grouped together into 'A' Teams – the combat units of the Green Berets.

These teams are then parachuted into the forests of North Carolina, where they pit their skills against the 'aggressor' forces from the 82nd Airborne Division. Gathering about itself a group of 'natives' (random selection of soldiers), the A Team must hone this unlikely looking force into a capable guerrilla unit within one month. Not surprisingly, the failure rate is high, often as much as 77 per cent.

The Green Berets are undoubtedly a warrior elite, yet, as US experience in Central America clearly shows, they can only be as effective as the local forces they have trained. The current situation faithfully mirrors that of Vietnam during the tragic US involvement in that country, for although the US-trained counter-insurgency forces are militarily effective in the short term, the problem remains ultimately a political one.

In the meantime, the Green Berets, along with the other Special Operations Forces, form the scalpel of overseas deployments – in preference to the blunter tools of conventional warfare. Whether used as storm troops in a hostage rescue mission, as military training teams in a low intensity conflict, or as the 'guerrilla' element in any future struggle, the Green Berets remain an integral and increasingly active element in the US order of battle.

THE AUTHOR David Esler is a freelance journalist who has written a number of articles on United States involvement in Central America.

FORTRESS CRETE

With Crete earmarked as a refuelling and support station for the Allied campaign in Greece, the island's population was swelled by the arrival of 42,000 British troops following the collapse of the Macedonian front in April 1941. Possession of Crete, however, would provide German planners with air and sea bases capable of threatening Allied operations in the Middle East and on 20 May 22,000 German troops invaded the island. By 2 June the garrisons at Retimo, Heraklion and Maleme had been taken, forcing the Allies to evacuate to Egypt. However, German losses in the airborne invasion were so severe that plans to use Crete as a base for further airborne operations were dropped. Instead, a garrison of 30,000 troops remained on the island as a deterrent to Allied intentions in the Balkans. Although Cretan resistance to the occupying German forces failed to reach the same scale as that on the Greek mainland, the partisans never totally succumbed to their oppressors. Guided by SOE agents and Leigh Fermor, they set up a chain of safe-houses and radio stations, affording shelter to members of the resistance and enabling them to monitor German troop movements. Letters could be carried by partisan 'runners' if the use of radio was deemed too dangerous.

In February 1944, Irish Guards Major Leigh Fermor successfully kidnapped the German general Heinrich Kreipe from the occupied island of Crete

IT WAS BITTERLY COLD and dark in the Wellington bomber as it left Egypt and roared its way through the night across the southern Mediterranean, heading for Crete. But four men, crouched in the flimsy canvas seats bolted to the deck of the aircraft, had little thought for this; all their attention was riveted to the crazy mission that lay ahead. Leading this unlikely-looking four-man team was Major Patrick Leigh Fermor, with Captain Billy Stanley Moss as his second-in-command. The other two men were Cretans, Manoli Paterakis and Georgi Tyrakis, both of whom were experienced agents of the SOE, the British Special Operations Executive. It was the night of 4 February 1944, and their mission was no less than to kidnap General Wilhelm Müller, commander of XXII Bremen Panzer Division based at Heraklion in Crete.

KIDNAPPED

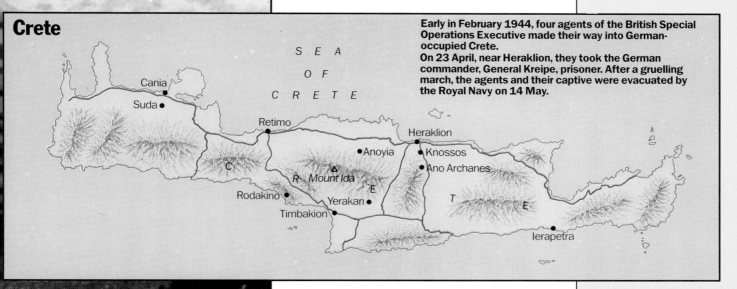

Crete

S E A
O F
C R E T E

Cania
Suda
Retimo
Heraklion
Anoyia
Knossos
Ano Archanes
C
R
Mount Ida
E
Rodakino
Yerakari
T
E
Timbakion
Ierapetra

Early in February 1944, four agents of the British Special Operations Executive made their way into German-occupied Crete.
On 23 April, near Heraklion, they took the German commander, General Kreipe, prisoner. After a gruelling march, the agents and their captive were evacuated by the Royal Navy on 14 May.

A highly efficient, but brutal officer, Müller had masterminded the Brandenburgers' capture of the British garrison on Leros in November 1943. During his rule over Crete, Müller had acquired a fearsome reputation as he subjected the population to torture and forced labour, and ordered the wholesale destruction of villages in retaliation against the resistance fighters. Should the kidnappers succeed, it would lower the morale of the German forces in the area and boost the confidence of the Cretans.

Below them lay the jumping zone, the Lasithi Plain, surrounded by desolate mountains. Known locally as the 'Valley of a Thousand Windmills', the plain was situated in the heart of the 169-mile-long island of Crete. The order came, 'Stand by to jump!' A gap in the mist, the green light flashed on, and Leigh Fermor flung himself into the blackness of the aircraft's slipstream. At the first tug of his chute opening, he glanced upwards over his shoulder, but the aircraft was already hidden in a thick mist. Despite several attempts, the pilot was unable to drop the three other agents, and the young major drifted down alone to his rendezvous with the partisans waiting below. They hurried him to one of their huts, where he was soon warming himself by an olive-wood fire, gulping down raki, a fierce local brew distilled from vine leaves.

Leigh Fermor was confined to the hut for two months before being joined by his companions. Further attempts at a parachute drop had been foiled by dense ground fog, and it was eventually decided to send the rest of the team by boat, with arms and equipment for the operation dropped by air. This meant a two-day trek to the southern shore of the island beyond Kastamonitza. As they landed from their rubber dinghy, the three other agents were greeted with the news that their target had been altered. General Müller had been replaced by General Heinrich Kreipe, newly arrived from the Russian front. Travelling by night and hiding among the olive groves during the day, they trudged their way up the mountainous slopes towards Kastamonitza, where they were to lodge in the security of a shepherd's cave.

Far left: General Kreipe, having commanded divisions on the Leningrad and Kuban sectors of the Russian front, was awarded the Knight's Cross and transferred to Crete for a 'rest cure'. Left: A heavily armed German unit scours the Cretan countryside in pursuit of the partisans.

FREELANCE WARFARE

The Special Operations Executive (SOE) was established in 1940 as an independent secret service responsible to the minister for Economic Warfare. Its purpose was to encourage, organise and supply the partisan groups that existed in countries under German occupation. On the creation of SOE, Churchill commented: 'And now set Europe ablaze.' SOE missions were set up in Lisbon, Stockholm, Berne and Cairo, to guide counter-espionage and guerrilla warfare.

Divided into six sections, the SOE despatched over 1800 agents during the war, with top priority given to the Greek islands, Crete, the Balkans, central Europe and France.

Recruitment was strictly informal, with potential agents being approached following a careful assessment of their suitability. Training was closely related to techniques that would be required in the field: parachuting, explosives, firearms, reconnaissance, radio operation and forgery. On Crete itself, the SOE established a communications network in direct contact with Force 133 at the Cairo mission. Some agents were volunteers from the army, equipped with a special knowledge of the area, while others, such as Paterakis and Tyrakis, were native to the island and specially trained at SOE bases in Britain.

The second night of the march found them at Skonia, a remote mountain village, free of Germans, where they were feasted in a taverna. Black olives, feta cheese and the inevitable roast lamb was washed down with raw red wine, ouzo and raki. Toast followed toast in the Greek fashion and it soon developed into a party as the whole population of the hamlet, including the two village policemen, trooped in to greet the agents. At Kastamonitza, which they reached at daybreak, it was a different story. There they spent their time behind tightly shuttered windows, constantly on guard; the village was crawling with German soldiers from a convalescent home that had recently been set up there.

While they were lying low in Kastamonitza, Micky Akaumianos, the chief SOE officer on the island, arrived with false papers and passports. The following day, he and Leigh Fermor took the local bus to Heraklion, the capital. Meanwhile, Moss and a group of partisans were to set up base in the rugged mountains above the village. Heavily disguised as local Cretan countrymen, Leigh Fermor and Akaumianos arrived safely at Heraklion and walked the four-and-a-half miles to Knossos. Here General Kreipe had his headquarters in the Villa Ariadne, built by Sir Arthur Evans, the British archaeologist who had excavated the ancient palace. Now, surrounded by barbed wire with four guard posts, and patrolled by guards armed with machine pistols, the villa was a daunting place – hardly a candidate for a direct assault.

'I then shouted, "Hande hoch" with one hand thrusting the automatic against his chest...'

Akaumianos and Leigh Fermor stayed with the Cretan's parents, who lived in a farm adjoining the villa, while they closely observed the general's movements and the routine of the guards. It soon became obvious that any kidnapping attempt would have to take place during one of the general's frequent excursions from the Villa Ariadne and, eventually, they hit on a bold plan to snatch Kreipe when he was returning at night from the officers' mess at Ano Archanes, 12 miles from the villa. The kidnappers decided upon a hair-pin bend on the Ano Archanes road, where Kreipe's Opel would have to slow down to a walking pace.

Meanwhile, Moss and his partisans, an ill-disciplined crew, shaggily-dressed in sheepskins and armed to the teeth, had made their headquarters in a cramped, damp cave, high on the mountainside, where each day they were supplied with food and drink by nearby shepherds. On Easter Sunday, Leigh Fermor and Akaumianos joined them and set out the detailed plan. Moss and Leigh Fermor, dressed in German military-police uniforms supplied by Akaumianos from some mysterious source, would set up a road block at the hair-pin bend and stop the general's car. After effecting the snatch, Kreipe would be bundled back into the car and from there they would have to bluff their way past any sentry points they encountered while travelling through Heraklion. The partisans, under their leader, Bourdzalis, would be responsible for looking after any German patrols in the area. The Opel would finally be abandoned and the group would continue their journey to the south coast on foot, where they were to be picked up by a British naval launch. That night they moved to the small village of Skalini, three miles from the point of the kidnapping. Here, Leigh

Fermor was forced to dispense with Bourdzalis and his men, who could not be prevented from roaming about the countryside, attracting attention and alerting the whole area.

At 1730 hours on 26 April, the two Englishmen, sporting close-cropped hair and German uniform, set up their road block. Several hundred yards up the road Paterakis, Tyrakis, Akaumianos and the more disciplined partisans lay in wait, ready to warn the agents of the Opel's approach. The time was 2130. On a signal from the partisans they leapt from their position, waving their red lamps, and shouting for the car to halt. Walking calmly to his appointed door, Leigh Fermor was able to recognise the Knights Cross on Kreipe's uniform. Kreipe reached for identification. As Leigh Fermor later wrote:

'I opened the door with a jerk – the cue for the others to break cover – and the inside of the car was flooded with light. I then shouted, "Hande hoch" [Hands up] with one hand thrusting the automatic against his chest and the other pulling him out of the car.'

With strict formality, Leigh Fermor informed his captive, 'General, you are a prisoner of war in British hands.' The astonished Kreipe was quickly overpowered, trussed up by Paterakis and Tyrakis, and tossed into the back of the car. A knife at his throat ensured his silence.

The kidnapping had gone off without a hitch, over within 70 seconds, and at 22 control points the officer of the guard saluted at the sight of the general's pennant on the car and waved them through. Moss was at the wheel and Leigh Fermor sat beside him muffled in Kreipe's greatcoat and cap. At the Retimo crossroads Kreipe was unceremoniously bundled out of the car and marched along a goat track towards Anoyia by Moss and the two Cretans. Before following, Leigh Fermor drove the car a mile or so down the road to the beach, abandoning it with a letter stating that General Kreipe had been kidnapped by British commandos, without any assistance from the Cretan population, and was on his way to Cairo. For authenticity he left a green beret, a number of Players cigarette stubs and an Agatha Christie novel in the Opel. The following day the BBC were to broadcast that General Kreipe was on his way to Cairo, in a further attempt to throw the Germans off their trail.

Once it had been established that the general was indeed missing, the German authorities swung into action. The 30,000 troops on Crete were thrown into an island-wide search, with Fieseler Storchs combing the known mountain haunts of the partisans. A hastily put together and savage leaflet was distributed throughout Crete. General Bauer had taken command of the German garrison, and he was convinced that his predecessor was being held in one of the villages around Heraklion. The leaflet threatened that unless General Kreipe was released within three days, these villages would be razed to the ground.

The discovery of the abandoned Opel, coupled with the BBC announcement, deceived the Germans for a short time and the search was called off, but when one of their agents reported that Kreipe was still on Crete, the hunt was on again.

With a grumbling General Kreipe, the team made their way to Anoyia through rough country, reaching

the village at dawn on 27 April. The day was spent resting, and at sunset the kidnappers left the village and continued their climb up Mount Ida, towards the snow line. Marching until dawn before pausing at one of the partisans' caves, they received news that German infantry had been deployed on the eastern foothills and were beating their way upwards in a tight line towards them. A local shepherd led them to a damp, winding cave, where they spent a miserable night, huddled together for warmth and within earshot of the German patrols.

At first light on the 28th they were once again heading south, hardly cheered by the partisans' news that German troops had rushed in that direction and were now strung along the whole of the southern coast. From their next hiding place, a beehive-shaped shepherd's hut, they learned of a radio report from Cairo that on 2 May and each of the following four nights a British commando force, waiting

Below: Mount Ida's daunting snowline, over which the kidnappers were forced to climb (left). Above left: A disconsolate General Kreipe, flanked by Captain Moss (left) and Major Leigh Fermor (right). Above right: The general's escorts, partisans and officers. The tall, striking figure is SOE operative Manoli Paterakis. Leigh Fermor and Moss are sitting to his left.

offshore, would be ready to land on a south coast beach and clear a passage for the kidnappers. They were only a few hours march from the coast, all downhill, and it looked as if their hair-brained mission would succeed after all. Then they received a disturbing report: a traitor among the partisans had passed details of this plan to the Germans, and a force of 200 troops had been transferred to Saktouria, a village close to the escape beach. The commandos would be sailing straight into a trap. On 4 May Leigh Fermor and Tyrakis left for the nearest SOE radio post to warn Cairo that their intended escape route was blocked.

Since the southern slopes were packed with German infantry, Moss and his party moved westwards with the general, desperately trying to locate an unguarded beach which could be used as a pick-up rendezvous. If one was found, they would radio the position to Leigh Fermor who would contact Cairo and arrange for a fast naval launch. They soon discovered that the way west was cut off by large German search parties, and were forced to hide out for 24 hours. They then had no choice but to break out before they were completely surrounded. After several nightmare hours playing hide-and-seek with

A MAN WITH A MISSION

Patrick Leigh Fermor enlisted in the Irish Guards in 1939, having travelled for four years in central Europe, the Balkans and Greece prior to the outbreak of war. Promoted to lieutenant in 1940, his fluency in Greek and German, combined with a first-hand knowledge of the area, were key factors in his appointment as a Greek Liaison Officer. Serving with distinction in the Greek and Crete campaigns, Leigh Fermor remained on Crete after the Allies evacuated in 1941. With the support of SOE agents, he stayed for two years, helping to organise the local partisans in clandestine operations against the occupying German forces.

In 1943 he was promoted to major. In July of that year, only days before the Allied invasion of Sicily, he led a force of 23 SBS commandos in an attack against Crete's three airfields. This action helped to reduce the Luftwaffe's capacity to strike against the invasion force at Sicily, some 480 miles to the west.

Following in the fine British tradition of 'freelance warfare', the daring scheme to kidnap the German commander on Crete had been concocted during a cocktail party in Cairo by Leigh Fermor himself and a young captain in the Coldstream Guards, William Stanley Moss.

Leigh Fermor was awarded the DSO in 1944 in recognition of his work in Crete, and towards the end of the war he became a team commander in the Special Allied Airborne Reconnaissance Force operating in northern Germany. Well-known and much-loved by the Cretan partisans, Leigh Fermor was made an Honorary Citizen of Heraklion in 1947.

Above: Leigh Fermor and Micky Akaumianos.

Below: For General Kreipe, the war is over. The general, perhaps astonished at the bravado of his captors, offered little resistance during the hide-and-seek with German patrols which followed his kidnap. Despised by the partisans, the general was well aware of his fate should the kidnap attempt fail. Seen here bidding farewell to his escorts upon arrival at Mersa Matruh, Kreipe's right arm is in a sling following his stumble on the slopes around Rodakino.

With the Allies poised on the Gustav Line in Italy, waiting for a breakthrough, and plans for Operation Overlord already well advanced, British Headquarters in the Middle East had readily agreed to Leigh Fermor's bold scheme. Even had the mission failed, it may still have misled the German General Staff as to Allied intentions in the Balkans. As it turned out, the major's inspired efforts were rewarded by success.

stumbled, throwing the general and breaking his right shoulder. The precious time lost in patching him up made it touch-and-go whether they would rendezvous with the launch in time; its commander would certainly linger as little as possible in such enemy-infested waters. With a Cretan partisan going ahead to warn them of searching patrols, they took a long route through the mountain in order to avoid the tight German net stretched along the coast.

On the night of the 14th they were scrambling noisily down the rubble of a steep cliff to the escape beach; to their stretched nerves, the racket must surely be heard by every German within miles. Minutes after signalling the boat, which they hoped would be waiting offshore, they heard the sound of a launch's engines – friend or foe? There was the crunch of a rubber dinghy on the beach, and they were surrounded by black-faced commandos. 'Major Leigh Fermor?' came a voice from amongst them. Without ceremony, they were hurried into the dinghy and paddled out to the launch, which was waiting with engines throbbing. The anxious commander gave the order to open up the engines and they were on their way to Egypt, bounding through a more than choppy sea; flat out, nothing could catch them now.

Leigh Fermor and his team had pulled off a seemingly impossible kidnapping. They were met at Mersa Matruh, where Colonel Bamfield, CO of the commandos, officially received General Heinrich Kreipe. The war had ended for him, and he sat out the rest of it as a prisoner of war near Calgary in Canada.

THE AUTHOR Bernard Brett left the Royal Navy at the end of World war II, and has since written several books on ships, sea power and naval warfare. He is currently preparing a history of modern sea power.

searching patrols, they reached the remote village of Yerakari at the foot of Mount Ida.

By now, the unfit General Kreipe was totally exhausted and unable to travel any further on foot, so a mule was found to carry him up the steep mountain tracks to yet another lonely shepherd's hut. On 13 May Leigh Fermor arrived with the welcome news that an unguarded beach had been located and that a Royal Navy launch would rendezvous there to pick them up at 2200 hours on the following night. Once again they set off, scrambling down treacherous mountain tracks, making for Rodakino. At a particularly precipitous stretch of loose shale, the mule

In 1970, the US Special Forces led a daring attempt to free American prisoners held by the North Vietnamese

WHEN, ON 9 May 1970, an NCO of the USAF's 1127th Field Activities Group (1127th FAG), a special intelligence unit that correlated information about American POWs in North Vietnam, spotted what appeared to be a prison full of American POWs at Son Tay, some 37km west of Hanoi, from reconnaissance photographs, he started a chain of events that would eventually lead to one of the most daring

When intelligence reported that American POWs were being held at Son Tay in the heart of North Vietnam, the US Special Forces mounted an unprecedented rescue operation. After months of meticulous preparation, the attack was carried out on the night of 20/21 November. Below: As the assault teams raced for the objective, 7.62mm miniguns were used to blast the prison guards from their positions.

Special Forces operations of the entire war. Once the Joint Chiefs of Staff had evaluated the information from the 1127th FAG and decided that a rescue was desirable, both for the well-being of the prisoners and for the morale of American fighting men and civilians, the go-ahead was given for SACSA (the Special Assistant for Counter-insurgency and Special Activities), Brigadier-General Donald Blackburn, to begin planning a rescue mission to free the POWs held at Son Tay.

Various photo-intelligence sources, including the Big Bird reconnaissance satellite, the SR-71 Blackbird and Buffalo Hunter reconnaissance drones, were also made available to gather the information necessary for the raid. By 5 June, a full briefing had been given to the Joint Chiefs, and Blackburn had received permission to continue planning the raid. A little over a month later, on 10 July, the Joint Chiefs gave Blackburn the OK to begin implementing the plan.

Blackburn, a real fire-eater who had commanded Philippine guerrillas during World War II and the Special Operations Group in Vietnam, wanted to lead the raid himself, but because of his knowledge of sensitive intelligence matters he was precluded. Instead, the assignment went to Colonel 'Bull'

SON TAY
SON TAY RAIDER

The Special Forces deployed two types of helicopter in the Son Tay raid: the HH-53 Super Jolly Green Giant, and the HH-3 Jolly Green Giant. Built by Sikorsky, the HH-53 was designed as a heavy assault transport helicopter and when the machine entered service in late 1967 it was the fastest and most powerful helicopter in the USAF. Despite a maximum weight of 19,050kg when fully loaded with either 37 troops or 24 litters and four attendants, the HH-53 has a range of 870km when fitted with auxiliary fuel tanks and a speed of 300km/h at sea level.

During the attempt to free the prisoners, Super Jolly Green Giants were used in a fire-suppression role to take out enemy guard towers around Son Tay prison's perimeter wall. The HH-53s were fitted with three 7.62mm miniguns. Like the HH-53, the Jolly Green Giant was also designed by Sikorsky. A twin-engined all-weather search and rescue helicopter, the HH-3's first flight took place in 1963. Fully loaded, with a crew of four and up to 30 troops or 2270kg of cargo, the HH-3 has a maximum range of around 1000km. Operating from Udorn in Thailand or out of Da Nang in South Vietnam, the Jolly Green Giant was capable of reaching any part of the North and making the return journey.

During the Son Tay raid, the assault force's helicopters were refuelled during the flight to the objective. Below right: A Super Jolly Green Giant links up with an HC-130P version of the Hercules to replenish its fuel tanks.

Simons, a highly experienced Special Forces officer who had served under Blackburn and had a reputation for getting things done. The raiding force was known as the Joint Contingency Task Group (JCTG), and the mission itself was code-named Ivory Coast. An area of Eglin Air Force Base in Florida was set aside for training the JCTG. Although Major-General Leroy Manor, the commander of USAF special operations at Elgin, was put in overall command, Simons was his deputy and in charge of leading the raiding force.

Since the optimum time for the raid appeared to be between 20/25 October, when the weather and moon would be most favourable, both men began selecting their teams: Manor, the air and planning elements, and Simons, the actual assault force. At Fort Bragg, hundreds of Special Forces troopers volunteered for the JCTG only knowing that it was hazardous and that the 'Bull' would be commanding. Some 15 officers and 82 NCOs, predominantly from the 6th and 7th Special Forces Groups were chosen. As training progressed, the assault force, their back-ups, and the support personnel would be selected from these 97 Green Berets.

To carry out realistic training, a mock-up of the Son Tay compound was built at Eglin. So that Soviet spy satellites could not detect its presence, the mock-up was designed to be dismantled during the day and quickly set up at night for training. Since the raid itself would be at night, training at night on the mock-up was essential. As an additional training aid, a table-top model of the camp, costing some 60,000 dollars, was also built.

Detailed training of the raiding force began on 9 September. Two problems involving the elimination of guards at the prison arose during this period. Simons was dismayed to find that even his best marksmen were having trouble getting more than 25 per cent of their shots on target at night. This difficulty was solved, however, by going outside the normal Army supply channels to acquire 'Singlepoint Nite Sites' for the sharpshooters' M16s. The other problem involved the need to saturate the guard towers around the Son Tay compound with fire. To solve this problem an HH-53 Super Jolly Green Giant equipped with 7.62mm miniguns was given the mission of chopping the towers down with a hail of fire.

The assault force was formed into three groups: the compound assault force of 14 men, who would actually be deposited inside the prison compound by crash landing an HH-3 helicopter: the command and security group of 20 men; and the support group of 22 men commanded by Simons himself. Five HH-53s, which could be refuelled in-flight and the HH-3 would carry the assault force.

Beginning on 28 September, the assault force practised the actual assault with the air force crews

Son Tay
US Special Forces, 21 November 19[70]

In the early morning of **21 November 1970** a crack as[sault] group of US Special Forces staged a daring raid on a N[orth] Vietnamese POW camp only 23 miles from Hanoi. The POWs they hoped to free had been moved out – but th[e raid] was executed with verve and the force pulled out with[out] suffering a single serious casualty.

Song C[...]

The Son Tay Assault

Meadows' assault force

Son Tay POW camp

Sydnor's force

Son Tay City

Song Con

Canal

Simons' support group

'Secondary School'

'U/I Light Industry'

① ②

Key

→ Son Tay assault force

North Vietnamese POW camps

Assault force helicopter landing zones

Opium Den

Beer House

Cat House

Compound

Guard Tower

who would fly the helicopters and other aircraft, which included three C-130s (two of which were Combat Talons equipped for command and control) and A-1 strike aircraft. The landing and assault were rehearsed again and again, with many simulations being 'live-fire' run-throughs. Alternative plans were also produced in case one of the three teams failed to make it to the target.

As the rehearsals progressed, Simons, a firearms enthusiast and expert, ordered his supply people to come up with additional weapons and special equipment. Eventually, the teams were equipped with 12-gauge shotguns, 30-round M16 magazines, .45 automatic pistols, CAR-15s for the compound assault force, M-79 grenade launchers, LAWs, bolt cutters, cutting torches, chainsaws, and special goggles.

The Son Tay raiders

18 Nov 0300 The Son Tay assault force arrives at Takhli air force base in Thailand. The order to go ahead with the raid is given.

20 Nov The raiders transfer to Udorn air force base.

2318 The Son Tay raid is launched as the HH-53 helicopters and C-130 tankers leave Udorn.

21 Nov A-1 attack aircraft and a C-130 Combat Talon guide-plane leave Nakon Phanom and US Navy aircraft are launched from the Gulf of Tonkin to begin diversionary raids.

0218 (Son Tay time) An HH-53 gunship helicopter strafes the guard tower of the Son Tay compound. As the assault group goes in, Simons' support force lands 400m to the south at a military installation mis-identified as a 'secondary school'.

PRISONERS

During the dozen years of direct US involvement in Vietnam some 800 Americans were held captive by the enemy. The majority of the prisoners were aircrews shot down during raids over North Vietnam. The US captives were placed in several camps scattered throughout the North and their living conditions, although generally harsh and sometimes brutal, were survivable.

The North Vietnamese held the view that the prisoners were not POWs but criminals and that their treatment was 'lenient and humane'. Punishment, they argued, was only inflicted on men displaying an 'unprogressive or reactionary' attitude.

The US government was always trying to secure the release of the captives but, despite their softly-softly approach, negotiations were made difficult by Hanoi's reluctance to admit the presence of their troops in South Vietnam. Captives were occasionally released as in the late 1960s when three groups of three men were freed.

In 1970, US Special Forces launched the only attempt to free prisoners held in the North. Although the camp at Son Tay was empty, the raid forced Hanoi to improve the conditions of the captives. After President Nixon's 1972 visits to China and the USSR, and the failure of the North's spring offensive, representatives of both sides met during the Paris peace talks and agreed a timetable for the repatriation of prisoners.

The exchange of captives began in February 1973, just a month after the peace accords were signed.

Over the next two months, some 600 US prisoners were released. It is known that over 70 Americans died in prison and that, although escape attempts were common, only 30 men successfully evaded their pursuers.

Some men carried cameras to record the prisoners' living conditions. Many items used in the raid had to be acquired outside of the normal Army supply channels. To ensure communications during those critical minutes on the ground, the 56 men of Simons' assault force were given 92 radios: two AN-PRC-41s to maintain contact with the Pentagon via a radio link at Monkey Mountain in South Vietnam, 10 AN-PRC-77s for calling in air strikes, 24 AN-PRC-88s for communications between the various groups on the ground, and, finally, 56 AN-PRC-90 survival radios for escape and evasion.

Although the mission had not been approved by the target date of 20/25 October, Blackburn got the go-ahead to begin moving personnel to Southeast Asia in preparation for the mission on 27 October. On 1 November, Blackburn and Simons, among others, left for Southeast Asia to lay the groundwork for the raid. By the 12th, both Blackburn and Simons were back in the States as the raiding force prepared to head for Thailand. Six days later, a few hours after the raiders had left for Takhli RTAFB (Royal Thai Air Force Base) in anticipation of receiving orders to carry out the raid, President Nixon gave the 'go' order. The weather and moon had to be right for the raid to take place and conditions were deemed acceptable on the night of 20/21 November.

On the evening of 20 November, the raiders were shuttled to Udorn RTAFB from where the raid was launched at 2318 hours local time. Carrier aircraft from the *Oriskany*, *Ranger*, and *Hancock* were also launched a couple of hours later, during the early morning of the 21st, to create a diversion by staging a fake raid over Hanoi. At about 0218 on the morning of 21 November, the raid itself began. As a C-130 flare ship illuminated the area with flares, the HH-53 code-named Apple Three, opened up on the guard towers of Son Tay Prison with its miniguns, bringing them crashing down.

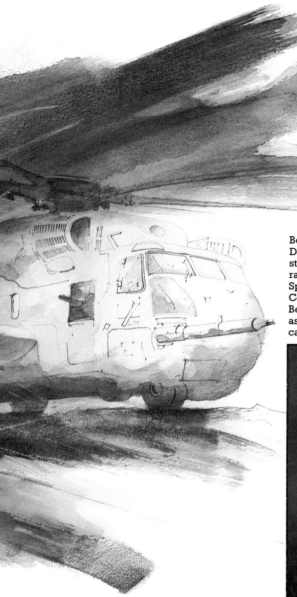

killed, preventing them from reinforcing the prison compound and taking the other raiders by surprise. Within 10 minutes Simons had cleared the area and his men had been lifted back to the Son Tay compound, where they assisted the assault and security elements in eliminating several guards.

Despite the smoothness of the assault, however, the raiders discovered that there were no POWs in the prison. They had been moved elsewhere some weeks before the raid. This development had not been picked up by the US intelligence, because no one had wanted to risk putting in any agents on the ground, and too much reliance had been placed on photographic intelligence.

Less than 30 minutes after the raid had started, the raiders were back on board their choppers and heading for Thailand. Casualties were light: only one raider had been wounded. The raid itself had gone almost perfectly. Even Simons' landing at the wrong complex was fortuitous as it allowed a surprise attack on an undetected enemy unit.

The raiders themselves had mixed reactions on the flight back to Thailand. They were disappointed that all of their training and effort had not resulted in the rescue of a single prisoner. However, they were also glad that they were all heading home, and justifiably proud of the precision with which the raid had been carried out.

The raid proved that the North Vietnamese were vulnerable to attacks close to home

The Son Tay raid was not a complete failure, despite the fact that no prisoners were rescued. It proved in very striking fashion that the North Vietnamese were vulnerable to attacks on installations close to home. As a result, the North Vietnamese had to tie down additional troops to guard sensitive areas, and they also lost some credibility with the Chinese and Russians, who feared that the US would continue to mount raids into North Vietnam. Indirectly, the raid also led to some improvement in the treatment of American POWs.

It should not be forgotten, either, that Simons' party had killed dozens of the enemy, many of them foreign advisors, without taking any losses themselves. The Special Forces troopers, and the air force and navy pilots had carried out their jobs with great skill. It was a classic raid – get in quick, hit hard, get out fast, inflict maximum casualties – but the intelligence had been wrong, a failure which clearly illustrated the fact that intelligence is critical to special operations, especially raids into enemy territory. It is still not known why the North Vietnamese moved their prisoners from Son Tay, but it may be speculated that a rescue attempt was foreseen as the US were steadily building up pressure for their release.

The final point proven by the Son Tay raid was one that Donald Blackburn had been making ever since being appointed SACSA. He argued that North Vietnam was vulnerable to hit-and-run raids by highly-trained special operations forces. Other such raids might have secured the release of many of the American POWs held by the Hanoi government.

Below: Brigadier-General Donald Blackburn headed the study team that developed the raid's operational plan. The Special Forces were led by Colonel Bull Simons (bottom). Below left: Three of the assault force pose for the camera.

Shortly thereafter, the HH-3 carrying the assault party, commanded by Major 'Dick' Meadows, landed inside the prison compound: the whole group pressed against mattresses to cushion them against the crash. The HH-3, known as Banana One came to rest amid branches, leaves, and other debris brought down by its whirling rotors during the crash descent. On landing, 'Dick' Meadows rushed out with his bullhorn shouting: 'We're Americans. Keep your heads down. We're Americans. This is a rescue. We're here to get you out. Keep your heads down. Get on the floor. We'll be in your cells in a minute.' The remainder of the assault party rushed into action, some men laying down suppressive fire, others streaking for the cellblocks to rescue the prisoners.

A few minutes later the command and security group landed just outside the prison's walls. The support group led by Simons himself, however, had landed 400m off course at what was identified on the raiders' maps as a secondary school. Instead of a secondary school, they found themselves outside a barracks housing Chinese or Soviet advisors to the NVA (North Vietnamese Army). School or not, though, Simons and his men proceeded to teach its denizens a lesson. Within minutes of touching down, many of the residents of the barracks had been

THE AUTHOR Leroy Thompson served in Vietnam as a member of the USAF Combat Security Police. He has published several books including *Uniforms of the Elite Forces* and *Uniforms of the Indochina and Vietnam Wars*.

AN INTERNATIONAL RESPONSE

Terrorism has been a significant part of modern life since World War II, but it was in the late 1960s that international terrorism first became a major problem for the governments and security forces of the West. Cheap and speedy travel enabled terrorists to roam the world at will, and groups have been able to create an international 'terror-network' along which money, weapons and their members move. In retrospect, it seems inevitable that anti-terrorist agencies had to liaise to meet the threat.

From 1976-80, Britain, West Germany and France agreed to increase co-operation in the fight against terrorism, but there was also a growing network of bi-lateral agreements – such as those between Britain and the Irish Republic, West Germany and Austria, France and Spain – that provided for the flow of information about active terrorist groups. There have also been close links between the British and American security services (MI5 and the FBI) since the Second World War. Security forces are at the sharp end of any counter-terrorist operation, and their ability to deal with outrages and to wrest the initiative from terrorists on a tactical level has been enhanced greatly by this prevailing spirit of international co-operation. Weapons tactics and experiences are exchanged on a regular basis – three SAS officers were on hand to help the Dutch authorities to free hostages held on a train by South Moluccans in May 1977, and two other men travelled to Mogadishu with GSG9. These links, the most obvious expression of the mood of the recent past, have significantly lessened the terrorist menace.

GSG9

Stun grenades, sub-machine guns, and the SAS all helped this crack German anti-terrorist squad storm a hijacked airliner at Mogadishu, in Somalia in 1977.

DRESSED in dark blue with green trousers, their faces blackened with camouflage paint and betraying little emotion, the commandos of the crack West German anti-terrorist squad Grenzschutzgruppe 9 (GSG9) edged warily to the rear of the hijacked Lufthansa Boeing 737. Some clutched automatic pistols, others cradled the Heckler and Koch MP5A2 sub-machine gun. One group moved to take up position under the aircraft's wings and nose, while another crouched in readiness beneath its tailplane. Metal ladders were propped gently against the fuselage, and magnetic charges were placed around the front and rear doors on the right-hand side of the aircraft. The men's leader, Colonel Ulrich Wegener, watched the preparations with grim satisfaction. Many questions ran through his mind, but two in particular plagued his thoughts – would his men's training prove equal to the task in hand, and could they rescue the 79 passengers and crew unharmed? The West German government had had major reservations about the creation of a specialist unit with a national role for, until 1972, all the states of the Federal Republic controlled their own police forces.

The massacre of Israeli athletes at the Munich Olympics in 1972, however, had highlighted the West German government's lack of preparedness for dealing with terrorism, and Hans-Dietrich Genscher, the Federal Minister of the Interior, was given permission to set up a special anti-terrorist unit. Although GSG9 was initially raised for use in this role, it has also evolved techniques to protect VIPs, guard sensitive government installations and carry out other covert operations. Wegener, recognised as an expert on terrorism, was ordered to take command of the new unit. He began gathering the men he needed during late 1972 and, after a period of tough training, they were ready for action by early 1973. That year, they adopted the distinctive green beret, that has been worn with pride ever since.

Wegener's experience had taught him that the success of any anti-terrorist squad depended on small, tightly-knit groups of men capable of infinite subtlety, and, when needed, extreme ferocity. He knew also that GSG9 had to have the best men, organisation and weapons, if the tragedy of Munich was never to be repeated. To apply for GSG9 a candidate had to have served successfully in the border police for over two years. After application, the next step is a three-day selection course that tests psychological aptitude, endurance, shooting skills, physical fitness and intelligence, and finishes with a medical examination. An interview with GSG9 officers concludes this stage, and about 66 per cent of the applicants are rejected. Successful candidates

Below: The creator of GSG9, Ulrich Wegener, was also the architect of their triumph in Somalia. His unit's cap badge, a gold eagle, is visible on his green beret. Left: The hallmarks of a crack anti-terrorist unit are agility, excellent gun skills and the ability to respond to any threat quickly. Left top: Rappelling from a border police helicopter enables GSG9 to deploy men on the tops of trains or buildings. These men are armed with Heckler and Koch MP5A2 and MP5A3 sub-machine guns. Left centre above: Mercedes Benz sedans are used in high-speed chases. Left centre right: Learning to shoot left-handed. Left centre left: Training to leap from high walls. Left bottom: A GSG9 squad waits to take its turn on an assault course.

move on to a five-month basic training phase, during which another 10 per cent usually fail regularly. This period concentrates on developing physical and technical skills, especially in shooting and the martial arts. The final training session lasts for three months and the men are taught specialist skills, particularly teamwork and small-unit assault tactics.

COLONEL ULRICH WEGENER

With his extensive police experience, Colonel Ulrich Wegener was the ideal choice as first commander of GSG9. After joining the border police in 1958, his training with the FBI and Israeli secret service made him something of an expert on anti-terrorist operations. Indeed, his involvement was so close that it was alleged that he took part in the rescue of hostages carried out by Israeli troops at Entebbe airport in 1976. Wegener's brief was to create a small, flexible squad able to operate in a wide variety of anti-terrorist and undercover roles. The original strength of GSG9 was set at 188, but the unit's size was raised to 219 men after 1977. GSG9 is organised into an HQ, communications and intelligence sections as well as engineer, specialist, technical and training units.

The brunt of any action, however, is borne by three or four strike units of between 30 and 42 men. Mogadishu in 1977 threw GSG9 into the public limelight, and Wegener became something of a national celebrity for his part in the assault. Promotion was rapid; in 1979 he was promoted to brigadier, and took overall control of the West German border police. Although his successors in GSG9, Klaus Blatte and, more recently, Uwe Dee, exercise day-to-day control over the unit, Wegener continues to make the decisions on its deployment.

Firearms training in GSG9 concentrates on hand-guns, sniper rifles, and sub-machine guns. GSG9 men are given shooting practice three half-days and one night per week, and they are instructed in the techniques needed to storm aeroplanes, trains, embassies, and other possible operational targets. At GSG9 base in St. Augustin is a $9m underground range which includes mock-ups of likely terrorist targets. Weapons training is extended to familiarise the GSG9 commando with not only the capabilities of the weapons he is likely to encounter in action, but also how to use any enemy weapon that might fall into his hands. Because they are so popular with terror-ists, special attention is given to the Soviet AK47 assault rifle and the Czech M61 Skorpion machine pistol. Special training in communications, first aid, skiing, mountaineering, heli-borne insertions (including rappelling) and high-speed driving, is tough, and instructors are on hand to give lessons in the day-to-day working of airports to enable GSG9 men to infiltrate the scene of a hijacking by passing themselves off as airport employees.

Thorough training, however, is only part of the story: to be wholly effective in anti-terrorist opera-tions the men of GSG9 have to work as a team. The spearhead of the squad is three special strike units. Each unit, made up of 30 men, is broken into a command section and five Spezialeinsatztruppen (SETs). As with the SAS four-man team, GSG9 finds that the small SETs are easier to command and control and give better mobility and greater flexi-bility in combat. The assault sections actually 'go in' to rescue hostages and the sniper SETs are used to take out terrorists at a distance.

To carry out missions, GSG9 is equipped with some of the most sophisticated weapons and equip-ment in the world. Originally, GSG9 used the Smith and Wesson Model 36 or 60 Chief's Special .38 revolvers and the 9mm Heckler and Koch. At Moga-dishu the Chief's Special was shown to be inadequ-ate for the job, however, and the main GSG9 hand-guns are now either the Model 19 .357 Magnum or the Heckler and Koch P9S or P7. The standard GSG9 sub-machine gun is the Heckler and Koch MP5A2,

often used in the silenced MP5SD version. Both these weapons can be used at night with the ZPP other low-light sights.

GSG9 has a large number of special transpo vehicles available, but the most interesting are th high performance Mercedes Benz 280SE sedar used for pursuit and rapid deployment. With a to speed of 201km/h and carrying sophisticated cor munications equipment, these vehicles are a pote weapon when used to chase terrorists on We Germany's extensive autobahn system. GSG9 sni ers also practice stopping vehicles by pouring fi into the engine compartment, and this tactic is oft carried out from helicopters with troopers using th MP5 sub-machine gun.

After years of patient and painstaking preparatic for the real thing, GSG9's chance to prove their valu as an anti-terrorist unit came on 18 October 1977 Mogadishu airport in Somalia.

Schumann's voice nervously reported that his aircraft had been hijacked

Five days before, at 1300 hours on 13 Octobe Lufthansa Flight LH181, Boeing 737 Charlie Ech lifted smoothly off the tarmac of Palma airpoi Majorca, under the control of Captain Jürgen Sch mann, and set course for the southern coast France. It never reached its destination; an hour late air traffic controllers heard Schumann's voice ne vously report that his aircraft had been hijacked ar that he had been ordered, under pain of death, to f to Rome. Almost immediately the near-hysteric voice of the terrorist leader, Mahmoud, broke i and, in halting English, announced their demand which not only included the release of the leaders the notorious 'Baader-Meinhof' terrorist grouj imprisoned in West Germany, but also a £9m ranson for the aircraft, its 79 passengers and crew.

In Rome, while the aircraft was being refuellec Schumann was able to drop four cigars from flight-deck window, a sign that the authorities co rectly read as meaning that there were four terroris

0208 Main attack goes in.

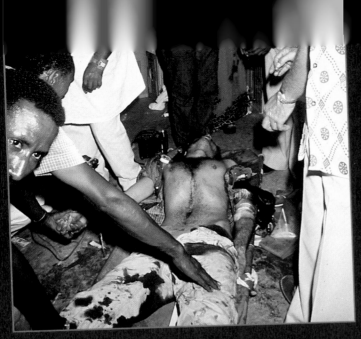

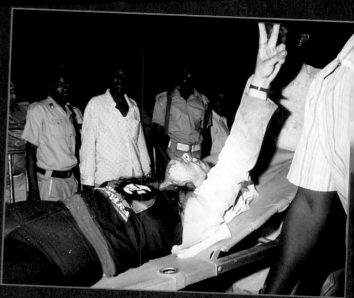

on board. Before they could make use of this vital information, Charlie Echo flew off, and headed for Cyprus. It was the first stage of a flight that would later take the aircraft around the Middle East, before it made a final landing at Mogadishu. By this stage, the German response was gathering momentum. Wegener, at the head of a GSG9 commando group, followed the terrorists first to Cyprus and then on to Bahrain, Dubai and the Republic of Yemen, from where he was forced to fly to Jeddah in Saudi Arabia after being denied permission to land. Meanwhile, Mahmoud had ruthlessly killed Schumann for allegedly communicating with the authorities in the Yemen, and it was left to co-pilot Jürgen Vietor to fly the refuelled aircraft to Somalia on 17 October. Warned of these developments, Wegener and his men followed the hijackers to their new destination. Time, however, was running out for the hostages.

Above, left and right: Death and defiance – the two faces of international terrorism seen at Mogadishu. One terrorist lies dying as a wounded comrade is taken away to hospital. The Palestinians' close links with the German Red Army Fraction led to their demands for the release of the Baader-Meinhof terrorists held in West German prisons.
Below: The assault, from a reconstruction by the magazine *Sterne*. It was actually an ignited oil drum rolled in front of the aircraft, and not a flare that distracted the terrorists and opened the assault.

e released.

D-ACE

0150 GSG9 moves into position.

D-ABCE

At Mogadishu, Mahmoud threatened to blow up the aircraft unless all his demands were met, and to emphasise the point he had Schumann's body thrown onto the tarmac. To gain a few precious hours the negotiators told him that 11 terrorists were being freed from prisons in West Germany, and Mahmoud extended his deadline for blowing up the plane to 0230 hours on 18 October. In the event, the offer to free the terrorists was a ruse, designed to buy a little breathing space. It was clear by this stage that the plane had to be stormed, and Wegener put the operation, code-named 'Magic Fire', into motion.

Towards midnight, a small group of GSG9 troopers crawled out into the desert. Lying behind a sand dune – some 30m from the aircraft – they studied the hijacked plane through infra-red glasses and relayed their findings back to Wegener in the control tower by walkie-talkie. The scouts confirmed that Mahmoud and another terrorist were in the cockpit of the aircraft, but could not give the precise location of the other two hijackers.

The two SAS men threw in their stun grenades which exploded with a roar

Armed with this vital information, Wegener called his men together, and gave his final orders. Once inside the aircraft, he would give the command 'heads down'. Anyone left standing was to be shot. He believed, correctly as it turned out, that the hostages would duck behind the seats and that the terrorists would be unable to cope with a surprise attack that came from all sides. At 0100 hours on 18 October specialists, armed with grenade launchers, and marksmen moved out into the desert. Two SAS men, Major Alistair Morrison and Sergeant Barry Davies, who had accompanied Wegener, set about preparing their own 'fireworks'. The operation began at 0150. While the two hijackers on the flight-deck were kept talking by the control tower, commando teams moved towards the aircraft to take up their attack positions. Then, at 0207, 23 minutes before Mahmoud's final deadline expired, a flaming oil drum was rolled onto the runway in front of the aircraft. Ladders were placed against its doors and magnetic charges gently put in place. The terrorists watched the fire suspiciously, but before they could react, there was a massive explosion. The doors had been blown, and the two SAS men threw in their stun-grenades which detonated with a deafening roar and blinding flash. The GSG9 men, who had kept their eyes closed for several seconds, then pushed their way into the aircraft.

Wegener crashed through the front door at the head of one group, two others clambered over the wings and a fourth entered from the rear of Charlie Echo. Immediately shots rang out. The passengers hit the deck as bullets whistled overhead. One terrorist died instantly. Mahmoud appeared in the

Below: The heroes of GSG9 return home to an ecstatic reception. Their action at Mogadishu was a turning-point in the war against terrorism but there was no time to bask in the glory. Below right: Back to training. Two men with blackened faces cover a colleague.

doorway of the flight-deck and was hit by a number of .38 bullets fired by the GSG9 pointman. They did not stop him. The terrorist leader flung two grenades that exploded harmlessly before he was cut down by a well-aimed burst of fire from a Heckler and Koch MP5. One of the women terrorists ran into a toilet, and was shot in the head by Wegener. As soon as the final hijacker was neutralised the hostages were evacuated to the safety of the airport buildings.

Five minutes later Mahmoud and two of his comrades lay dead or dying

The commandos of GSG9 had gone in at 0207 hours; five minutes later Mahmoud and two of his comrades lay dead or dying, and the fourth member of his team was being carried away seriously wounded. The victorious commandos sent out the code-word that signalled the successful completion of the mission, 'Springtime', and a little later the West German government received a brief message: 'Four opponents down, hostages freed, four slightly wounded, one trooper slightly wounded.' By 0513 the hostages and GSG9 were on their way back to Germany. They arrived back at Cologne in the early afternoon, and were given an ecstatic reception. Brass bands played and radio stations put on special programmes.

Although it has not been used again on full-scale international operations like Mogadishu, GSG9 has maintained its alertness by carrying out sensitive protective assignments, and performing other special and unpublicised missions. It did play an important part in apprehending two Red Army Fraction (RAF) terrorists at an arms cache in November 1982, but, in general, the experience and publicity it gained from the freeing of the hostages at Mogadishu has acted as a curb to terrorist activities in West Germany, and vindicated totally the concept of a nationwide anti-terrorist unit ready for action at a moment's notice.

THE AUTHOR Leroy Thompson served in Vietnam as a member of the USAF Combat Security Police. He has published several books on anti-terrorist methods, and is the author of *Uniforms of the Elite Forces*.

STING RAY

CODENAME STING RAY

The Marines landed in Vietnam in March 1965. Initially, they were employed in a defensive role protecting Da Nang airfield. Dissatisfied with this passive posture, the Marines were soon authorised to engage in active campaigning. The Viet Cong, however, proved elusive. They were seldom found concentrated, and when they were, the target was a fleeting one.

An exception to this was found in the case of reconnaissance units (badge above), since these teams were reporting frequent observation and contact with the VC. Such patrols made effective use of artillery and air strikes on these occasions. Gradually, the specific use of reconnaissance patrols to call in fire missions became routine. During 1966, this became a primary task for patrolling teams.

In July 1966, a small Recon team led by Sergeant Orest Bishko caught a VC company in the open and decimated it with artillery fire. This use of recon was formalised under the codename Sting Ray, and two artillery pieces were assigned in direct support of each active Recon team.

Between 1966 and the departure of the Marines from Vietnam in 1971, Sting Ray techniques were modified, refined and polished, giving credence to the comment made in 1966 on early Sting Ray operations: 'Recon elements are a truly deadly force in hiding among enemy units with this [Sting Ray] capability in hand.'

Previous page. Above: A Cobra gunship, silhouetted against the dawn sky. Below: Lance-Corporal Dowell en route to the insert on 'Charlie Ridge', an M79 'blooper' nestling in his lap.

When US forces in Vietnam required a positive fix on enemy positions, Marine Reconnaissance teams were called in with devastating results

THERE WAS no warning. Death came quickly and violently to the six Viet Cong (VC) as they stood near the hidden entrance to a cave. With their American enemies miles away and their position seemingly inaccessible on the remote mountainside, the VC had felt safe. The Americans were concentrated in the lowlands to the east, and, while the marines did occasionally penetrate the mountains, the VC knew that the chance of discovery was remote. Even the prying eyes of reconnaissance aircraft posed little threat, with good camouflage discipline and nature's canopy of jungle growth providing visual sanctuary. Periodically, an artillery round would disturb the tranquillity, but the Americans seemed to be firing blindly. Their H & I (Harassing and Interdiction) bombardments accomplished little more than to shatter the eerie calm of the forest.

The Viet Cong had no reason to believe that the rounds that exploded around them were anything other than random shots. Their error was fatal. Perhaps in that final second of life, as the fiery shards from high explosive shells devastated their position, the guerrillas recognised the random shots as spotting and adjustment rounds. For the past 17 hours, the Viet Cong cave had been under the watchful gaze of seven sets of eyes. Like their opponents, the marines were also adept at blending into the forest environment. The time was 1046; the date 23 December 1970. The six VC who were not to see Christmas had been victims of a 'Sting Ray'.

There was nothing occult about a Sting Ray. The name was a generic term given to supporting arms missions (air, artillery and naval gunfire) called in on unsuspecting communist forces by highly trained

marine reconnaissance teams, operating by stealth deep in the heart of enemy territory. Apart from their intrinsic military value, Sting Rays were psychologically demoralising to VC and NVA (North Vietnamese Army) forces because they descended unexpectedly, and with great accuracy, on areas thought to be safe and unobserved.

The seven-man reconnaissance team, one of several that made up the Reconnaissance Battalion, Marine Division, was known by the call sign 'Swift Scout'. Led by Corporal James Combs, the team had been secretly inserted into the area by helicopter early on the morning of 21 December. Its mission was 'to conduct reconnaissance and surveillance operations within your assigned haven to detect VC/NVA troop movement or arms infiltration and be prepared to call and adjust air/artillery on all targets of opportunity.'

Swift Scout was operating in a sensitive area known as 'Charlie Ridge' which ran eastwards from the Laotian border to the fertile plains surrounding South Vietnam's principal northern city, Da Nang. During the latter part of 1970, the NVA was using the ridge as an infiltration and logistic pipeline to its VC compatriots in the lowlands. A network of jungle trails with hidden way-stations had been set up along Charlie Ridge to support this effort, though successful marine operations in the area had reduced VC and NVA capability to small-scale raids on isolated villages and posts. For the communists, the use of Charlie Ridge was essential if they were to continue their desperate hit-and-run strategy. Armed with this knowledge, Combs was well aware that the enemy would react swiftly and violently should his recon team be spotted.

When the team had been inserted, two days earlier, it had quickly moved a safe distance from the

Below: With Swift Scout safely inserted onto Charlie Ridge, Corporal James Combs signals the helicopter to take-off. Combs is flanked by Dowell (left) and Dorn (right). Left: Disembarking from their helicopter (below), recon marines move off in search of the elusive Viet Cong (above).

Below: Calling up fire support. All of Swift Scout's transmissions were monitored by the Reconnaissance Battalion Combat Operations Centre. Following standard procedure when a team made enemy contact, the watch officer alerted the Division Fire Support Co-ordination Centre and the Marine Air Wing. Immediately, all unengaged artillery batteries were informed of a stand-by fire mission, and the two A-4 Skyhawk attack aircraft at Da Nang airfield were briefed of a possible mission.
Below right: Armed and ready – Private First Class Owens.

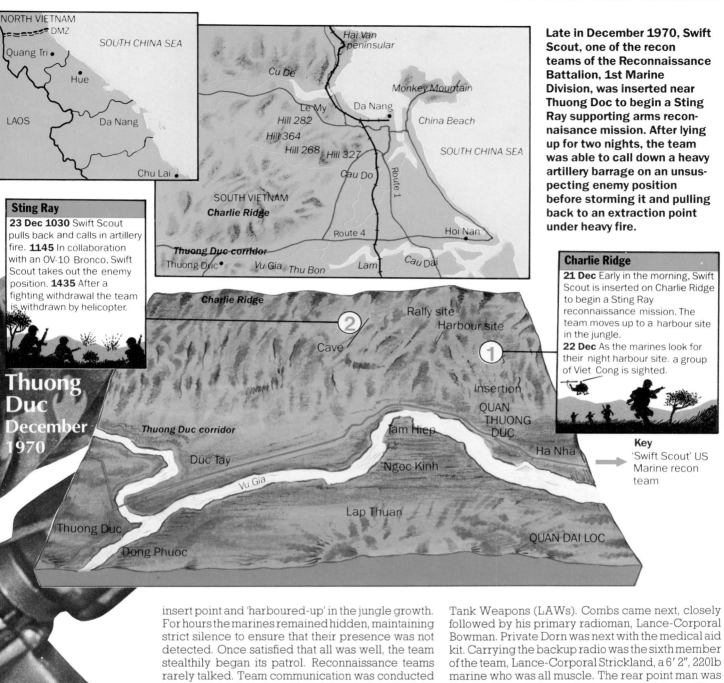

NORTH VIETNAM
DMZ
SOUTH CHINA SEA
Quang Tri
Hue
LAOS
Da Nang
Chu Lai

Hai Van
peninsular
Cu De
Monkey Mountain
Le My
Da Nang
Hill 282
China Beach
Hill 364
SOUTH CHINA SEA
Hill 268 Hill 327
Cau Do
Route 1
SOUTH VIETNAM
Charlie Ridge
Route 4
Hoi Nan
Thuong Duc corridor
Thuong Duc
Vu Gia
Thu Bon
Lam
Cau Dai

Late in December 1970, Swift Scout, one of the recon teams of the Reconnaissance Battalion, 1st Marine Division, was inserted near Thuong Doc to begin a Sting Ray supporting arms recon-naisance mission. After lying up for two nights, the team was able to call down a heavy artillery barrage on an unsus-pecting enemy position before storming it and pulling back to an extraction point under heavy fire.

Sting Ray
23 Dec 1030 Swift Scout pulls back and calls in artillery fire. **1145** In collaboration with an OV-10 Bronco, Swift Scout takes out the enemy position. **1435** After a fighting withdrawal the team is withdrawn by helicopter.

Charlie Ridge
21 Dec Early in the morning, Swift Scout is inserted on Charlie Ridge to begin a Sting Ray reconnaissance mission. The team moves up to a harbour site in the jungle.
22 Dec As the marines look for their night harbour site. a group of Viet Cong is sighted.

Thuong Duc
December 1970

Charlie Ridge
Rally site
Harbour site
2
Cave
Insertion
QUAN THUONG DUC
Thuong Duc corridor
Tam Hiep
Ha Nha
Duc Tay
Ngoc Kinh
Vu Gia
Thuong Duc
Lap Thuan
QUAN DAI LOC
Dong Phuoc

Key
'Swift Scout' US Marine recon team

insert point and 'harboured-up' in the jungle growth. For hours the marines remained hidden, maintaining strict silence to ensure that their presence was not detected. Once satisfied that all was well, the team stealthily began its patrol. Reconnaissance teams rarely talked. Team communication was conducted by a system of touch and hand signals, and, as they moved along, Combs would periodically designate a rally point by a gesture. Should contact be made with the enemy, an 'immediate action' drill would occur – the team would open fire, falling back through itself to the last designated rally point. These locations were selected on their defensive merits and, once at the rally site, the team would establish a 360-degree defence.

As Corporal Combs led his team through the jungle, he was tense but confident. He had 16 of these patrols under his belt and this was his third as team leader. The other members were also veterans of this type of warfare; training and operating together for months, they had been honed into a skilled and deadly team. Like fingers on a hand, each had a different function, but all acted in silent harmony. Corporal Wells was acting as point man, followed by Lance-Corporal Dowell, who carried an M79 gre-nade launcher – the 'blooper' – and two Light Anti-

Tank Weapons (LAWs). Combs came next, closely followed by his primary radioman, Lance-Corporal Bowman. Private Dorn was next with the medical aid kit. Carrying the backup radio was the sixth member of the team, Lance-Corporal Strickland, a 6′ 2″, 220lb marine who was all muscle. The rear point man was Private Owens, the coolest man on the team. On a previous mission, a lost VC had accidentally blun-dered into the team's night harbour site. Without uttering a word, Owens had stood up, walked over to the startled soldier, throttled him into unconscious-ness, gagged, tied him up, deposited him in the centre of the harbour site and silently resumed his place. It all took no more than a minute, and, as Bowman was later to report: 'That bastard Owens wasn't even breathing hard.'

On 21 December and for most of the following day, the team came across no evidence of VC/NVA activity or presence. Throughout both days, the marines worked their way uphill to the west and, by late afternoon on the 22nd, Combs thought the team's four-day patrol would come up with a zero. As evening came on, the team began to look for a night harbour site. In the process, Wells, on point, sudden-ly froze. Instantly, his team members hunkered down to provide 360-degree protection.

Left: As Swift Scout races through the undergrowth, relentlessly pursued by the Viet Cong, a Cobra gunship, piloted by 'Scarface 5', unleashes fire on the enemy. Using the smoke as a reference point, the Cobra directs Combs and his men to a suitable extract point. Once the reconnaissance team has been lifted clear, two A-4 Skyhawks (right) scream in on the crater with 250lb drag bombs and napalm. Below: Dripping with sweat, Lance-Corporal Strickland primes a grenade during Operation Stingray.

About 200m above the marines were five enemy ldiers, including one woman, emerging from a everly concealed cave. Two had AK47s and mbs assumed the others had pistols, although he uld not be sure. As darkness crept through the ngle, the team moved to its right and established a rbour site within view of the cave. Following ndard procedure, the team sat shoulder-to-shoul-r, back-to-back in a circle facing outwards, each o men covering a third of the surroundings. mbs, as team leader, faced the direction of eatest threat. No conversation was allowed and all mmunication had to be through touch and tap. A 50 r cent alert was maintained, which enabled one n in each pair to doze in the sitting position – oviding he didn't snore. The harbour-up proce-

re was not a comfortable one, but it was effective – the event of trouble the team had only to pitch ward into a firing position to cover an attack from y direction. Usually the greatest discomfort came m cramped legs, the mosquitoes and the necessi-to relieve oneself in place if the call of nature manded. It was a long and nerve-racking night. At dawn, the team broke harbour and moved to ncealment within 100m of the cave. During the xt two hours, the marines observed 22 enemy ving in and out of the area. Combs came up on the lio net and initiated a request for fire. His plan was se an offset (flank gun) to fire spotting rounds so as to endanger the team or alert the enemy. Once ed, the adjustments would be entered into the Fire ection Center computer back at the artillery ttery. The request for a six-gun 'fire for effect' on target would be on hold until deemed propitious Combs. Following the spotting rounds, activity ased around the cave site. For two more hours, as a nt drizzle fell through the jungle canopy, Combs l his men continued to observe.
By mid-morning, activity at the cave began anew. o Viet Cong left the cave and headed west. Others uld exit and look around, before returning to their eaway. At about 1030 a cluster of six stood at the rance. The team could hear them chattering and ghing, unaware of the imminent holocaust. The e had arrived for Sting Ray to commence. Cautiously, the team withdrew downhill and to the st of the cave. Once in a protected position, Combs

completed his fire mission to the waiting artillery battery on a fire base in the lowlands: 'Fire for effect'. After a brief pause, the team could hear the distant rippling booms as six 155mm howitzers opened up. Almost immediately, the marines heard the swish of the incoming rounds followed by a series of explosions that made the ground jump under them. The team could not see the cave at this point. For safety reasons, Combs had distanced Swift Scout from the target – but the marines could see the smoke and debris billowing upward between the trees. Several shouts echoed through the forest and then silence.

The team gingerly moved back towards their objective, not yet knowing if the bombardment had hit any of the enemy. As they approached their observation point, the smell of explosives was overpowering. Getting within 50m of the cave, Swift Scout could make out two VC hauling the body of one of their comrades back into the cave.

Dowell was to pump 40mm rounds from his M79 'blooper' into the mouth of the cave

For a moment, Combs was uncertain what to do next. He had a number of choices. He could try to kill those in the cave while they were still in shock, but this violated recon policy of avoiding firefights. Besides, it risked stirring up a hornet's nest if there were more VC/NVA in the area. Fairly certain that the team's presence was unknown, he knew he could withdraw and try to take out the cave with an air strike. This course of action he quickly rejected as the target would be tough to identify for the pilots, and the odds of destroying the cave, even if it could be spotted, were low. A third course of action would be to call in the heliborne infantry Quick Reaction Force (QRF). However, with no suitable landing zones nearby, the communists would almost certainly be long gone by the time the QRF arrived. As Combs was pondering the options, an OV-10 Bronco of VMO-2 Squadron buzzed overhead.

The presence of the Bronco, with its full load of rockets and machine-gun ammunition, decided the issue as far as Combs was concerned. Turning to Bowman, he motioned for the radio and then signalled the team of his decision to take the cave out. Dowell was to pump 40mm rounds from his M79 'blooper' into the mouth of the cave, while Dorn was to use the two LAWs for added effect. Wells was to concentrate on the entrance with M16 fire. Bowman, Strickland and Owens were to provide the initial cover, and, when the cave had been saturated, they would come in on it from the right side while Dowell and company reverted to a covering role.

Swift Scout began to move into position while Combs came up on the radio to inform the Reconnaissance Battalion Combat Operations Center (COC) and the Bronco pilot of his intended course of action. By 1145 the team was in position, with Dowell, Dorn and Wells 35m from the entrance. On Combs' signal, the base of fire opened up and two LAWs, six blooper rounds and two M16 magazines were emptied into the cave. Firing ceased while Bowman and the other two made for the entrance. Bowman tossed a grenade into the cave. After the explosion Bowman entered the mouth, with the others in trace. It was at this point that the sharp staccato of an AK47 was heard issuing from the left, along the trail used by the two enemy soldiers earlier that morning.

Combs yelled, 'Rally', and Strickland grabbed Bowman by his harness and yanked him out of the

MARINE RECON OPERATIONS

From the outset of the US involvement in World War II, the Marines had reconnaissance units to provide 'eyes and ears' for the ground combat commander.
The specialised reconnaissance operations in Vietnam were largely the result of Lieutenant-General Bernard Trainor's experience as an exchange officer with the Royal Marine Commandos in 1958-9. He had become familiar with the commando reconnaissance techniques used during the Cyprus Emergency (1955-9), and on returning to the US 1st Marine Division, as a company commander in the 1st Reconnaissance Battalion, he championed the British techniques.
The idea was to establish a clandestine network of small, radio-equipped teams well beyond friendly lines. Remaining hidden, they could provide 24-hour observation and reporting in their assigned area. Stealth, small size and the avoidance of contact with the enemy were key elements of this approach to reconnaissance. The concept was tested in mountains, desert, jungle and on more conventional terrain. By 1961, the technique was adopted and refined, using helicopters as the primary means of team delivery and recovery.
When the Marines entered Vietnam in 1965, however, uncertainty led to an initial misuse of Recon teams – as raiding and screening units.
A belief in the safety of numbers resulted in teams of up to 24 men – too large to hide and too small to fight on their own. Gradually, confidence in the original concept returned and the small-team (five to seven men) approach was reinstated. It proved to be highly successful. Procedures and techniques were refined and, by the time of the US withdrawal from Vietnam, Marine Recon teams operated almost at will behind enemy lines.

cave. All team members opened fire in the direction of the intrusion. Strickland threw a CS grenade and, as the team moved off to its rally point, Combs popped a red smoke grenade to mark the area and radioed the circling Bronco to take it under fire. As the team withdrew, enemy fire came from a new direction – up-slope. Swift Scout knew that there were at least two VC/NVA elements on their trail.

Thirty kilometres to the northeast, the Reconnaissance Battalion COC was monitoring the team transmissions. As Swift Scout beat a hasty retreat, 'emergency extraction' procedures were initiated in the event that the team had to be rescued. Out of breath, the team reached its rally point, and set up an all-round defence. The excellent coverage of the target area by the Bronco's rockets and machine guns had allowed the team to break contact. It now remained to be seen if the Swift Scout marines could remain undetected in their concealed position. A calm settled over the forest, broken only by the whine of the Bronco's engines as it made dummy firing runs, having expended its ordnance.

Suddenly, about 50m beyond the team's position, an enemy soldier was spotted moving through the undergrowth, carrying an AK47. Dorn blew him away with one shot from his M16. Combs was now convinced that there were a lot more hostile elements in the area than those seen around the cave and, as return fire searched out the area and two hand grenades exploded harmlessly down-slope, he requested an emergency extract over the radio. The enemy had so far failed to gain a positive fix on Swift Scout, and it was obvious that the automatic weapons fire that was issuing from all directions was designed to draw a response from the marines, thereby disclosing their position.

By the time the emergency extract request was made, a relief Bronco from VMO-2 was on station, and the distinctive *whoppa-whoppa* sound of approaching Cobra gunships could be heard in the distance. The emergency extract request had been approved, and the team was directed to proceed to any clearing which would permit a Special Patrol

Insert and Extract (SPIE) operation. The CH-46 helicopters with the call sign 'Peach Bush' took aboard the trained extract team from the Recon Battalion Command Post and departed for the beleaguered Swift Scout.

The jungle canopy prevented the pilots of the Bronco and the Cobras from locating the team on the ground and providing either support or directions to an extract location. For its part, Swift Scout had no idea of the nearest clearing which could allow an extract, and the use of smoke to mark the marines' position would have revealed their location to the enemy with suicidal results. Whispered communications were conducted between Combs and his airborne comrades. The Cobra section leader 'Scarface 5', used the almost dissipated red smoke initially used to identify the cave area for the Bronco as a reference point. He then indicated to the team that a large bomb crater was located at two o'clock uphill of the reference point, at a distance of about 300m from the smoke.

Thirty minutes later, the marines spotted the clearing made by the bomb crater

The team acknowledged and began to E&E (escape and evade) in that direction. The going was tough and Swift Scout was prepared to fall back on the rally point to fight it out if their movement was blocked. Thirty minutes later, the marines spotted the clearing made by the bomb crater. Simultaneously, however, they were spotted by the VC/NVA and a spirited firefight broke out. Moving by bounds, the team made for the protection of the crater when, suddenly, Strickland screamed that he had been hit. All hands went to ground to provide covering fire for the downed marine, who was conscious, but yelling that he was blind.

Straddling on all fours over the wounded marine

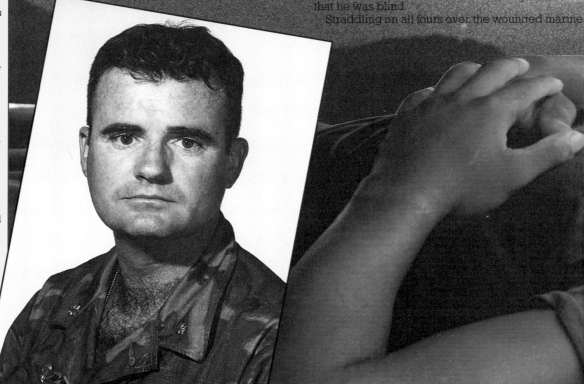

Bowman used his snap link to fasten himself to Stickland's harness, and tried to drag him to the cover of the crater. A moment of panic ensued when Bowman realised that Strickland's size, weight and equipment made movement through the undergrowth impossible. He called for help. Wells crept over and the two began tugging at Strickland. It was no go. They could only move him inches at a time. Strickland kept muttering, 'I'm blind.'

The extract officer rushed to the stern ramp and opened fire on full automatic with his AR15

In desperation, Bowman uncoupled and the two team members rolled Strickland face down. They then took one of their climbing ropes and attached one end to their wounded colleague. Bowman and Wells then scrambled the remaining distance to the crater. Once there, they tugged and hauled Strickland on a very bumpy journey to the hole. The need for secrecy gone, Combs threw out two smoke grenades to help cover his team's movement, and to signal location to the aircraft circling overhead. Enemy fire was heavy, but it was all coming from the west, indicating that Swift Scout had broken clear of the enemy search cordon. Combs gave a spot report over the radio and requested gun-runs west and southwest of the smoke. As the first Cobra rolled in, the remaining team members broke for the relative safety of the crater. The OV-10 Bronco and Cobras now had a positive fix on the team, and felt free to shoot up the forest around them.

At this point, the well-drilled extract procedure got underway. The Peach Bush CH-46 helicopters had already arrived and had been orbiting to the south of the ridge during the marines' race to the crater. The primary bird, piloted by Lieutenant-

Colonel Ken Keck, flew to the crater and, under the suppressive fire of the Scarface Cobras and its own .5in side guns, hovered above the team and dropped the SPIE rig. Usually, a team SPIE 'hook up' took a matter of seconds, but the unconscious Strickland delayed matters. Heavy enemy fire was directed at the extract helicopter and a ruptured hydraulic line sprayed fluid throughout the interior. Anxious seconds ticked by as the team struggled with Strickland, aware that the Scarface Cobras were running low on ammunition. Their peril further increased when two daring enemy soldiers emerged from behind some boulders on the lip of the crater – too close for the Cobras to fire upon them without fear of hitting Swift Scout. The extract officer rushed to the stern ramp and opened fire on full automatic with his AR15. Both green-clad soldiers crumpled among the rocks. By this time, the entire team was hooked up. The extract officer gave a thumbs up and the damaged CH-46 was up and away, with Swift Scout dangling 120ft below the helicopter. Combs checked his watch and mentally recorded the extract time as 1435, 23 December 1970. He then began to frame his thoughts for the mission debrief.

Reports of the emerging extract were being monitored at 1st Marine Division Headquarters, and as Swift Scout dangled in mid-air, en route to safety, the QRF platoon from the 1st Marine Regiment was launched by helicopter to follow up on the recon contact. However, all was quiet – the VC/NVA were long gone.

In April 1971, the 1st Reconnaissance Battalion left Vietnam and returned to the United States as part of 'Vietnamization' – the handing over of responsibility for the war to the South Vietnamese.

THE AUTHOR Lieutenant-General Bernard Trainor was the extract officer who shot the two VC/NVA at the lip of the crater. He went on to become a three-star general in the Marine Corps and retired from active duty in 1985.

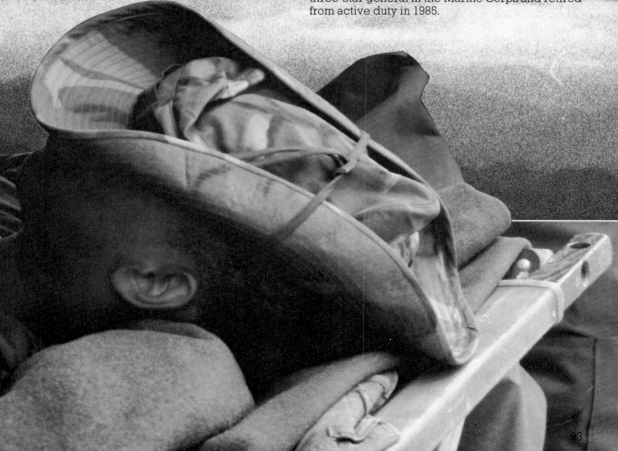

Many of the partisan groups in the Mediterranean lacked the punch of heavy weapons. That was where the Raiding Support Regiment came in

BY SEPTEMBER 1943 the land war in the Mediterranean theatre had moved from North Africa to Italy and Sicily. This left only about 800 suitably trained men available to GHQ Middle East when it was given the task of harassing the Germans still occupying the Balkans and Greece. These 800 men mostly belonged to small units such as the Special Boat Squadron and the Long Range Desert Group, so the decision was made to gather them into a new formation called the Middle East Raiding Forces. To this organisation was soon added a new unit: its role was to support commando raids and underpin partisan activities with heavy weapons.

The name of the new unit, the Raiding Support Regiment (RSR), described its role exactly and a call went out from Middle East Command for volunteers for 'duties of a hazardous nature'. Over 3000 men from 60 different regiments applied and one of the first tasks of the newly appointed commanding officer, Lieutenant-Colonel Sir Thomas Devitt, Bart, was to interview and select suitable officers. Being an international rugger player, he not unnaturally chose those who were keen on that game. One, Jack Gage,

was an Irish international, while others had played for clubs in Britain and South Africa. A training camp at Azzib in Palestine was established, a programme of strenuous physical training, including 24-hour mountain marches with heavy loads, was instituted, and all were given parachute training. By the end of the year a motley collection of men had become a disciplined and energetic unit that was raring for action.

The regiment was organised into a headquarters commanding five batteries, and it is safe to say that never before in the history of the British Army had a regiment of this nature been formed with such a mixed complement of weapons. A Battery consisted of 12 Vickers and MG-42 medium machine guns; B Battery contained 18 3in mortars; C was a light anti-aircraft battery with 18 0.5in Browning machine guns; D was an anti-tank battery with four Italian 47/32mm anti-tank guns; and E was a mountain battery equipped with four 75mm pack howitzers. This, at least, was the theoretical establishment, but weapons and equipment were in desperately short supply and when C Battery, in February 1944, was sent to support No. 2 Commando on the island of Vis, off the Yugoslavian coast, it was still untrained in the use of its weapons as none, up to that point, had ever

QUIT YOU LIKE MEN

Background: A 25-pounder is manhandled over difficult terrain during operations on the Yugoslavian mainland in 1944. Below: Members of E Battery, Raiding Support Regiment (RSR), in the spring of 1944, when the RSR supported No.2 Commando's raiding operations in Yugoslavia, the Dalmatian islands and Albania from its bases on the island of Vis and in southern Italy. Bottom right: A raiding craft, its decks crowded with guns and troops, heads back to Vis after a raid on the Yugoslavian mainland. Left: After coming ashore in Albania, commandos prepare to move inland to rendezvous with Albanian partisans.

THE RAIDING SUPPORT REGIMENT

Soon after the formation of the Raiding Support Regiment (RSR), Lieutenant-Colonel Sir Thomas Devitt announced a competition for the design of a cap badge. As rations were critically short in those early days, one wag submitted a drawing of a skeleton holding a mess tin, but the winner was Captain D.C. Rose. In his design, a winged, mailed fist stood for armed help from the air (all members of the RSR were trained parachutists), while the bare hand grasping it represented the poorly-armed partisans; the turret from which the hand extended signified that the partisans were beleaguered in their mountain strongholds.

The design decided upon, Devitt now had to think of a suitable motto. Eventually, he picked out 'Quit You Like Men, Be Strong', which came from the First Epistle of St Paul to the Corinthians. However, this proved to be too long and was shortened to 'Quit You Like Men', with the inevitable result that the unit became affectionately known as 'The Quitters'! Devitt now drew a complete sketch of the proposed badge, but when it was found that the cost of producing such an elaborate design in metal would be excessive, he sat down and embroidered the first one himself in coloured silks on a white handkerchief. This was submitted to the supplier of SAS cap badges, who then reproduced it. The badge (above) was worn on a beret of the same beige colour as that issued to the Special Air Service (SAS).

been issued to it! Later, the battery was joined by a Troop from E Battery. Both supported numerous commando raids on the Dalmatian Islands to such good effect that three RSR officers were decorated with the Military Cross.

On 11 April 1944 the regiment was moved to Bari, situated on the southeastern coast of Italy, and from here it helped support a number of raids into occupied territory, under the aegis both of Land Forces, Adriatic, and Force 266, the cover name given to SOE (Special Operations Executive) operating in the area. These operations were undertaken by the remaining Troop of E Mountain Battery, and by one Troop from each of B and D Batteries.

One of the largest of these raids was one carried out on the Albanian mainland in support of the partisans operating in that area. In all, 180 men from the RSR, with four 75mm guns, four anti-tank guns, six medium machine guns and six 3in mortars, supported No.2 Commando and other units when they attacked four German strongpoints northeast of the

Right: All members of the RSR underwent parachute training before embarking on active service with the unit. Bottom: Men of Force 133, the Special Operations Executive group working with Greek partisans, on the move with a mule column near Mount Olympus. RSR officers parachuted into Greece to make contact with this group. Below right: During operations in Albania, radio contact was maintained with patrols from forward positions. Bottom right: The Albanian partisan officer Lieutenant Mitro Nika (left) indicates German positions.

Raiding Support Regiment 1944-45

town of Spilje. Unfortunately, the Allied plans were betrayed to the Germans, allowing them to reinforce their positions so that none of the objectives could be reached. But the enemy was so weakened by the fighting that shortly afterwards all four positions fell to the partisans, who were then able to enter the town.

All these commando raids landed from the sea. But while they were taking place, some members of the RSR became involved in what originally had been considered one of its main roles – that of dropping behind enemy lines in support of partisans who were engaged in harassing the Germans. In April 1944, six men of the unit were parachuted into Greece to contact both the Military Mission officers from Force 133 (the cover name for SOE controlled from Cairo) and the partisans; after that they were to make preparations for the arrival of the rest of the force. This last was to include both Troops of A Battery, the two remaining Troops of B Battery and the one remaining Troop of D Battery, all of whom were to be divided in mixed proportions over three different areas. Eventually, nearly 200 RSR personnel were infiltrated from the sea to support the partisans.

The six men had to be entirely self-sufficient and could expect to be cut off for at least six months

The officers chosen to parachute into these three areas were Major Douglas Unsworth, Major Norman Astell and Captain Jack Gage, each one to be accompanied by an NCO. Astell dropped into the northern area, north of Salonica; Unsworth into the central area in the vicinity of Mount Olympus; and Gage further south into countryside around Lamia. Devitt told them:

'Your orders are to reconnoitre the main roads and railways in your area. To ascertain the strength and morale of the enemy; to build up food supplies for your men when they arrive; and finally to check for suitability certain targets which have been chosen by British liaison officers who are already in Greece, for a final assault on the Germans when they withdraw.'

The small party was given 10 days of intense briefing in Cairo. They were to live off the land, and their diet was to consist mainly of beans and black bread although, on rare occasions, they might be supplied from the air. Medical supplies were very limited. They would be given gold sovereigns and some drachma, with which mules and food could be bought. To travel around they were only to walk, or ride their animals. The liaison officers from the Allied Military Mission already established in the areas would do everything they could to help, but the six men had to be entirely self-sufficient and could expect to be completely cut off for at least six months. They were also briefed on the complicated situation in Greece, where the Military Mission of around 100 officers was attempting to conciliate between the two largest guerrilla organisations. These were the communist-inspired ELAS, led by General Serafis, and the pro-British EDES, commanded by General Zervas, and they were already fighting each other rather than the Germans. Additionally, the relationship between the villagers and the partisans was not always a cordial one.

Unsworth and Astell were dropped in April and were soon followed by their detachments. One bombardier later described how each man's kit was carefully compiled:

'One quarter-pound tin of tobacco, one toilet roll, one book, thin, which would give a Troop library of 25 volumes. The book was a very good idea. My copy was a wartime edition on very flimsy paper and I was able to use the leaves to roll cigarettes with when our proper fag-paper became exhausted. My idea of the perfect reading for a lonely mountain residence was "The Life and Impressions of Ethel Mannin", so that my cigarettes were practically self-igniting ... We even had an escape kit, complete with everything that the well-dressed escaper could desire. In it were compasses, gold sovereigns, a map and files.'

The compass was in two parts and as each could pass for a button it was sewn onto the flies of the men's trousers.

All three parties were soon to be harassed by big sweeps carried out by crack German troops. One group was hunted by over 12,000 of them moving into the mountains of central Greece from nine different directions. The search went on for 11 days, forcing the Allied detachments to march by night and hide by day, covering in all nearly 130 miles to escape capture. But the Germans did not have it all their own way; one large group was surrounded in a mountain village and plastered with RSR mortar bombs and machine-gun fire.

Because of the intense pressure on them, the two northern groups were not able to be as active as the RSR group fighting with the guerrillas in the mountains around Lamia, even though Gage's group was the last to parachute in. Adverse weather conditions had delayed his drop until the beginning of May, but the subsequent actions of his group well illustrate the kind of war in which all those fighting behind the lines in Greece had to engage.

It was quite a task to move a convoy of 200 mules, 200 muleteers and 50 British personnel

During the weeks following his arrival, accompanied by his faithful interpreter Dimitri, Gage reconnoitred his area and prepared the way for the men who were later to join him. In mid-June he crossed to the west coast to meet a small force of Americans and RSR personnel who needed to be guided to their destinations. The following month his own troops arrived and it was quite a task to move a convoy of 200 mules, 200 muleteers and 50 British personnel across a half-starving and devastated enemy-occupied country. But somehow, with the aid of both ELAS and EDES – and the £5000 in gold sovereigns that the whole undertaking cost – he managed it without being detected by the Germans. After being involved in a few skirmishes with the enemy, including an ambush of a German armoured train, Gage received from Cairo the codeword 'Noah's Ark'. This was the signal to set up his small force in ambush positions by the main Salonika-Athens road, where the maximum damage would be done to the

Top right: Men of the RSR and the US Operational Group pose with Greek partisans beside a banner incorporating their three national flags. Centre, far right: Men of the RSR in Athens shortly before the outbreak of civil war in Greece. Above centre: General Saraphis of ELAS (left) and General Zervas of EDES (right) with General Scobie, commander of the British troops in Greece.

retreating Germans.

The withdrawal started on 9 September, and with the help of the partisans Gage and his men shot up any German convoys that tried to negotiate the road that wound through their pass. This went on for some time, the Germans trying first one tactic and then another, but on the whole being thwarted in their attempt to withdraw northwards in any numbers.

The actions of this long-running ambush are well described in Gage's report for 16 September:

'MG sections have fired about 7000 rounds and mortars about 750 bombs. Still cold and wet. Convoy of 50 trucks delayed all day by sections. It is difficult to say what damage we are inflicting on the Hun. We must be causing more than we realise as he takes all sorts of precautions before attempting to get past our ambushes. Puts out 88mm guns, mortars and MGs and plasters the hills. Then

always waits for whole convoy to get through each ambush before moving on. The whole operation takes him seven or eight hours for a normal half an hour. Also he has wasted a couple of days trying to spot us. Mines and demolitions are also doing considerable damage.'

Those that did escape still had the other RSR detachments to cope with as they drove towards Yugoslavia. But after 10 days, despite constantly blowing holes in the road and shooting up anything that moved on it, Gage's group was obliged to withdraw for the Germans had built up an overwhelming superiority in numbers in order to remove them. However, the men continued to harass the enemy with lightning strikes on their convoys.

One of Gage's officers, Lieutenant Hoey, was especially audacious during this time. On 22 September he took his section of heavy machine guns forward to an exposed position north of the town of Dhomokos. From this vantage point, he shot up a German convoy of battalion strength, preventing it from moving for 12 hours and inflicting many casualties. In the following days his section penetrated the German positions guarding the road no less than three times, again inflicting heavy casualties. For these actions, and for entering

Background: The rooftop position held by men of 2 Independent Parachute Brigade comes under fire from ELAS forces during bitter fighting in the streets of Athens. Above far left: Members of ELAS, the communist group that attempted to seize power when the German occupation ended, carry away a dead comrade.

Lamia while it was still occupied and firing a Bren gun into two truck-loads of troops, he won the MC.

The following month Gage received orders to move into Lamia immediately it had been evacuated. Accordingly, on 19 October he and his men moved down out of the mountains and took over a hotel for the night. The next day they were joined by British paratroopers and the SBS, who were moving up from Athens. It was later reckoned that Gage's men had held up a complete division for a week, and Gage himself calculated that during the seven months he was in Greece he had walked over 2000 miles! For his leadership he was later awarded the MC.

The record of the RSR in Greece is an outstanding one. Its casualties had been light – four killed, four wounded and six taken prisoner – but it had managed to wreak havoc among the enemy. Seventeen vital bridges had been destroyed, as had a mine, a dam, and five petrol and ammunition depots, while hundreds of yards of railway line had been torn up on 18 separate occasions. Five trains had been shot up and 150 vehicles knocked out. The total enemy killed amounted to 300, with many more being wounded.

More members of the RSR, including Major Astell, were killed by Greeks than by Germans

Most of the personnel from the original RSR groups in Greece were withdrawn at the end of November, though some were moved to Athens in anticipation of the trouble that was to come. On 4 December civil war erupted, with the ELAS and EDES forces fighting each other in the streets of the Greek capital. Now British troops were also regarded by ELAS as the 'enemy' and it is a tragic fact that more members of the RSR, including Major Astell, were killed by Greeks than by Germans.

One of those who were involved in the conflict was an RSR captain, Peter Street. Since the previous April he had been leading his sections of mortars and anti-tank guns in ambushes against the Germans in central Macedonia and was to be awarded the MBE for doing so, but by December he had joined a small detachment of the RSR in Athens. The fighting was bitter, but on 4 January 1945 he was able to write:

'Big attacks with 2 Indep Para Bde. RSR again spearhead attack. Hard going but objectives reached and captured. Lieut. Keane killed. 12 ORs wounded. 16 ELAS killed including two Germans, 31 prisoners. Attack a great success. ELAS finished as fighting force in Athens area.'

The war was now nearly over for the Raiding Support Regiment, but some members still saw action when supporting the commandos at Lake Comacchio and joint SBS/LRDG operations in Istria on the Italian-Yugoslavian border. Another of the RSR's officers, Captain Newton, was awarded the Military Cross for bravery during the battle for the Argenta Gap.

Within three months of the German surrender the regiment had been disbanded. In the decades that have followed it has become perhaps one of the least known fighting units of the British Army – and yet it had more than measured up to its motto, 'Quit You Like Men'.

THE AUTHOR Ian Dear served as a regular officer in the Royal Marines, 1953-56. He is now a professional writer on military and maritime subjects and is author of *Ten Commando*, a book on No. 10 (Inter-Allied) Commando, which is to be published later this year by Leo Cooper Ltd.

FREEDOM FIGHTERS

The Spanish Civil War attracted volunteers from all over the world to fight for the Republican cause. At Jarama, the British Battalion of the International Brigades fought a bitter encounter against the Nationalist troops of General Franco

Left: Page from a Welsh volunteer's identity card pay book. Above: Republican troops are issued with archaic and often temperamental rifles. Background picture: British volunteers of the International Brigades in September 1938.

EARLY ON 11 FEBRUARY 1937 Tom Wintringham, newly appointed CO of the British Battalion of the XVth International Brigade, was summoned to a Brigade orders meeting. There, the commander of the XVth Brigade, a naturalised Russian known as Colonel 'Gal', outlined the dispositions of the three battalions under his command for the impending battle: the French on the right, the British on the left, with a mixed force of Czechs, Austrians, Italians and assorted Balkans to be held in reserve. The Spanish Civil War, which broke out on 18 July 1936, had reached a critical phase: the Nationalist forces under General Francisco Franco had launched a major offensive to the south of Madrid, hoping to cut off the Republican troops in the beleaguered capital from the important sea port of Valencia on the Mediterranean coast. The International Brigades were assigned an important role in defending the Madrid-Valencia road which lay astride the Jarama valley. The Nationalists' plan was to cross the Jarama river and then cut the road; if successful, this thrust would gain them a significant strategic victory, further isolating Madrid from the rest of Republican Spain.

The British Battalion, consisting of some 600 men, was a newly formed unit within the International Brigades, only having come into being in January 1937, even though a steady trickle of volunteers had arrived in Spain since the fighting had begun in

THE INTERNATIONAL BRIGADES

When civil war broke out in Spain in 1936 several states in Europe showed an immediate interest in the struggle. This was soon to develop into the provision of military aid – Germany and Italy supporting the right-wing Nationalist movement while the Soviet Union sent arms and equipment to the Republican Government. The origins of the International Brigades are less than completely clear, although Maurice Thorez, head of the French Communist Party, developed the idea into a reality. Throughout the war, the communist party remained the single most important element in the organization and direction of the Brigades, although many of its members were not communist and represented a wide spectrum of political viewpoints. In addition, a considerable number of volunteers (as many as 5000 men) remained outside the structure of the International Brigades, fighting instead within the many left-wing groupings that made up the Republican armed forces. Thus, for example, the writer George Orwell joined the POUM (Workers' Party of Marxist Unification) militia, an organisation invariably in conflict with its supposed communist ally.

The war in Spain soon proved to be a magnet for political idealists and adventure seekers,

Soldier of the XIIth (Garibaldi) Brigade, Spanish Civil War, 1936-38.

This trooper wears an army cap, Spanish-army leather equipment, khaki overalls, and espadrilles on his feet. The rifle is a Spanish 7mm model 1916 'short rifle'.

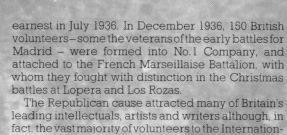

earnest in July 1936. In December 1936, 150 British volunteers – some the veterans of the early battles for Madrid – were formed into No.1 Company, and attached to the French Marseillaise Battalion, with whom they fought with distinction in the Christmas battles at Lopera and Los Rozas.

The Republican cause attracted many of Britain's leading intellectuals, artists and writers although, in fact, the vast majority of volunteers to the International Brigades varied: some were card-carrying members of the communist party, following orders to the men came from all parts of the United Kingdom, four areas counted for a significant part of the total: London, the valleys of South Wales, Manchester and Clydeside. Their reasons for joining the International Brigades varied: some were card carrying members of the Communist Party, following orders to support the threatened Spanish Republic, others

were political idealists who saw themselves fighting against the evil of fascism, while others welcomed an opportunity to escape the boredom of civilian life in the 1930s. Both Britain and France adopted a policy of 'non-intervention' in the war and actively discouraged the movement of volunteers, even to the point of arresting men they could prove were in the process of joining up. The typical route for British volunteers was to take a quiet weekend excursion to Paris (for which no passport was needed) and report to the French Communist Party Headquarters, where transport and guides would be arranged to get them to Spain. As the Franco-Spanish border was closed, the volunteers had to face the Pyrenees, an ordeal that left a lasting impression on many would-be recruits. A future battalion CO, Fred Copeman, recorded his impressions of the mountain crossing:

'God, when we arrived at the Pyrenees...I'd

and large numbers of men were volunteering for service in the Republican cause within months of the outbreak of war. Altogether some 35,000 men saw service with the International Brigades, although at any one time maximum strength was never more than 18,000 men. The French formed the largest national group, followed by Germans, Poles, Italians, British, Americans and Yugoslavs.

The first of the brigades, the XIth Brigade, was formed in October 1936, followed a month later by the XIIth, or Garibaldi Brigade, so named because of the large number of Italians in this formation. Over the next few months the XIIIth, XIVth and XVth Brigades were

established, to be joined by the 150th and 129th Brigades in the summer of 1937. The French communist leader Andre Marty became the Brigades' controller, while military command was invested in the hands of General 'Kleber', a veteran soldier from Hungary who was subsequently to fall foul of Stalin and be shot on his orders. The International Brigades were withdrawn once it became clear that the war was lost for the Republicans. Although on the losing side, they played a vital role in the early stages of the conflict, notably in the defence of Madrid, and in gaining some breathing space for the Republicans to recruit and organise their own armed forces.

The Spanish Civil War
July 1936-Mar 1939

When Civil War broke out in Spain during July 1936, the country divided between the Nationalist north and southwest, and the Republican strongholds of Madrid, southeastern Spain, the Basque country in the north, and Catalonia and Aragon in the northeast. As the Nationalists advanced through Aragon and Catalonia, and attempted to encircle Madrid, the International Brigades stiffened the Republican defence.

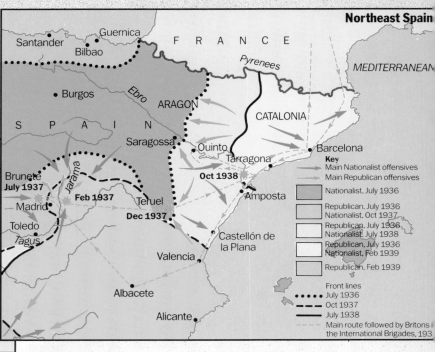

Northeast Spain

Spain
July 1936

Key
Republican, July 1936
Nationalist, July 1936

Key
Main Nationalist offensives
Main Republican offensives

Nationalist, July 1936
Republican, July 1936
Nationalist, Oct 1937
Republican, July 1936
Nationalist, July 1938
Republican, July 1936
Nationalist, Feb 1939
Republican, Feb 1939

Front lines
•••• July 1936
– – – Oct 1937
— July 1938
— Main route followed by Britons in the International Brigades, 193

Bottom left: Moorish troops regroup after a victorious encounter. Bottom centre: British soldiers at machine-gun practice. Bottom right: A British anti-tank section at the Battle of Jarama. Below: Republican troops advance.

never climbed before in my bloody life. For every mountain you climbed there was another bugger; you wondered when the hell you were going to get there.'

...he mountains were bad, the volunteers also had to ...dge fascist patrols who were helped by right-...ng French sympathisers. Some men were smug-...ed into Spain by boat and ship, although a con-...derable number of stowaways were caught and ...turned to their home port.

...Once in Spain, the British volunteers were sent to ...bacete, mid-way between Madrid and Valencia, ...here they received some rudimentary training and ...re kitted out with uniforms, equipment and ...eapons. The issue of weapons was a major prob-

Commanders of the British Battalion. Bottom: Sam Wild (wearing a beret), commander from March 1938. Centre: Fred Copeman lead the battalion until falling severely ill at Teruel in 1938. Right: Tom Wintringham was commander at the battle of Jarama.

Below: Troops of the International Brigades pay their last respects to British Battalion members who fell at Jarama in early 1937.

lem. Not only were they in short supply, but those available often verged on the obsolescent – sometimes single-shot rifles of various types and calibres, requiring their own special ammunition. One recruit's account of his rifle allocation was typical:

'They were real ancient ones. What I got was an old German gun dated 1878. It was a single-loader. There was a great big pile of cartridges on the floor, not in clips, just in a big heap. What you did was to just pick out handfuls and see if they would fit the breech. You put them in one at a time to see if they'd fit. They were all different kinds – some rimless, some rimmed. I'm sure the gun I had would never have fired anyway.'

During January 1937 the British Battalion underwent a brief but intensive training programme; rumours that the battalion would soon be going into action heightened the urgency of the training. Some men had experience of service life in the British Army and

Royal Navy (with a few having fought in World War I but most had no military experience at all, and so the training was necessarily rudimentary and strictly functional. At the end of January the training for wai came to an abrupt end with the order for the battalion to proceed to the front and take up its position for the defence of the Madrid-Valencia road.

The Nationalists crossed the Jarama river at dawn on 11 February and a force of Moors (Moroccan Moslems), slit the throats of the French Battalion's sentries, allowing the main body of Nationalist troops to advance close to Republican positions before being observed. This also left the British in a dangerously exposed position. Wintringham received orders to swing round and attack the Nationalists without delay in order to relieve the hard-pressed French. Despite misgivings – fuelled by the lack of support from artillery and machine guns – the British commander sent his men forward. By contrast, the assaulting columns of Nationalists were well supplied with artillery, including guns from the crack units of the German Condor Legion. The British inevitably suffered heavy casualties. As the other units from the International Brigades fell back, the British Battalion was forced in turn to adopt a new position, on a projection later called 'Suicide Hill'.

On the morning of 12 February the Nationalists advanced towards the Republican positions and, as he had been during the previous day, Wintringham was ordered to counter-attack. This time, however he refused to throw his troops forward, despite repeated requests which eventually turned into threats of immediate arrest. As the man on the spot Wintringham rightly saw that the International Brigades should fight a defensive battle with only small limited counter-attacks, and these should be properly supported with sufficient firepower. The key elements in the British positions were their Maxim machine guns – old, heavy weapons but capable of sustained long-range fire – which were ideal for defensive warfare of this nature. The Nationalist attacks were repeatedly thrown back in the face of a hail of bullets from the machine-gunners on Suicide Hill.

As the day wore on, the Moors spearheading the Nationalist attack were able to work around the British flanks, enfilading their positions with accurate rifle fire. At the same time, ammunition for the machine guns ran out and the Nationalists began to apply renewed pressure on Suicide Hill; for the British it was a time of crisis. Fred Copeman, at the time a machine-gun section leader in No.1 Com-

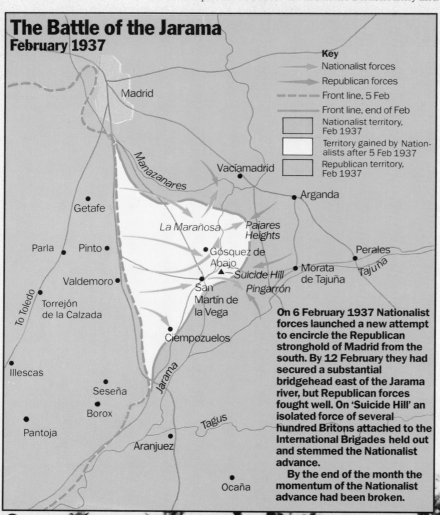

The Battle of the Jarama
February 1937

Key
→ Nationalist forces
→ Republican forces
--- Front line, 5 Feb
--- Front line, end of Feb
Nationalist territory, Feb 1937
Territory gained by Nationalists after 5 Feb 1937
Republican territory, Feb 1937

Madrid
Manzanares
Vacíamadrid
Arganda
Getafe
La Marañosa
Paiares Heights
Parla
Pinto
Gósquez de Abajo
Perales
Valdemoro
Morata de Tajuña
Tajuña
▲ Suicide Hill
San Martín de la Vega
Pingarrón
Torrejón de la Calzada
To Toledo
Ciempozuelos
Jarama
Illescas
Seseña
Borox
Tagus
Pantoja
Aranjuez
Ocaña

On 6 February 1937 Nationalist forces launched a new attempt to encircle the Republican stronghold of Madrid from the south. By 12 February they had secured a substantial bridgehead east of the Jarama river, but Republican forces fought well. On 'Suicide Hill' an isolated force of several hundred Britons attached to the International Brigades held out and stemmed the Nationalist advance.

By the end of the month the momentum of the Nationalist advance had been broken.

ove left: British volunteers
ernicasim in July 1937,
ore the battle of Brunete.
ove centre: British troops
y a well-earned rest – a
nce for a smoke, and to
d letters from home.
ove right: A Russian
xim, as used by the British
inst the Moors at Suicide
. Below: Coming home.
ish volunteers, taken
oner by Franco's
ionalist forces, arrive at
don's Victoria station.

Although the majority of those who fought in Spain were ordinary working men, the Republican cause attracted a very large number of writers, poets and other intellectuals who had made the decision to make a practical military contribution to the fight against fascism.

In Europe during the 1930s many intellectuals were left-wingers, and a substantial number belonged to the Communist Party. Once the communists had decided to come to the aid of the Republican Government, many communist intellectuals quickly threw in their lot with the International Brigades. One such volunteer was the poet John Cornford, who was killed early on in the war and became something of a romantic hero as a result.

And yet many famous names associated with the Spanish Civil War were never in the International Brigades at all, the war attracting droves of journalists and 'visitors' to the conflict. These people ranged from the writer Ernest Hemingway, to committed left-wing journalists such as Arthur Koestler and Willie Brandt.

Below: George Orwell, author of *Animal Farm* and *1984*, who fought with the anarchist POUM.

pany, discovered new supplies of ammunition and began organising men to carry the boxes forward to the machine guns. Copeman's good fortune was, however, countered by disaster, for the machine-gun battery was overrun by a Moorish attack. In a desperate hand-to-hand fight, six of the guns were salvaged and dragged back to a new site, and resupplied with the ammunition found by Copeman.

400 Moors had advanced up the slope of Suicide Hill; less than half staggered back

Taking command of the Maxims, Copeman made ready for a new attack which the Nationalists could be seen preparing. Copeman and his machine-gun crews watched the Moorish troops massing silently for the assault. The Moors' reputation for brutality was well known to all Republican troops and to be captured by them almost inevitably meant death through mutilation. During the battle Copeman encountered one such instance:

'I remember hearing a kind of squealing and then this head bobbed over the wall. It was a boy of about sixteen, a good-looking lad. The Moors had gouged out his eyes. I can still feel that right to the bone, even after all this time. We went to help him but he died almost immediately.'

Amid the high-pitched battle cries of the Moors and the fire from a German anti-tank battery, whose shells were landing uncomfortably close by, Copeman steadied his men. 'Not a shot until I give the word,' he called. 'All guns to sweep the line together

from left to right.' Only when the Moors were clearly visible was the order given to fire. The shock of the bullets ploughing through the ranks of the marching troops stopped them dead in their tracks – in many cases, literally. Up to 400 Moors had advanced up the slope of Suicide Hill; less than half staggered back but the guns kept on firing, their crews singing and laughing with relief and exultation at this single-handed destruction of the Nationalist attack.

During the lull in the fighting that followed the Nationalist repulse, Copeman and other more senior officers attempted to restore order to the battered British positions, which included rounding up 'stragglers' who could be a considerable distance from the front line. While the battalion officers met to plan the improvement of their defences they found themselves victim of a clever Nationalist ploy. From the direction of the valley below, the Republican anthem of the 'Internationale' could be heard. Gradually about 40 men in International Brigade uniforms emerged from the valley floor, cheerfully waving rifles, before walking past the British front line to where the machine guns were sited. At that moment the bogus British troops raised their rifles and at a stroke captured the guns and their bewildered crews, too startled to offer resistance. Fighting broke out again and the British, now deprived of their Maxim machine guns, fell back exhausted, hungry and demoralised by this set-back. Of the 600 men who had gone into battle two days earlier only 180 remained. Their position looked hopeless but the company commanders and 'political commissars' managed to rally them. Yet again, the remnants of the battalion took up their positions, where they were

joined by a mixed band of rear-echelon and lightly wounded troops from the International Brigades. A counter-attack was planned and, edging round to the Moors' exposed flanks, the brigaders flung themselves at the enemy. Despite some limited success, the outnumbered British troops again found themselves isolated from other Republican units as the Nationalists closed in around them. Now down to about 100 fighting men, the long-suffering British Battalion looked doomed. Fortunately, reinforcements arrived in the form of an augmented brigade of Spanish Republican forces on the British left flank. Surprised and exhausted, the Moorish troops began to fall back. As darkness fell they were in full retreat. The following day the Republicans began to dig in and a trench stalemate ensued. The focus of the war then moved to other fronts. Franco's plan to cut the Madrid-Valencia road had been thwarted and the International Brigades were justly awarded most of the credit. Within the brigades, the British Battalion's steadfast defence of Suicide Hill against superior enemy forces was an outstanding achievement.

The survivors of the British Battalion were repatriated, receiving an unofficial heroes' welcome

After spending several months in the trenches, the British Battalion was withdrawn to take part in a major Republican offensive at Brunete, a few miles west of Madrid, which was intended to divert Nationalist forces away from the north of Spain. The Brunete offensive was of limited value however, and hit the British Battalion particularly hard; casualties were high and many good officers were killed. The tide of the war was moving inexorably in favour of the Nationalists; a further Republican offensive at Teruel in December 1937 saw initial success turn to failure and heavy casualties for the British. The Battle of the Ebro (July-August 1938) was another diversionary attack in which the British Battalion was heavily engaged, but ultimately for no lasting gain. The fighting on the Ebro marked the end of the International Brigades' contribution to the war and in September 1938 the Spanish Republican Government began to withdraw the foreign volunteers from the ranks of its armed forces. Slowly the survivors of the British Battalion were repatriated, receiving an unofficial heroes' welcome on their return to England. Altogether, well over 2000 Britons went to Spain; over a quarter were to die there, while more than 1000 were to return severely wounded.

THE AUTHOR Adrian Gilbert has edited and contributed to a number of military and naval publications. His book *World War I in Photographs*, which is to be published this year, covers all aspects of The Great War.

Left: Republican troops tend to their wounded at the battle of Brunete in July 1937. Below: Men who fought and were sympathetic to the Republican cause who have since risen to great heights. Clockwise from top left: Willie Brandt, the West German Chancellor; President Tito of Yugoslavia; the author, Ernest Hemingway; and the journalist, Arthur Koestler.

EXTRACTIONS

The rapid evacuation of a recon team from a combat zone was of paramount importance to the outcome of an intelligence mission.

As with insertions, helicopters were usually used. Flying low and fast, pilots would drop into a landing zone at a steep angle to recover the team, the whole operation completed in a matter of seconds.

On many occasions, however, it was impossible for the choppers to land due to enemy ground fire or the lack of a suitable clear site, and other techniques were developed to overcome this potentially deadly problem. Next to helicopter landing, rope ladders proved the most successful method of extraction. Dropped from a hovering aircraft, each ladder could support the weight of up to three team members at one time.

The other means of effecting an extraction was by using a nylon webbing rig. Much like a simplified parachute harness, the wearer could, by attaching the rig to a rope hanging down from the helicopter, be drawn quickly aloft. The existing McGuire rig, however, proved unsatisfactory and staff members at the 5th Special Forces Group Recondo School designed an improved rig named STABO, after the initials of its five creators.

Use in the field soon established that the STABO rig was easier to use and more reliable than its predecessor. An added advantage was that team members were also able to use their weapons when being extracted by the STABO rig.

THE SECRET WAR

Taking the counter-offensive against communist forces, the Green Berets initiated a whole series of clandestine operations in Vietnam

SIX CLAYMORE mines erupted simultaneously across a 75m section of jungle track. Those Viet Cong (VC) not killed outright hit the deck as a barrage of CAR-15 automatic fire and rounds fired from sawn-off M79 grenade launchers added to the cacophony of battle. Only one guerrilla survived the deadly storm and, as he lay pressed to the cool, jungle earth, a menacing, green-clad snatch squad, consisting of a Green Beret officer, a South Vietnamese officer and interpreter, raced across the track to corner their prey.

Dragging the prisoner to his feet, the squad headed for cover and began to move back to the pre-arranged RV, their line of withdrawal covered by the other members of the 12-man recon team. To

Their ranks filled with the toughest, most proficient fighting men in Southeast Asia, the US Special Forces reconnaissance teams waged a ceaseless undercover war against the communist guerrillas operating in the depths of the South Vietnamese jungle. Trained in all the arts of jungle warfare, small teams, comprised of local tribesmen and the cream of the US armed forces' crack units, plunged into enemy territory for weeks on end, gathering intelligence, laying ambushes and grabbing prisoners, before hot-footing it back to base. Although often ordered to avoid contact, most recon teams were walking arsenals (right), armed with CAR-15 carbines, grenade launchers and Claymore mines. Casualty evacuation (left) was all part of a team's daily routine, and many a downed pilot owed his life to the timely arrival of a recon patrol.

prevent an enemy follow-up, the two flank parties activated the 60-second delay fuzes on a pair of Claymores. Less than an hour later, the team was back at base; their captive handed over for interrogation.

The VC were learning that it was hard to hide from the recon teams, who would often appear from nowhere in the gloom of the South Vietnamese jungle to wreak havoc and then fade back into the countryside, their mission accomplished. 'Sat Cong' (kill communists) was the motto of many recon teams.

The central co-ordinating body, responsible for organising and evaluating the performance of field teams, was the Military Assistance Command Vietnam, Studies and Observations Group (MACV/SOG). More commonly known as the Special Operations Group, SOG was activated in 1964 and through MACV was directly accountable to the US Joint Chiefs of Staff, through the Special Assistant for Counter-Insurgency and Special Activities.

Activated in 1964, Delta was a self-contained group specifically created to carry out hazardous intelligence gathering and hunter-killer missions against the communist forces operating in the South Vietnamese border areas.

Unlike the other Greek letter projects (Omega, Sigma and Gamma) Delta was run jointly by both US and South Vietnamese Special Forces. As the project grew in size and the scope of its work expanded, Delta's operations were controlled by Detachment B-52.

Under B-52, Delta was organised into 12 (later 16) reconnaissance teams, each made up of two US Special Forces and four indigenous personnel. The other undercover teams within Delta were known as 'Roadrunners'. Dressed as guerrillas, these groups comprised four locals and worked along known enemy infiltration routes.

Delta also had its own quick reaction force, the 91st Ranger Battalion (Airborne) of the South Vietnamese Army. Flown into action by 281st Assault Helicopter Company, the rangers were used to neutralise guerrilla bases and units.

When Delta reached full strength, the US Special Forces were working with nearly 1200 indigs, drawn from the Nung tribe. The other Greek letter projects also included ethnic Cambodians, Chams and Montagnards.

Aside from the more warlike activities, Delta was also closely involved in the training of other recon teams at the Recondo School. Above: the US Special Forces shoulder flash.

Although the most widely known functions of Special Forces teams in Vietnam were training and advisory, the Green Berets were also heavily committed to several types of undercover operations, both within and far beyond the borders of South Vietnam. Many of these missions involved the collection of detailed and up-to-the-minute intelligence within enemy-controlled areas. However, Special Forces teams also had a much more aggressive role to perform. Assassination, sabotage, psychological warfare, snatches and rescue missions all fell within the scope of Special Forces 'black ops'.

When established, SOG was a joint-services outfit drawing on the cream of all four branches of the US armed forces. Some of the toughest, most resolute fighters available were recruited: Navy SEALs, Marine Recons, air jockeys from the 90th Special Operations Wing and, above all, members of the Green Berets. Highly-trained 'indigs' (indigenous personnel) from local tribes were also attracted to SOG. Crack helicopter crews were always available to insert and extract SOG teams in enemy territory, and certain naval craft were also on hand to carry out clandestine insertions into North Vietnam.

The newly-created SOG also attracted some of the finest, most experienced senior officers available. Men like the redoubtable Colonel Donald Blackburn, whose behind-the-lines experience in the Philippines during World War II was to prove invaluable, and Colonel John Singlaub. Another legendary Special Forces officer who served with Blackburn was 'Bull' Simons who organised many of the covert operations into Laos, Cambodia and North Vietnam.

At its peak, SOG consisted of around 2000 US personnel and 8000 indigs. A percentage of the Americans in SOG were drawn from the 5th Special Forces Group (5th SFG), but in Vietnam were assigned to a shadowy organisation known as the Special Operations Augmentation. In practice, however, SOG also contained members of both the 1st and 7th Special Forces Groups who carried out SOG missions while on six-month TDY (temporary duty) tours in country.

RTs usually took their names from snakes or US states, such as RT Anaconda or RT Montana

SOG's headquarters was located close to Saigon near the town of Tan Son Nhut. Although particular missions were normally planned at this HQ, they were generally launched from forward sites originally called Forward Observation Bases (FOBs), but later known as Command and Control (CC) Sites. Other types of special operations were carried out by Mobile Launch Teams; from Ban Me Thuot, Kontum, Khe Sanh and Da Nang.

In November 1967, the co-ordination of SOG missions devolved to three CC units, each responsible for a particular combat zone. Command and Control North (CCN) was based at Da Nang to oversee missions into Laos and North Vietnam, Command and Control Central (CCC) was based at Kontum to carry out operations in the area where the borders of South Vietnam, Laos and Cambodia met, and the third body, Command and Control South (CCS), was based at Ban Me Thuot for ops into Cambodia.

The primary operational unit of each CC site was known as a Spike Recon Team, consisting of three Special Forces and nine indigs. Recon Teams (RTs) usually took their names from snakes or US states, such as RT Anaconda or RT Montana. At the peak period of SOG activity operational RTs numbered around 70. The RTs were backed up by Hatchet Forces which comprised five Special Forces personnel and up to 309 indigs. These teams were well-trained and experienced, specialists in ambushing enemy troops infiltrating into South Vietnam. RTs, however, were only the eyes and ears of the undercover forces, and it was the Hatchet Force and the four SLAM (Search–Annihilate–Mission) companies that provided the cutting edge to their activities. Acting on information provided by the RTs, these rapid reaction forces were often inserted by helicopter to attack enemy bases or lay ambushes.

Often confused with SOG, but having a similar role, were the 'Greek letter' projects: Delta, Sigma, Omega and Gamma. These four projects grew out of Operation Leaping Lena in which US Special Forces personnel trained local troops to carry out long range recon patrols. Leaping Lena evolved into Project Delta, the first and most famous of the Greek projects.

Captured enemy clothing and equipment was carried on ops to disguise a team's true identity

During the early stages, only one Special Forces A-Team was attached to Delta, although by the early 1970s almost 1000 men were involved in operations. Unlike SOG, however, Project Delta drew most of its personnel from the 5th SFG (Airborne). Delta was organised into 12 tight-knit, highly skilled reconnaissance teams made up of two Green Berets and four indigs each. Delta also had six (later expanded to 12) Roadrunner teams, each consisting of four indigs) whose role was to move along the enemy's infiltration routes disguised as guerrillas, report back to base, and call up the 'killer' element of the project: a South Vietnamese Ranger battalion. The 281st Assault Helicopter Company provided Delta with its own organic lift capability.

When Project Delta began, the infiltration of recon and Roadrunner teams was effected by parachute, often at night, but helicopters and other means were also used later. Fighting or reconnoitring the jungle was both time consuming and strength sapping, and it proved vital that the teams were well-supplied with every type of combat necessity. To disguise the exact location of a team, elaborate deception measures were devised to mask the influx of supplies. Both Delta and SOG teams were often resupplied by dropping fake bombs or napalm canisters containing supplies and equipment in the vicinity of their area of operations.

Delta proved to be so successful that it was expanded to include over 1200 indigs, and three other projects, Sigma, Gamma and Omega were activated between 1966 and 1967. Although the four projects concentrated on the unglamorous task of intelligence gathering, targets of opportunity were attacked if encountered.

Although the precise details of the missions undertaken by the various recon forces remain shrouded in official secrecy, certain aspects of their field procedures can be gleaned from available material.

To carry out their highly dangerous missions, the various recon units were equipped with a variety of specialist weapons and equipment. Uniforms, for example, were never standardised; jungle fatigues either dyed or splattered with black paint, were

often worn by both the Special Forces and the indigs. Bandannas were used to cover the face and break up the tell-tale silhouette of a recon member. Captured enemy clothing and equipment was also carried on ops to disguise a team's true identity. Frequently, USAF survival vests were worn, their pockets stuffed with a bewildering variety of essential escape and evasion aids.

Recon teams paid particular attention to their footwear. Jungle boots or 'Bata' sneakers were popular, and a type of shoe with rubber moulds of Vietnamese bare feet attached to the soles was experimented with but proved to be extremely uncomfortable and became little more than a novelty item. In fact, the footprints left by these shoes when worn by a Green Beret were so much larger and deeper than those left by a guerrilla that the enemy was rarely fooled.

Other items of specialist equipment, however, were more realistic and of lasting value. STABO rigs, which allowed a team member to be lifted into a chopper while still firing his weapon, were much prized, particularly as many recons were often hotly pursued by guerrillas as they withdrew. A few extractions were even made by skyhook, a device consisting of a large balloon and harness which could be snatched aloft by a low-flying aircraft.

Although recon teams often avoided 'live' contact with the enemy, many were still walking arsenals. The most common sidearm was the handy Browning 9mm pistol or the .22in Ruger automatic with silencer, used to take care of VC sentries with the minimum of fuss. Larger weapons included the CAR-15 version

Above: Taking the fight to the Viet Cong on their own ground was a tough way to go to war. Every recon had to learn to move with speed and stealth to prevent detection. Teams avoided well-worn paths or river crossings as the VC often rigged these points with booby traps, trip wires attached to grenades, or punji sticks plastered with human excrement. **Below:** 'Bull' Simons, one of the Special Forces 'greats'.

of the M16, the Swedish K 9mm sub-machine gun and a variety of carbines. Additional weaponry might include a sawn-off M79 grenade launcher. Usually affixed to a team member's webbing and loaded with a canister round, they could be used as a giant 'shotgun' to clear an enemy patrol from a trail.

Armed with this deadly array of ordnance, the various recon teams tended to follow a similar pattern when in the field. After arriving at a FOB, the RT commander, often a junior officer, would brief the local officers on the precise aims of his op, the strength of his team, its area of operations and the methods of insertion and extraction to be used.

Just before last light, the recon team would be assembled at the base's landing zone to rendezvous with their helicopters – their weapons, radios and equipment checked and cleaned, their faces blacked up with cam cream. Insertions at dusk were favoured as pilots were able to fly to the landing site and escape back before the inky Vietnamese night shrouded both them and the recon team in its embrace.

On landing, the team leader would gather his men, take bearings and then plunge into the jungle. During movement to the objective, the team took great care to avoid VC booby traps, mines and punji stake traps. Stealth was vital: hand and arm signals were used instead of voice commands, radio messages were kept as short as possible, and all weapons and equipment were taped and padded to minimise noise.

Sites for setting up camp or receiving supplies were always arranged and plotted before a mission.

RECON INSIGNIA

Most recon teams in Vietnam were named after either a US state or snake and, although risking official censure, all had personalised badges (above) made up by local tailors. Popular aggressive emblems included skulls, tigers, birds of prey and even alligators. Worn on the upper arm, the badges were worn not only as a means of identifying a particular unit, but also as a mark of their individuality.

A team's main needs were for a site that was defensible, with good cover and ready access to water. However, as a recon was essentially aggressive, few teams ever occupied a bivouac for more than a few hours. Any longer, and the VC were likely to be snapping at the team's heels.

The key part of any reconnaissance was gathering intelligence and every team member was fully trained in interpreting and reading the signs left by the enemy. Even the most seemingly inconsequential find might yield extremely valuable information. On one occasion a recon team discovered numerous piles of fresh elephant dung below a ridge line. Further investigation on the crest revealed recently abandoned gourds and small rifle pits. Piecing all the evidence together, it was estimated that a VC force of approximately battalion strength, using elephants for transportation, had occupied the site within the last 48 hours. From the direction of the tracks leading away from the position, the team was able to plot the route taken by the enemy. If the contact had been fresher, the team leader would have called in either a 'killer' force or an air strike to take care of the enemy.

Footprints were another valuable source of intelligence and recons were taught to identify the number of people in an enemy patrol, the direction of movement, and even the type of load being carried. Under normal conditions, spaced footprints with unusually deep toe marks indicated that the person leaving the prints was carrying a heavy load. Team members were also trained to take into account the effects of wind, rain and sunlight on tracks.

If it became clear that a particular trail was in constant use, the recon team might lay an ambush or carry out a snatch to capture a guerrilla. To avoid

After completing a mission, the top priority of every recon team was to get back to base. Team leaders would call-up helicopters on the radio net (below, far left). Exfiltrations from the countryside (below right) were fraught with danger as the VC often booby-trapped landing zones. If air evacuation was impossible, the teams had to walk home (below left). Speed was always vital as the intelligence gathered from captives (below, far right) gave the US Air Force the chance to hit hard at enemy positions (main picture).

getting involved in a firefight, teams often left the enemy a calling card: Claymore mines with a delay fuze, M14 mines planted in a triangular pattern across the track, or trip wires attached to fragmentation grenades.

After completing an operation, the recon teams would rendezvous at a pre-arranged landing zone for extraction. Again, helicopters were the favoured method of departure from the patrol area. If time permitted, the pilots would bring their choppers in to land, but if the enemy was in hot pursuit of a team, other, faster methods such as the STABO rig would be used. Back at base, the team leader would be debriefed and the information collated and assessed.

Although the scale and frequency of recon and 'killer' missions in Vietnam varied from month to month, most units spent up to 60 per cent of their tours

of duty in Vietnam on active operations.

Despite the frequent success of recon teams, they could never off-set the US armed forces inability to come to grips with waging a war against an unconventional enemy, and as the American commitment in Vietnam was wound down, many of the Special Forces teams were deactivated. By the early 1970s, the four Greek letter projects, arguably the finest realisation of the recon idea, had been disbanded, and the other long-range penetration units were being withdrawn. Nevertheless, the concept had proved a valuable part of the US counter-insurgency effort.

THE AUTHOR Leroy Thompson served in Vietnam as a member of the USAF Combat Security Police. He has published several books on the Special Forces and is the author of *Uniforms of the Elite Forces*.

SECRET RECONNAISSANCE

Sixteen months before the beginning of the Sinai Campaign of 1956, six Israelis were inserted deep into Egypt to make a vital reconnaissance

ON THE PLEASANT late autumn afternoon of 29 October 1956, 16 Douglas DC-3 Dakotas droned towards the eastern end of the Mitla Pass to the east of Suez. Then, in the fading light, the sky became dotted by the smoothly opening parachutes of 395 Israeli paratroopers. It was the sudden, bold opening move of what was later to be known as the Sinai Campaign. On the following morning, this body of paratroopers was to participate in one of the bravest and most costly engagements in the history of the Israeli Defence Forces (IDF). For a loss of 38 men, the paras were to inflict 260 casualties on the opposing Egyptian forces.

In the period just preceding the Israeli invasion of the Sinai peninsula, tension had been escalating rapidly between Egypt and Israel. Fedayeen terrorist groups based in the Gaza Strip were being encouraged by Egypt to attack civilian targets in Israel. Elat port on the Gulf of Aqaba was blockaded by Egypt to prevent free Israeli navigation to the Red Sea and the Suez Canal, and Egyptian guns had been set up at Ras Nasrani, overshadowing Israel's only southern route to Africa and the Far East. After Egypt signed treaties with Jordan and Syria, the economic boycott had tightened. But most threatening of all to Israeli security, in 1955 Egypt signed an agreement with Czechoslovakia for the supply of arms. Despite Israel's own arms build-up, this contract, when completed, would so alter the arms balance between Egypt and Israel that Israel's security could not be guaranteed.

Alarmed by these circumstances, General Moshe Dayan, then Chief of Staff of the IDF, presented a plan of retaliation before the Israeli cabinet. He suggested that Sharm el Sheik, a point on the southern tip of the Sinai peninsula that overlooked the Tiran Straits, should be seized in an airborne operation and a land-bridge established northwards to Elat, arguing that Israel could thus ensure herself free

Right: A Piper aircraft flies over vehicles of the Israeli 9th Infantry Brigade as they advance towards Sharm el Sheik in the south of the Sinai peninsula. That the brigade could advance in confidence in the unknown Egyptian territory was due to a secret reconnaissance mission led by Lieutenant-Colonel Asher Levy (below left). Far left: Israeli command cars penetrate into the waterless mountains.

passage to the Red Sea and severely hamper Egypt's preparations for war. However, the Israeli cabinet did not believe that the time was right and it rejected the plan, codenamed Operation Omer, stating that, 'Israel will act where and when she will find it suitable.'

More than a year later, Israel's opportunity to act appeared suddenly when Egypt's president, Gamal Abdel Nasser, nationalised the Suez Canal Company. Having gained the agreement of Britain and France, Israel launched an attack on a scale much bigger than envisaged for the original operation. Rapidly following the successful para drop on the Mitla Pass at 1700 hours on 29 October 1956, two companies of the 9th Infantry Brigade, commanded by Colonel Avraham Yoffe, captured Ras el Nakeb, just across the border from Elat, which was the starting point of the coast road to Sharm el Sheik. On 1 November the rest of the 9th Infantry Brigade began the march to Sharm el Sheik. Only 100 hours passed between the opening move and the securing of Sharm el Sheik and Israeli victory.

It was known by only a handful of men at that time that the brigade's march to Sharm el Sheik had been made possible by an undercover reconnaissance mission which had been carried out a full 16 months

Bottom left: Operation Yarkon, in which the Israelis confirmed that a road route existed between Elat and Sharm el Sheik, was a high priority in 1955. Both General Moshe Dayan (right) and General Chaim Bar-Lev, commander of the 27th Armoured Brigade, were closely involved in its planning. Bottom right: Their mission completed, the six patrolmen (front row) are photographed at Elat with all their support personnel. General Dayan is seated on a vehicle to the left. Below: Israeli infantrymen await the order to attack Egyptian positions on 30 October 1956.

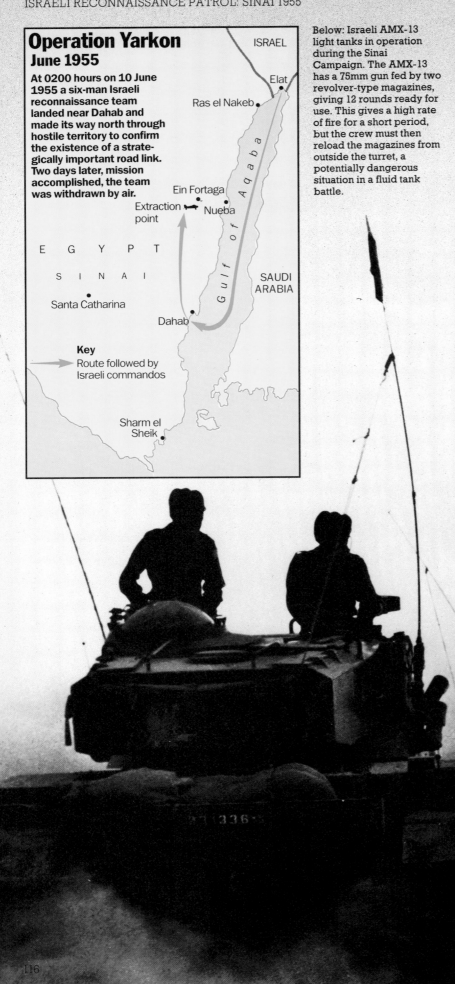

Operation Yarkon
June 1955

At 0200 hours on 10 June 1955 a six-man Israeli reconnaissance team landed near Dahab and made its way north through hostile territory to confirm the existence of a strategically important road link. Two days later, mission accomplished, the team was withdrawn by air.

Key

→ Route followed by Israeli commandos

Below: Israeli AMX-13 light tanks in operation during the Sinai Campaign. The AMX-13 has a 75mm gun fed by two revolver-type magazines, giving 12 rounds ready for use. This gives a high rate of fire for a short period, but the crew must then reload the magazines from outside the turret, a potentially dangerous situation in a fluid tank battle.

earlier. Even fewer knew that of the six men chosen for the operation, one was in the leading armoured car of the column, and another was commander of a unit in the brigade.

From its conception, General Dayan's plan for Operation Omer had raised an important unanswered question. Although aerial photographs showed that there was a route suitable for an advancing army from Elat to Sharm el Sheik, no-one knew whether it was passable to armoured vehicles. Without a serviceable road, the plan would be impracticable and another method of attack, such as an amphibious operation, would need to be considered. Dayan needed an answer quickly, and the only way to get it would be to mount a reconnaissance patrol deep behind enemy lines. When he informed the Israeli prime minister, David Ben-Gurion, that it would be better to cancel the operation if a patrol could not be authorised, Ben-Gurion finally agreed. Immediately Dayan picked up the phone to the Operations Officer. 'Okay,' he said, 'Green light.'

Operation Yarkon, as the reconnaissance patrol came to be known, was designed to integrate aerial, marine and infantry forces. As such, it was the first 'combined operation' to be executed by the young Israeli Army. The six members of the patrol were all hand-picked volunteers: commander of the force was Lieutenant-Colonel Asher Levy, then of the famous 5th 'Givati' Brigade; second-in-command was Major Emmanuel Shaked. The others were Lieutenant Yigal Talmi (the communications officer), Lieutenant Aharon Lubliner, Second-Lieutenant Yoram Lipsky and Sergeant Duban Simhoni.

'The operation was to be carried out in June, a very hot month in the Sinai desert, and we were going to walk very long distances'

The aerial photographs and French maps possessed by the Israeli group showed one route running south from Ras el Nakeb towards Ein Fortaga and then turning west. Another route climbed from Sharm el Sheik to Dahab and then also turned west. The big question was whether the two routes joined, for the aerial photographs suggested only that the intervening area was a canyon. The mission of the six men was to cross the unknown area and report back. The task would take three days and it was imperative that they should not be discovered, for the capture of Israeli military personnel so deep in Egyptian territory could easily lead to an Israeli-Egyptian war.

Lieutenant-Colonel Levy has described the process leading up to the patrol:

'Immediately after the participants were chosen we began a long series of exhausting training sessions. We went on long marches to improve our level of fitness. The operation was due to be carried out in June, a very hot month in the Sinai desert, and we were going to walk very long distances.'

The operational outline had three parts, each involving a different form of transport. The six men would be brought to shore just south of Dahab by a fisherman's boat, to be landed in a rubber dinghy. From the landing point they were to march very quickly into the mountains, for 17km, then pass northwards to Ein Fortaga where they would prepare a landing area for six small Piper aircraft which would then fly in to evacuate them. Lieutenant-Colonel Levy recollected asking how the men were to know whether the ground was suitable for a Piper to land. He was told, 'Dig your heel into the ground. If it doesn't sink in too deep, then it's okay!'

One problem faced by the men was that of ensuring an adequate supply of water during the mission. They could not carry all the amount needed, and the sources in the desert were extremely unreliable. The only possible solution was to parachute water containers down from an aircraft of the Israeli Air Force. This task was new to the pilots and several unsuccessful drops were made before they found a solution. A device was used to delay the opening of the parachute after the cargo had dropped from the plane, and soon safe landings were being achieved within pinpoint landing zones of no more than 100m diameter.

Following the four months of special training leading up to the mission two preliminary reconnaissances were made, one by air over the ground they were going to cover, and one by sea, to measure the sailing time between Elat and Dahab. The captain of the *Elat*, the boat which took them both on the initial reconnaissance and on the mission, was Naftali Rosen, who has recalled:

'When I look back on the mission, I cannot understand how we managed to complete it, with the means we had and the conditions we faced. The boat we had was nothing more than a disintegrating barge, and our only navigation system was a magnetic compass. The men were totally unready for such a trip at sea. They were sick all the time, especially on the way back when we tackled bad weather. Even Colonel Chaim Bar-Lev, who had joined us, was throwing up like hell!' The initial sea reconnaissance ended at Elat, with most of the men finding it very hard to stand on their feet.

At 1000 hours on 9 June 1955, the *Elat* set course for the mission proper. Colonel Bar-Lev remained behind to fly with the Dakota. At first the sailing was smooth, but the weather changed and a storm broke, wildly rocking the old craft. As if this was not enough, an Egyptian gunboat was sighted patrolling the area, but the two boats passed each other without making contact. At nightfall they identified the lights of a second ship, and in order to avoid contact they changed course towards the Saudi Arabian shore.

The bad weather and the evasive course of the *Elat* caused a serious delay. The landing was scheduled to take place at 2200 hours, after which the men were to march fast towards the mountains until dawn, and

THE SINAI CAMPAIGN

The nationalisation of the Suez Canal Company on 26 July 1956 by Egypt's president, Gamal Abdel Nasser, was accompanied by the deployment of Egyptian forces to the Canal Zone to protect it from potential Anglo-French attack. This move was fortuitous from the Israeli point of view, for it weakened the Egyptian presence on the Israeli border, just at a time when Israel was preparing a pre-emptive strike on Egypt in order to destroy a growing military threat and re-open her blocked access route to the Red Sea.

The Israeli attack, codenamed Operation Kadesh, was planned in three phases. In Phase One, a deep left hook was to capture the Mitla Pass, thus cutting one of the main lines of communication between Suez and the Israeli border, while simultaneous attacks were to hold down Egyptian units elsewhere. Phase Two was designed to destroy the Egyptian frontline units in direct conflict. In Phase Three, Egyptian resistance in the Sinai and on the Gaza Strip was to be cleared, the equipment of the broken enemy formations captured, and the Egyptian guns on the Tiran Straits neutralised. Preceded by an airborne assault, Phase One was successfully implemented on 29 October 1956. On 31 October, Anglo-French air forces attacked the Canal Zone, forcing the Egyptians to fight on two fronts. In a series of hard-pressed assaults the Israelis completed Phase Two by the end of 1 November, breaking the back of Egyptian resistance in Sinai.

Mopping up was commenced, and the last Egyptian outpost, at Sharm el Sheik, was taken on 5 November.

The Sinai Campaign was an undoubted success for the Israelis. The Tiran Straits were reopened and the United Nations Emergency Force was inserted as a neutral buffer between Egypt and Israel.

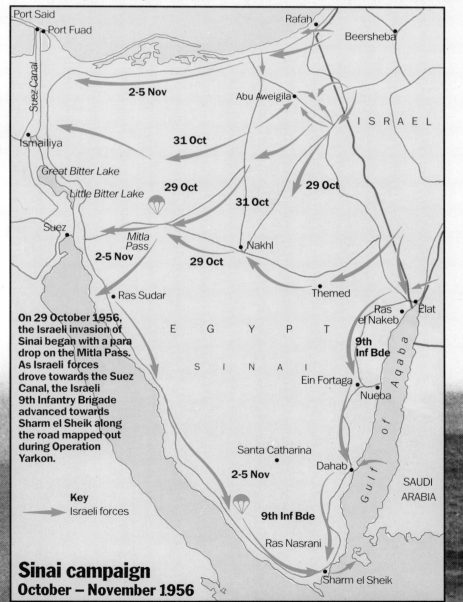

2-5 Nov

31 Oct

29 Oct

29 Oct

31 Oct

2-5 Nov

29 Oct

On 29 October 1956, the Israeli invasion of Sinai began with a para drop on the Mitla Pass. As Israeli forces drove towards the Suez Canal, the Israeli 9th Infantry Brigade advanced towards Sharm el Sheik along the road mapped out during Operation Yarkon.

9th Inf Bde

2-5 Nov

9th Inf Bde

Key
→ Israeli forces

Sinai campaign
October – November 1956

Below: Israeli machine-gunners ready their Czechoslovakian Model 37 (ZB 53) heavy machine guns for desert operations. Fed by 100- or 200-round belts, the Model 37 can be fired at two different cyclic rates, 500 or 700 rpm. Inset right: Israeli tanks raise great clouds of sand as they race to gain control of key positions in the Sinai. Inset left: Sharm el Sheik falls to the Israelis. Enclosed under guard by circles of loosely strewn barbed wire, Egyptian prisoners of war await their fate after the successful Israeli feat of arms. They were finally released when the US guaranteed Israel free passage through the Tiran Straits.

Colonel Bar-Lev had given express orders – if not on the beach by midnight – return! Yet when they approached Dahab it was already 0200 hours on the 10th. Lieutenant-Colonel Levi has stated, 'We decided to go on with the mission. One of the reasons, and not the least one, was our reluctance to climb back on that crummy barge…!'

They landed on the beach just one hour before daybreak. Exhausted as they were from the prolonged sea journey, they set off quickly towards the mountains, and by dawn they were at the mouth of the canyon identified in the aerial photographs. In accordance with the plan, they radioed just one codeword – 'Opening'. They expected no answer, and they learned only later that no-one received their call and that for many hours they were considered missing. Only when the water-carrying Dakota identified their lights the following night was it finally confirmed that they were alive.

As the day wore on, the heat became unbearable. They decided to begin walking before nightfall and, with the coming of darkness, they lit the green and red torches that marked the drop zones for the water canisters. Lieutenant-Colonel Levy commented:

'We were very glad to hear the plane coming. Not much water remained in our canteens. We saw the first load being ejected from the aircraft and counted: one…two…three. After three seconds the delayed opening of the parachute should have taken place. Nothing happened! The device didn't work and the precious water fell out of the sky like a bomb!'

A second attempt to parachute down a canister ended like the first. Colonel Bar-Lev then ordered the third load to be dropped without the device, but the wind carried the parachute a great distance.

Only the fourth and last load of water reached the men.

In the terrible blazing heat of the next day the men tried to bury the water containers to keep them cool, but the burning ground made the task impossible. Aware that their mission hung in the balance, the six men determined to complete their task, and they navigated a precise path through the canyon, finally confirming that armoured vehicles could traverse the ground.

On the third day of the patrol, word was received at Elat that the men had been detected by bedouins and that a company of Sudanese infantry was on their trail. The six Pipers were immediately despatched to evacuate the scouts before the Sudanese company made contact, an event which would have caused a severe diplomatic incident. Led by Hanoch Keret, the planes took off. One lost its way immediately after becoming airborne, yet all eventually succeeded in navigating to the pick-up point. Hanoch Keret remarked, 'The end of the "runway" marked by the men was blocked by a sheer rock face. But, whatever the consequences, I decided to land, and so did all of us.' Wheeling round, the Pipers collected the men and bore them back to Elat.

The six men of the patrol were each awarded citations by General Moshe Dayan. But their real reward came 16 months later, when the 9th Infantry Brigade rumbled over the route they had reconnoitred to conquer Sharm el Sheik.

THE AUTHOR Aharon Lapidot is a major in the Israeli Air Force and has been editor of the Israel Air Force Magazine since 1982. He has written many articles and several books on aspects of the Israeli Defence Forces.

The US Army Special Forces, the Green Berets, were regarded with suspicion by the US military establishment – until they showed what they could do in Vietnam

SINCE 1945 most of the world's armed forces have had to adjust to fundamental changes in the art of warfare. In the aftermath of World War II, nationalist movements in various colonial possessions began to employ guerrilla tactics against their colonial masters and few of the major powers were equipped to deal with this threat. It soon became clear that large conventional units were unable to defeat totally the guerrillas and that small teams of highly-trained specialists were better suited to playing the insurgents at their own game, and winning. The United States was one of the first countries to tap the potential of this new type of fighting man.

Deadly exponents of the new art of unconventional warfare, the men of the US Army Special Forces are tough professionals whose combat skills have been honed to perfection in one of the world's most exhaustive and thorough military training programmes. The few men who get through the course truly earn the right to wear one of the most revered symbols of any crack fighting force – the green beret.

The present-day Special Forces, formed in 1952, can trace its lineage back to the Office of Strategic Services (OSS). Active during World War II, the OSS was instrumental in the creation of guerrilla-style forces to attack and harass the enemy's weak points. One formation in particular, Detachment 101, working with Kachin and Jingpaw tribesmen in Burma, fully proved the value of such clandestine operations.

The commander of the new unit, designated the 10th Special Forces Group (Airborne), was an OSS veteran, Colonel Aaron Bank. With boundless energy,

GREEN BERETS

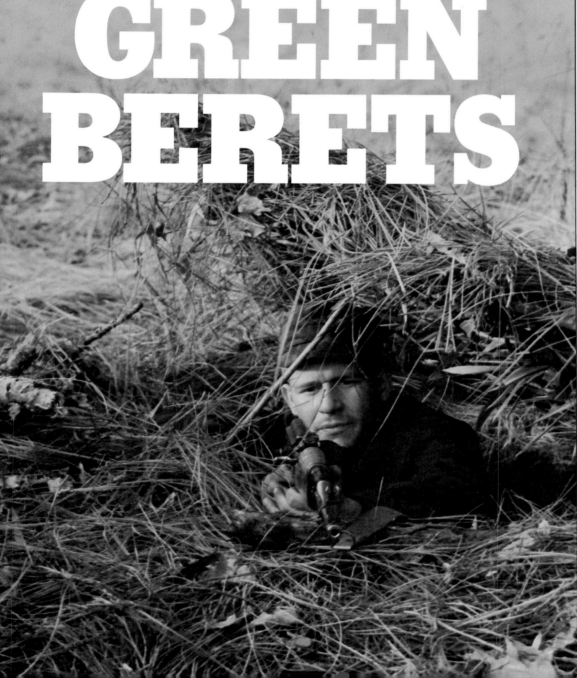

THE GREEN BERET

In 1954, a year or so after the formation of the Special Forces, a committee of officers and NCOs met at Fort Bragg in North Carolina and chose the green beret as a suitable headwear for members of the new unit. Based on the beret worn by the British Royal Marine Commandos, the berets were first worn publicly in June 1956. The following December, the 77th Special Forces Group (Airborne) ordered all its personnel to wear the beret.

The Special Forces' adoption of a distinctive emblem, however, brought them into conflict with senior officers who ordered the beret to be replaced. Despite a vigorous campaign to retain the beret, the ban remained in force until 1961.

In October 1961 President John F. Kennedy, a keen supporter of Special Forces, visited Fort Bragg and reviewed the 5th and 7th Special Forces Groups. At Kennedy's request, the troops wore the green beret at the ceremony. Believing that the beret would be a suitable mark of distinction, the President then ordered the reinstatement of this Special Forces emblem.

Above: The US Special Forces insignia, as worn on the front of the green beret.

Left: Members of the US Special Forces are trained to work with a wide range of foreign weapons, including the ubiquitous AK-47, favoured smallarm of communist guerrillas the world over.

Bank immediately began to formulate the role of the Special Forces, defining their mission as: 'to infiltrate by land, sea or air, deep into enemy-occupied territory and organise the resistance/guerrilla potential to conduct Special Forces operations, with emphasis on guerrilla warfare.' With the help of some early volunteers, Bank developed a training course in unconventional warfare that formed the basis of the present-day programme. Bank's original course, however, has been constant-

ly updated to accommodate changes in the type and areas of operations that might be faced by members of the Special Forces.

At the outset very few officers outside the Special Forces' base at Fort Bragg in North Carolina were even aware of its existence. Most of those regular army officers who did know about the Special Forces viewed their psychological and guerrilla warfare missions with distrust. The US Army of the 1950s was geared to conventional warfare in Europe rather than unconventional operations, and even the early Special Forces viewed their role in the limited context of behind-the-lines operations in Europe. At this time, few people realised the importance that counter-insurgency work would soon assume.

However, many early members of Special Forces were especially well-qualified to carry out operations in the Soviet Union's satellite states: many had been born in Eastern Europe and had entered the US Army under the Lodge Bill which allowed foreigners to gain American citizenship by serving in the US armed forces.

By the mid-1950s, members of the Special Forces were involved in training programmes with other NATO units such as the British SAS

In September 1953, the 77th Special Forces Group (Airborne) was activated from elements of the 10th SFG (Airborne). Elements of the 10th also became the nucleus of the Special Warfare Center, while the remainder of the unit, some 782 men, deployed to Bad Tolz in West Germany, where they would be closer to the action should war break out.

The 10th Special Forces in Germany were designed to be ready to move into Hungary, Czechoslovakia, Romania, East Germany or Poland should hostilities break out. As one would expect of troops trained to work with the local population, the Special Forces in Germany were soon widely accepted by the Germans in the Alps, who aided the Green Berets against conventional ground troops during military exercises. Even though the US Seventh Army in Germany was well-trained and highly professional, Special Forces-led 'guerrillas' harassed them continuously during these manoeuvres. By the mid-1950s, members of the Special Forces, especially the 10th SFG (Airborne) were involved in exchange training programmes with other NATO special units such as the British Special Air Service.

Most US commanders in Germany, however, did

Above: An instructor gives a recruit a few tips on the finer points of survival techniques. Left: Learning the ropes. A member of the 77th Special Forces Group practises abseiling at Camp Hale in Colorado. Opposite page above: Before candidates are allowed to put theory into practice, they have to attend study classes. Here, men get to know the lay-out of a para-rig. Opposite page below: Sudden death for a 'guerrilla' on the 'manhunt' course.

not really understand the Special Forces' role in any future war. Many would have gladly traded the 'Sneaky Petes' for a few more tanks. As a result, by the mid-1950s, Special Forces' strength in Europe had been more than halved to less than 400 men.

Back at Fort Bragg the 77th SFG (Airborne) continued to train in the skills of guerrilla warfare and psychological operations. By June 1957, elements of the 77th had moved to Okinawa in the Pacific where they formed the nucleus of the 1st Special Forces Group (Airborne). Just as the 10th SFG (Airborne) specialised in Europe, the 1st SFG (Airborne) trained for service in the Far East. Indeed, the 1st was soon training troops from South Vietnam, Thailand, Taiwan and the Philippines. The 1st also established their own jump school on Okinawa to give basic parachute training to American and foreign troops. Although they were still viewed with suspicion by many senior officers, by 1960 the three Special Forces groups had a combined strength of about 2000 hard-core professionals.

In the late 1950s and early 1960s, the Special Forces began to turn their attention to the wars of national liberation – the communist-backed insurgencies taking place in the Third World. As the reigning US experts on guerrilla tactics, it was natural that the Special Forces should become highly proficient in the techniques of anti-guerrilla or counter-insurgency warfare. Since gaining the trust of the population and, in many cases, training them to defend themselves is an important part of counter-insurgency warfare, the Special Forces' ability to work with the indigenous population and provide various types of training made them well-suited for the new counter-insurgency role. However, it was essential that a tougher, more exhaustive training course be devised to prepare the Green Berets for this new sphere of operations.

With the inauguration of President Kennedy in 1961, the US Special Forces gained a supporter in their new Commander-in-Chief, who believed that counter-insurgency operations were vital to the strategic interests of the United States. Kennedy's interest in the Third World was reflected in the formation of the Peace Corps and in the increased size and deployment of Special Forces. To meet the manpower requirements caused by this rapid expansion, the Special Warfare Center at Fort Bragg increased the number of its graduates from under 400 to over 3000 per year and developed an even more rigorous training programme.

New recruits face one of the most stringent selection courses ever devised; as many as 75 per cent fail to make the grade

New recruits, tough and in peak physical condition, are always high-school graduates and some have college degrees. However, there is no direct entry into the Special Forces – candidates are drawn from the US armed forces and, with an average of three years' service behind them, most are in their early 20s. Most are airborne-qualified but few have combat experience. After arriving at Fort Bragg training school, they face one of the most stringent selection courses ever devised: a three-stage programme in which their mental and physical abilities are evaluated. As many as 75 per cent of candidates fail to make the grade.

The first 31 days of the course are given over to developing stamina and basic combat skills. During

ORGANISATION

The basic operational unit of the US Special Forces is the A-Detachment. More commonly known as the A-Team, the detachment is led by a captain and consists of two officers and 10 enlisted men in total. Each member of the team is a specialist in a particular field: medical, engineering, intelligence, communications or weapons.

When an A-Team is engaged in raising and training a counter-insurgency force, each Green Beret uses his skills to teach local recruits basic combat skills. In theory, each A-Team is capable of raising a guerrilla unit of up to 1500 men within a single month.

Four A-Teams are controlled by a B-Detachment. Commanded by a major, a B-Team comprises six officers and 18 other ranks. On active service, however, B-Teams can operate independently in a more war-like capacity. In Vietnam, for example, B-Teams were actively engaged in raising cadres for the South Vietnamese Army's airborne and ranger units.

Each group of three B-Teams is controlled by a Special Forces Company. Usually called a C-Detachment, each company consists of 19 men, six officers and 13 NCOs, led by a lieutenant-colonel. C-Teams assign objectives to other detachments in the field and assess intelligence gathered.

During the early 1960s, when the Special Forces' responsibilities were being expanded, Special Action Forces (SAF) were created to augment the skills of the A, B, and C-Teams. Each SAF includes a Civil Affairs Group, a Psychological Operations Battalion, an Engineer Detachment, a Medical Detachment and an Army Security Agency unit.

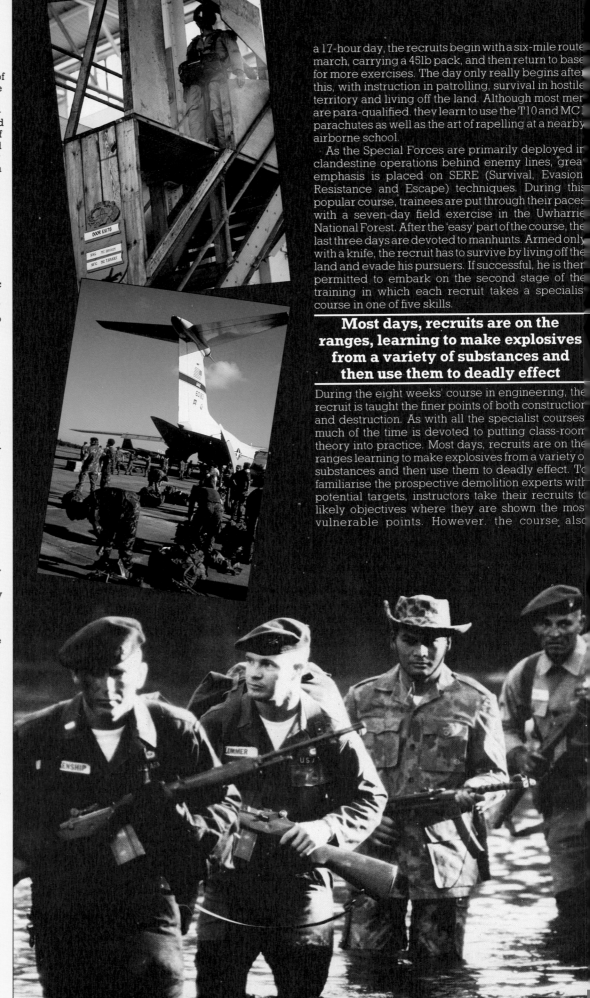

a 17-hour day, the recruits begin with a six-mile route march, carrying a 45lb pack, and then return to base for more exercises. The day only really begins after this, with instruction in patrolling, survival in hostile territory and living off the land. Although most men are para-qualified, they learn to use the T10 and MC1 parachutes as well as the art of rapelling at a nearby airborne school.

As the Special Forces are primarily deployed in clandestine operations behind enemy lines, great emphasis is placed on SERE (Survival, Evasion, Resistance and Escape) techniques. During this popular course, trainees are put through their paces with a seven-day field exercise in the Uwharrie National Forest. After the 'easy' part of the course, the last three days are devoted to manhunts. Armed only with a knife, the recruit has to survive by living off the land and evade his pursuers. If successful, he is then permitted to embark on the second stage of the training in which each recruit takes a specialist course in one of five skills.

Most days, recruits are on the ranges, learning to make explosives from a variety of substances and then use them to deadly effect

During the eight weeks' course in engineering, the recruit is taught the finer points of both construction and destruction. As with all the specialist courses, much of the time is devoted to putting class-room theory into practice. Most days, recruits are on the ranges learning to make explosives from a variety of substances and then use them to deadly effect. To familiarise the prospective demolition experts with potential targets, instructors take their recruits to likely objectives where they are shown the most vulnerable points. However, the course also

eft: During a parachute raining course in anama, a Green Beret rom the 7th Special orces Group Airborne), dressed in IELO (High Extraction, ow Opening) gear, repares to practise oor exits from an ndoor gantry. Once the nen have attained the igh level of proficiency emanded by the pecial Forces, they are llowed to make their rst 'live' jump. Centre eft: Green Berets wait o board a C-5 Galaxy ransporter. Below left: Men of an A-Team on a ERE (Survival, Evasion, esistance and Escape) ourse. The Green erets are equipped vith M14 rifles. Right: wo men learning the elicate art of house learance – a skill that vas much in demand uring the Vietnam War.

involves construction, and trainees are taught how to build bridges, dams and stockades.

The weapons specialists take part in eight weeks of intensive instruction that familiarises them with over 80 different types of modern smallarm. Particular emphasis is placed on marksmanship, and proficiency in the building and use of less conventional weapons such as crossbows. Specialists are also taught the tactical use of their weapons: at squad, platoon and company levels. A candidate must also learn how to teach his skills in the field to friendly forces.

As the Special Forces are expected to go 'native' and operate independently for long periods, they also learn how to work with a wide variety of communications equipment. To pass this course, candidates have to be capable of sending and receiving Morse code at a minimum rate of 18 words per minute. First-rate soldiers are expected to service their equipment in the field and recruits are taught to repair and maintain both transmitting and receiving sets. The disruption of the enemy's communications equipment is also seen as an invaluable skill and prospective specialists have to become adept in this field.

Candidates who opt for the medical specialist course undergo the longest and most difficult training programme. Lasting up to 50 weeks, the course trains the men to deal with most types of combat wound, as the Special Forces are expected to wage 'hearts-and-minds' programmes, to win the trust of the indigenous population, they also learn how to cope with more common ailments and diseases. It is

believed that candidates work with animals during the programme and, if the 'patient' dies, the recruits are thrown out of the Special Forces.

The fifth specialist course concentrates on developing a recruit's intelligence-gathering skills. Particular attention is focussed on establishing intelligence networks, the organisation of guerrilla forces and the interrogation of enemy suspects.

US soldiers play the part of untrained 'natives' and the Green Berets are expected to knock them into shape within a month

Following the completion of the second stage of basic training, the trainees are brought together to learn the basic operational procedures of Special Forces working in the field. After an initial period of theoretical training at Camp Mackall, the recruits are formed into teams and then dropped into the heart of the Uwharrie forest. Once in position, they have to evade the enemy, in the form of aggressor forces drawn from the 82nd Airborne Division, and form guerrilla units. The guerrillas, a random selection of US soldiers, play the part of untrained 'natives' and the Green Berets are expected to knock them into shape within a month. Capture, or failure to raise a guerrilla force, spells the end of the course for the candidate. The successful completion of the course allows the trainees to wear the much-coveted green beret.

After completing their basic training the Green Berets continue to acquire additional skills during

A GLOBAL ROLE

In the years following the creation of the US Special Forces in 1952, the Green Berets underwent a prolonged process of reorganisation and expansion. In September 1953 men from the original unit, the 10th Special Forces Group (Airborne), were detached to form the nucleus of the 77th Special Forces Group (Airborne) and the Special Warfare Center. The remainder of the 10th was despatched to West Germany.

In June 1957 elements of the 77th moved to Okinawa to form part of the 1st Special Forces Group (Airborne). Specialising in the Orient, the 1st was soon training troops from Vietnam, Taiwan, Thailand and the Philippines. By 1960 the three Special Forces Groups had a combined strength of about 2000 hard-core professionals.

The inauguration of President John F. Kennedy in early 1961 led to the expansion of the Special Forces. The 77th became the 7th Special Forces Group (Airborne) in May 1960, and a month later the 1st, 7th and 10th formed the 1st Special Forces (Airborne). As US involvement in Southeast Asia grew, four new groups. the 3rd, 5th, 6th and 8th. were created between September 1961 and March 1964.

Each group was given special responsibilities in a particular strategic area: the 3rd was orientated towards Africa, the 5th was assigned to Vietnam, the 6th was created for operations in the Middle East, and the 8th operated in Central and Southern America. By this stage, each Special Forces Group consisted of 1500 men divided between 36 A-Teams, nine B-Teams and three C-Teams.

their attachment to US military commands throughout the world. Graduates from the Fort Bragg school are usually cross-trained in some other skill. This is seen as being vital to the performance of Special Forces units operating in the field as the loss of one specialist might jeopardise the other members of the team. As the Green Berets are geared up to conduct missions in any part of the world, each man is also taught the specialist techniques needed to survive in every type of environment.

As the teams are likely to work with indigenous populations, particular emphasis is placed on the teaching of languages and training local forces. In general, at least one member of a Special Forces' team should be fluent in the native language. Those teams intended for service in Latin America or Europe find it easier to reach the required level of proficiency than those scheduled for deployment in the Middle East, Africa or Southeast Asia. However, there are now a number of Thai or Vietnamese speakers in the Special Forces because of the Green Berets' involvement in the Vietnam war.

When involved in organising and training local forces for defence or counter-insurgency operations, each member of the Special Forces team has a particular job. Two officers, the operations sergeant and the two weapons experts attached to each team, teach basic tactics, the use of weapons and operational procedures. An intelligence sergeant is on hand to prepare the locals to supply useful information and counter enemy subversion, while the communications expert spends his time training them to use basic radio equipment. The medical specialist

instructs the local recruits in basic hygiene and first-aid. As part of the hearts-and-minds aspect of Special Forces operations, the team's engineer is on hand to assist and direct building programmes. In his more warlike capacity, he trains the local forces in the use of explosives and booby traps. Teams are expected to be able to set-up and train a battalion-sized counter-insurgency force within a month of making contact.

Some team members also become highly trained snipers and each student is expected to achieve a kill from 1800ft

The Special Forces' preparations for war continue during peacetime, with members learning the dangerous arts of insertion into enemy-occupied territory. The most common methods used are HELO (High Extraction, Low Opening) and HEHO (High Extraction, High Opening). During a HELO insertion, the Green Beret parachutes from 35,000ft and free-falls to the minimum safety height before opening the parachute canopy. Before trying a real HELO jump, each man is taught the correct procedures for stabilising his parachute in high winds, in a wind tunnel. HEHO is a method of entering enemy territory by gliding down undetected. By dropping at a rate of around half-a-mile per 1000ft of descent, a Green Beret should be able to travel a considerable distance from the jumping-off point.

Top: A DC-3 of Air America, a CIA-sponsored airline, being loaded with military supplies for use by Laotian tribesmen. As US involvement in Southeast Asia was stepped up in the early 1960s, the Green Berets were sent in to train civilian defence forces. Bottom: Turning tribesmen into fighters: villages being taught to strip, clean and reassemble US-supplied smallarms.

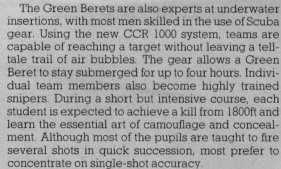

The Green Berets are also experts at underwater insertions, with most men skilled in the use of Scuba gear. Using the new CCR 1000 system, teams are capable of reaching a target without leaving a telltale trail of air bubbles. The gear allows a Green Beret to stay submerged for up to four hours. Individual team members also become highly trained snipers. During a short but intensive course, each student is expected to achieve a kill from 1800ft and learn the essential art of camouflage and concealment. Although most of the pupils are taught to fire several shots in quick succession, most prefer to concentrate on single-shot accuracy.

Like all elite formations, the Special Forces have placed a high priority on creating the all-round soldier: a man capable of operating both as an individual and as part of a small team. By necessity, the Green Berets' training programme has been specifically created to weed out the poor candidates and identify those men able to cope with the rigours of unconventional warfare and behind-the-lines work. Despite the diversity of basic training, the US Special Forces never rest on their laurels; they are always looking to improve upon their skills and are prepared to make use of any new combat techniques that become available. Only by maintaining the highest state of readiness can the Green Berets hope to succeed in the twilight world of counter-insurgency and behind-the-lines operations.

THE AUTHOR Leroy Thompson served in Vietnam as a member of the USAF Combat Security Police. He has written several books on anti-terrorism, and is the author of *Uniforms of the Elite Forces*.

The first photographs to be taken from an airborne platform were the work of French photographer Felix Tournachon, who obtained good views of Paris from the basket of a balloon in 1856.

Six years later his technique saw its first military application when aerial photographs of Richmond in Virginia were used during the American Civil War. Identical prints overlaid with a grid were held by balloon observers over the town and by army headquarters on the ground, and any movement seen from the air was signalled down and pinpointed by reference to the grid.

Still photographs were first taken from an aeroplane in 1909, and in 1913 the British Royal Flying Corps installed a camera in a Farman aircraft. Photographic reconnaissance aircraft were widely used over the trenches in World War I, and increasingly sophisticated combinations of oblique and horizontal camera angles were used to gain the maximum useful information.

Between the wars, airborne cameras were mainly used for aerial mapping, and immediately World War II began they again became extremely important to the intelligence networks of both sides. Although the Luftwaffe had excellent equipment the RAF made far better use of techniques of stereoscopic viewing (analysis of overlapping, paired photographs) and photo-interpretation.

Since the war, reconnaissance has advanced out of all recognition. The first major breakthrough was in high-altitude photography, leading to the deployment of the USAF's Mach 3 SR-71 Blackbird in 1966, which also carried radar and infra-red reconnaissance systems. Today, the threats of ground-to-air and air-to-air missile attacks have made reconnaissance increasingly the preserve of satellites and remotely-piloted vehicles.

HIGH-SPEED SPIES

Streaking into enemy air space in specially-modified Spitfires, the Photographic Reconnaissance Unit of the Royal Air Force kept close tabs on the German war effort

naissance aircraft were all converted bomber types which retained their defensive armament to enable them to fight their way to and from their targets. As Longbottom pointed out, the guns and gunners imposed a weight penalty that brought the recon

IN AUGUST 1939, shortly before the outbreak of World War II, Flying Officer Maurice 'Shorty' Longbottom presented a memorandum on strategic aerial reconnaissance to the Air Ministry in London. In it he stated:

'... this type of reconnaissance must be done in such a manner as to avoid the enemy fighters and AA defences as completely as possible. The best method of doing this appears to be the use of a single small machine, relying solely on its speed, climb and ceiling to avoid detection.'

Longbottom's idea was for lone, unarmed, high-speed and high-flying reconnaissance aircraft to make a sortie into enemy territory avoiding the defences whenever possible. Today his concept is so firmly accepted that it would not raise an eyebrow, but in 1939 it was a radical departure from accepted thinking. At that time long-range recon

Above: A Spitfire bearing the code letters LY of the Photographic Reconnaissance Unit soars high at 30,000ft. Over enemy territory the pilot would take steps to avoid being betrayed by his condensation trail. Left: The Belgian village of Bulligen (above centre in photograph) photographed in November 1939 with a 5in telephoto lens from 33,000ft. Bottom left: On 18 November 1939 a Spitfire took off from Seclin in France on the first Spitfire photo-reconnaissance mission. Bottom right: A pilot and his observer are briefed before their flight.

naissance aircraft down to within range of the very defences they sought to avoid.

Longbottom believed that the ideal aircraft for long-range reconnaissance was a high-speed, single-seat fighter like the Spitfire, stripped of its guns and radio and fitted instead with cameras and additional fuel tanks. His argument was that the removal of the guns, radio and other unnecessary equipment would reduce the weight of the Spitfire by 450lb. Since it had already been discovered that 480lb could be added to the weight of the fighter version of the Spitfire without impairing its ability to take off, the removal of armament and other gear meant that over 900lb of lift capacity could be made available. If this was used to carry cameras and extra fuel, the reconnaissance Spitfire would have a range of 1500 miles, three times that of the fighter version.

The Air Ministry read Longbottom's paper with interest but at first nothing could be done to prove or disprove his arguments. At the outbreak of war the Royal Air Force (RAF) was desperately short of modern fighters, and all its Spitfires were allocated to Fighter Command for the defence of Britain. There was great reluctance to divert any of these precious aircraft to other roles, no matter how persuasive the arguments might seem on paper.

The breakthrough for Longbottom's ideas came in October 1939, when it was gradually realised that daylight photographic reconnaissance over Germany was too risky for conventional RAF reconnaissance aircraft. Even during shallow penetration missions the squadrons involved were suffering severe losses. Two Spitfires were consequently released for the reconnaissance role and delivered to Heston airfield, north of London. At Heston, a secret reconnaissance unit, commanded by Wing Commander Sidney Cotton and known by the cover-name 'Heston Flight', prepared the Spitfires for their new role. Appropriately, one of the officers posted to the unit was 'Shorty' Longbottom himself.

There was no time for the extensive modifications necessary to get the optimum performance out of the Spitfire in the new role. The urgent priority was to modify one to take photographs of enemy territory as soon as possible, and thus prove that Longbottom's proposals were sound. Two cameras were fitted in place of the guns in the wings of each Spitfire, set to look vertically downwards. The Spitfires were then 'cleaned up' in the Heston workshops to give them the last ounce of speed. The empty gun ports were sealed with metal plates, then all joints were filled with plaster of Paris and rubbed down to give the

LENSES IN THE SKY

Pilot Officer Gordon Green joined the Photographic Reconnaissance Unit at Heston in December 1940 and began flying Spitfires on operations in the following February from Benson airfield:

'The technique of high-altitude photography from a single-seater like a Spitfire was largely a question of experience, for a great deal depended on being able to judge where the cameras were pointing. One flew alone to the general area of the target, then tipped the aircraft on its side to check one was properly lined up. Once that was done it was a question of holding the aircraft dead straight and level for the photographic run. Until one learned the art it was all too easy – if, for example, one had a bit of a bank on – to come back with a lovely line of photographs of the ground a couple of miles to one side of the intended target.

'A big worry over enemy territory was that one might start leaving a condensation trail without knowing it, thus pointing out one's position to the enemy. To avoid that we had small mirrors fitted in the blisters on each side of the canopy, so that one could see the trail as soon as it started to form behind. When that happened one could either climb or descend until the trail ceased. If possible, we liked to climb above the trail's layer, because then fighters trying to intercept us had first to climb through the trail's layer themselves and could be seen in good time. It was all rather like a fox hunt – either the fox got away unscathed or else it was caught and killed. There was rarely anything in between.'

aircraft the smoothest possible finish.

Wing Commander Cotton had observed that a distant aircraft seen from below invariably appeared as a dark silhouette against the lighter background of the sky, unless sunlight was glinting off the machine. While nothing could be done about sun glint, he noticed that light-coloured aircraft were less visible at long distance than dark ones. Cotton had his Spitfires painted in the shade of pale green which he thought would make them least conspicuous from below.

In the autumn of 1939 Cotton's unit was renamed 'No. 2 Camouflage Unit' to explain the odd colouring of its aircraft. One aircraft was detached to Seclin near Lille in France to begin operations and on 18 November Longbottom, now a Flight Lieutenant, took off on the first Spitfire reconnaissance mission. His target was the German city of Aachen and some fortifications nearby, but at 33,000ft he found navigation more difficult than expected, and he returned with photographs of the Belgian side of the frontier to the south of Aachen. This problem was quickly solved and four days later Longbottom successfully photographed the Belgian-German border east of Liège. During the six weeks that followed, cloud cover prevented high-altitude photography of enemy territory, but at the end of December the Spitfires

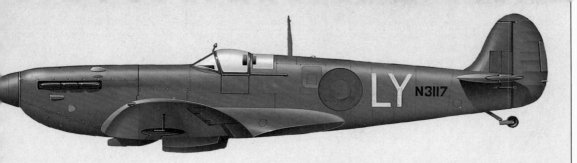

resumed operations and returned with photographs of Aachen, Cologne, Kaiserslautern, Wiesbaden, Mainz and parts of the Ruhr. Significantly, all of this was done without loss or even interference from German fighters or anti-aircraft guns.

The feasibility of Longbottom's concept had been proved beyond doubt, but much remained to be done. From 33,000ft the 5in focal-length cameras carried by the Spitfires produced pictures of such a small scale that they gave little indication of troop positions, even after prints had been blown up as large as the grain of the film would allow. Roads, railways, villages and major fortifications could be picked out but anything smaller was likely to be missed. The answer was to fit cameras with longer telephoto lenses which would give better definition of features on the ground. Additional fuel tanks also

The *Freya* radar at Cap de la Hague (top left) and the *Würzburg* radar at St Bruneval (centre left) were both photographed by 'dicing' Spitfires. The *Würzburg* was photographed by Flight Lieutenant Tony Hill (bottom left). Background: Smoke rises from the *Scharnhorst* and the *Gneisenau* at Brest.

had to be fitted to increase the range of the Spitfire.

During 1940, progressive increases in fuel tankage enabled the reconnaissance Spitfires to penetrate deeper and deeper into enemy territory. In February the limit from bases in England was Wilhelmshaven; in April the Spitfires reached Kiel; in October Stettin on the Baltic was photographed, and in November a Spitfire photographed Marseilles in the south of France. Better cameras for high-altitude work also appeared, first with 8in then 14in, 20in and 36in telephoto lenses.

Vertical photography from high altitude was the best way to cover large areas or cities on clear days, but other techniques were needed to take close-ups of small targets or if there was complete cloud cover. Cotton's unit pioneered low-altitude oblique photography, using cameras looking sideways from the aircraft. The oblique camera proved its value during an early mission in July 1940, when Flying Officer Alistair Taylor ran past Boulogne at 300ft and photographed the harbour despite a 700ft cloud base and heavy rain. Low-altitude photography of small targets, nicknamed 'dicing' on account of the risk from enemy defences, became an important new role for the Spitfires.

As the unit became more experienced, its aircraft were repainted in new and more effective colours according to their specialised roles. Those fitted

SPITFIRE SPYPLANES

Until the introduction in 1941 of the photographic reconnaissance variants of the Spitfire Mark V, the PR Mark IV and PR Mark VII, most British missions were carried out in PR versions of the first Spitfire to be mass produced, the Mark I.

The first adaptation, the Spitfire PR Mark IA, carried two F24 cameras under the wing. The PR Mark 1B was similar except for the addition of a 29-gallon fuel tank just behind the pilot's seat, to increase the aircraft's range.

The Spitfire PR Mark IC was developed by Heston Aircraft Limited and was the first version to carry cameras in the fuselage.

The pink-painted low-altitude reconnaissance Spitfire (below and bottom left) was equipped with two F24 cameras mounted to point eight degrees to port and eight degrees to starboard of vertically downward. Paired photographs could thus be taken and later viewed stereoscopically by the photo-interpreter. Mounted above these cameras was a third F24 which was set to photograph obliquely

through an observation port. Exposed at low level, this camera's film provided an invaluable supplement to the 'bird's eye' views secured by the other two. At high altitudes the oblique camera was of little value, and the blue-painted high-altitude reconnaissance Spitfire (top left) did not carry one.

Left: A loaded camera is manoeuvred into the fuselage of a Spitfire. Below left: This typical reconnaissance photograph, taken in 1940 of Detmold aerodrome near Hanover, has been subjected to scrutiny by interpreters. Their analysis is shown next to the photograph. Below right: Interpreters examine photographs taken during a night reconnaissance for evidence of troop movements.

DETMOLD AERODROME

(A) Crops (B) Small hillock being removed and ground levelled to make an extension to the aerodrome (C) Building under construction (D) Motor transport sheds (E) Hangars on which a novel form of camouflage has been attempted (F) Shelter trenches (G) Compass swinging base (H) Barracks and crew quarters (I) Tennis courts (K) Numerous small trees have been planted between the buildings (L) Aircraft, including two Heinkel 111s, two Junkers 52s, a Dornier and a number of small machines.

ith long focal-length vertical cameras were
ainted a medium blue to make them as incons-
cuous as possible at high altitude; those with
blique cameras used for low-altitude dicing were
ainted a pale shade of pink, barely off-white, to
ake them difficult to see from below against a cloud
ackground. However, this latter scheme made the
pitfires highly conspicuous from above if there was
o cloud cover.

Throughout 1940 the Spitfire reconnaissance
rce was continually being expanded and reorga-
sed. In January, No.2 Camouflage Unit was desig-
ated the Photographic Development Unit (PDU),
ly to be renamed the Photographic Reconnaiss-
ce Unit (PRU) in July. By that time it operated 12
econnaissance Spitfires of different types under
Ving Commander Geoffrey Tuttle, who had re-
aced Cotton the previous month. In November the
nit was redesignated yet again as No.1 Photo-
raphic Reconnaissance Unit, to distinguish it from
her PRUs being formed. In December it left Heston
r the larger airfield at Benson near Oxford which
offered much better facilities.

Throughout the dark days of 1940 and 1941 PRU
Spitfires brought back a wealth of information on
what was happening on 'the other side of the line'.
Initially their main priority was to keep a careful
watch on German preparations for the invasion of
Britain, but when that danger receded there were
plenty of other urgent tasks. In the spring of 1941
there was a requirement for PRU Spitfires to fly out
sorties each day to check that the German battle-
cruisers *Scharnhorst* and *Gneisenau* were still in
Brest harbour: the Admiralty needed to know as
soon as possible if they had set out for another
Atlantic foray against Allied shipping. These operations were so important that Spitfires were sent in
pairs to give the greatest chance of securing photographs. A blue-painted aircraft flew over at high
altitude in case there were clear skies over the
harbour, while a pink aircraft went in below
cloud if there was sufficient cover. Six-tenths
cloud was the no-man's-land figure: too much to
allow much chance of a successful run from high
altitude, too little to hide a Spitfire going in low.

One man who flew to Brest to photograph the
German warships was Pilot Officer Gordon Green:
'During the early missions to cover Brest we lost

about five pilots fairly quickly. After the firs couple had failed to return, the Flight Comman der, Flight Lieutenant Keith Arnold, asked Ben son to send some reserve pilots and they dul arrived. They both took off for Brest the evenin they arrived, and neither came back. That was very sobering incident.

'There were times when I knew real fear. Whe one was 15 minutes out from Brest on a low altitude sortie, one's heart was beating away an as the target got nearer one's mouth got com pletely dry. Anyone who was not frightened at th thought of going in to photograph one of the mos heavily defended targets in Europe was no human.'

In the autumn of 1941, No. 1 PRU received the firs twin-engined Mosquitoes modified for reconnaiss ance. Able to fly as fast and as high as the Spitfire, bu with a considerably greater range and a two-ma crew to make accurate navigation easier, the new aircraft brought with it a considerable increase i reconnaissance capability.

By the summer of 1942, No. 1 PRU had a strength o 53 Spitfires and 12 Mosquitoes modified for recon naissance operations. These aircraft could reach th furthest extremities of Hitler's European empire, an had the speed and altitude performance to do s without incurring undue risk. By then the pioneerin days were over, and this type of reconnaissance ha become an accepted and important part of the Roya Air Force's capability. 'Shorty' Longbottom's far sighted concept had been developed to its logica conclusion.

THE AUTHOR Alfred Price served as an aircrew office in the RAF for 15 years, specialising in aircra weapons and tactics. He has written extensively o aerial warfare and amongst his published works i *Instruments of Darkness*, a history of electroni warfare.

In the course of developing the Mosquito, three prototypes were built – the fighter, the bomber and the unarmed photo-reconnaissance plane. Seen below is Mosquito W4051, the prototype of the aircraft that were delivered to Benson in November 1941. Above: Cameras are loaded aboard a Mosquito.

DANGER
UXB

THE ROYAL ENGINEERS

The Corps of Royal Engineers is one of the oldest units in the British Army, tracing its ancestry to the establishment of the Board of Ordnance by Henry VIII in 1518.

In 1717, it was reconstituted as a Corps of Engineers, and in 1772 the construction of the fortifications on Gibraltar resulted in the formation of the Soldier Artificer Company – the first permanent engineer soldiers of the army.

The Corps of Royal Engineers was awarded the Royal title in 1787, and although its structure altered considerably during the following century, in 1856 the Royal Sappers and Miners were absorbed into a single Corps of Royal Engineers. From this date until the end of World War II, the Royal Engineers carried out their wide-ranging duties in every theatre of operations. The construction of bridges, temporary harbours, roads, airstrips, buildings, minefields and a host of associated tasks were the responsibility of the Corps, in addition to the bomb and mine-disposal duties at home and abroad.

In 1948, Royal Engineer units were grouped under the command of a senior officer and a centralised headquarters, with 23 Engineer Regiments originally being retained. The present-day Corps of Royal Engineers has four types of engineer regiment, three of them – the Armoured Engineer Regiment, the Armoured Division Engineer Regiment and the Amphibious Engineer Regiment – attached to the British Army of the Rhine. The fourth, known as the Field Engineer Regiments, are based in the United Kingdom.

In addition, there are regiments responsible for specialised tasks such as explosive ordnance disposal (EOD). Today, this role is carried out by 33 Engineer Regiment (EOD), based at Lodge Hill Camp, near Rochester.

With the London Blitz came a new and lethal challenge for the men of the Royal Engineers – the unexploded bomb

Page 133: The shadow of the Luftwaffe over London during the Blitz. Not all the German bombs exploded however, and the dangerous and harrowing task of disarming the rogue bombs fell to the men of the Royal Engineers. Far left and left centre: Mission accomplished – with their fuzes deactivated, unexploded bombs are winched from their impact craters. Left below: London 1940. A 1000kg 'Hermann' is pulled from the earth after being disarmed by a Bomb Disposal Section. Left: The spirit of the Blitz. With casual indifference, a London child plays with his soap-box cart, unmoved by the police warning sign.

IN THE EARLY hours of 29 August 1940, a formation of German bombers neared its target – the Llandarcy oil refinery in Swansea, the largest establishment of its kind in the United Kingdom. The bomb doors crashed open and the cargo of high explosive was released, the fuze on each bomb being primed as it left the bay. Gathering momentum, the bombs began their inexorable descent. As they hit the ground, the air was thick with the sound of massive explosions, and seconds later the flames that engulfed the refinery could be seen licking the sky from a distance of 15 miles.

At 0900 hours on the 29th, Lieutenant B.S.T. Archer of the Royal Engineers, together with one sergeant and 14 sappers, received orders to defuze four unexploded bombs that were hindering efforts to control the fire at Llandarcy. When he arrived on the scene, Archer decided to tackle a bomb that had penetrated the ground beneath a fuel tank that, unlike others around it, had not ignited:

'It was a bad site to work on. Fifty yards away in one direction and 80 in another, a tank was on fire... as the flames on their tops worked their way down, they melted the steel walls so that the tanks flared like Roman candles... the sappers dug in relays, working as energetically as they could to reach the bomb before it exploded.'

Finally the 250kg device was uncovered. Using only a hammer and chisel, Archer removed the base-plate from the bomb and literally tore the fuze from the inside of the case. The operation had taken four and a half nerve-racking hours, and the men of the Royal Engineers had been all too aware that their chances of survival were slim.

Lieutenant Archer received the George Cross for his gallant action – these were the early days of bomb disposal, when such cold-blooded heroism captured the imagination of the British public and instilled in the Bomb Disposal Sections (BDSs) a sense of morale and loyalty that was to last through years of unstinting effort to foil the German armourers.

The hail of bombs that fell unmercifully on London and southern England from 1940 revealed to the authorities the inadequacy of British bomb disposal arrangements, particularly when it was realised that the Germans were employing a new type of weapon – bombs fitted with a delayed-action fuze. While most of the unexploded incendiary bombs could be rendered harmless if handled with care, these new weapons could lie dormant for up to 80 hours before detonating.

In February 1940 the War Office assumed responsibility for bomb disposal and, given their reputation for mastering the technical complexities of war, it was natural that the Royal Engineers should form the nucleus of the 25 newly formed Bomb Disposal Sections. Each section comprised one lieutenant, one sergeant and 14 other ranks, all of whom were assured that after six months of bomb disposal they could transfer to other duties. In July, the BDS organisation was expanded to incorporate 120 sections – 12 companies each comprising 10 sections. Their 'enemy' was a selection of bombs that varied from the 50kg high explosive to the awesomely destructive 1800kg 'Satan', but such was the loyalty engendered when working only one slip away from instant obliteration, that requests for transfer were few and far between. The experience of one newly commissioned officer in the Royal Engineers is typical. Finding himself posted to a bomb disposal unit, the officer was sent to the School of Military Engineering in Rippon to familiarise himself with the techniques of bomb disposal:

'I realised that I had happened on a trade where one's first mistake was likely to be one's last, and got down to the job in hand and worked hard ... Now I learnt how many cubic centimetres of fluid could be forced into such and such a fuze, and why you must never jump in a bomb shaft. I learnt about precautions, safety distances and how to spot whether a bomb had exploded... and came away confident of my capacity to produce an answer to any problem that was likely to confront me.'

'I realised that I had happened on a trade where one's first mistake was likely to be one's last'

Six weeks later, this officer had disarmed 15 bombs and, while his optimism remained, a later comment reveals the stress that the bomb disposal officers were exposed to on a daily basis:

'Should any man suggest that he took his first bomb without being frightened, I'd say that he was unwise to have done it under the influence of a stimulant, or else he's a liar.'

During mid-1940, enemy bombing was only sporadic, but in August the worst fears of the War Office were confirmed as the storm broke over London – the Blitz had begun.

In the early days, BDSs were operating virtually in the dark, uncovering the bomb, removing the fuze locking ring by the most primitive of methods, and finally pulling the fuze clear. The conventional bomb comprised four main elements: the outer bomb case, the fuze, the gaine and booster, and the high-explosive main filling. The fuze and gaine were enclosed inside a cylindrical fuze pocket stretching across the bomb case. Electrically activated, the fuze would 'spark off' the gaine, and the resulting explosion would detonate the main filling. Initially, the German armourers employed the relatively simple Type 15 impact fuze which, if it malfunctioned, could normally be dealt with using the steady nerves and rudimentary technical equipment of the bomb disposer.

The Type 17 fuze, however, presented the BDSs with a new and chilling problem. Designed to detonate the bomb after impact, this new fuze incorporated a clockwork mechanism that allowed a delay period of up to 80 hours before the bomb went off, though considerably longer if (as often happened) the clockwork mechanism jammed. Forced to wait the required 80 hours before tackling any bomb, on the premise that it could contain a Type 17 fuze, the workload of the Royal Engineers was staggering – by September 1940 there were more than 3700 unexploded bombs requiring their attention.

Casualties mounted steadily, especially after the Germans began to fit an anti-handling device, the ZUS 40 mechanism, on their bombs. The ZUS 40 prevented the extraction of the fuze, and, in areas where a controlled detonation of the bomb could not be tolerated, the Bomb Disposal Sections were tasked to render the explosive harmless while the fuze was still intact. This process was carried out by remote control, under the direction of the commanding officer. After drilling into the bomb case, the inert TNT would be emulsified using steam pressure. It was still, however, a hazardous task. Not only had the equipment to be fitted to the bomb, it had to be monitored, and the addition of the Type 50 fuze, which the Germans used to supplement the ZUS 40, meant that the slightest vibration could result in instant annihilation.

At times, the Royal Engineers seemed almost cavalier in their approach to their work, attempting to salvage bombs that could have been blown up on site – yet had it not been for their bravery in retrieving intact specimens, the scientists at the Bomb Disposal Committee (established to monitor new developments in enemy fuzes) would have been unable to instruct officers in the safest techniques of identifying and defuzing each new device that the German armourers came up with.

By the beginning of 1941, more than 8000 bombs had been successfully defuzed. Tragically, 123 officers and men had been killed, yet their sacrifice was not in vain – the Royal Engineers had played a crucial role in fostering the development of an efficient bomb-disposal network that spanned the whole country. Initially, the Royal Engineers received their training at RAF Melksham in Surrey, which had evolved into a central bomb disposal school for all three services. In September 1941 the first Royal Engineers bomb-disposal school was formed at Donnington.

The mechanics of German bomb armament. Right: A Type 17 fuze. This device featured a clockwork mechanism designed to detonate the explosive filling after the bomb had hit the ground. Below: A disarmed bomb with its fuze removed. Bottom right: A cutaway view of a bomb, showing the positioning of the fuze. Bottom centre: A variety of fuzes used by the German armourers. Bottom left: Dealing with a legacy of World War II in Sheffield. The technique of steaming out the explosive is still used today.

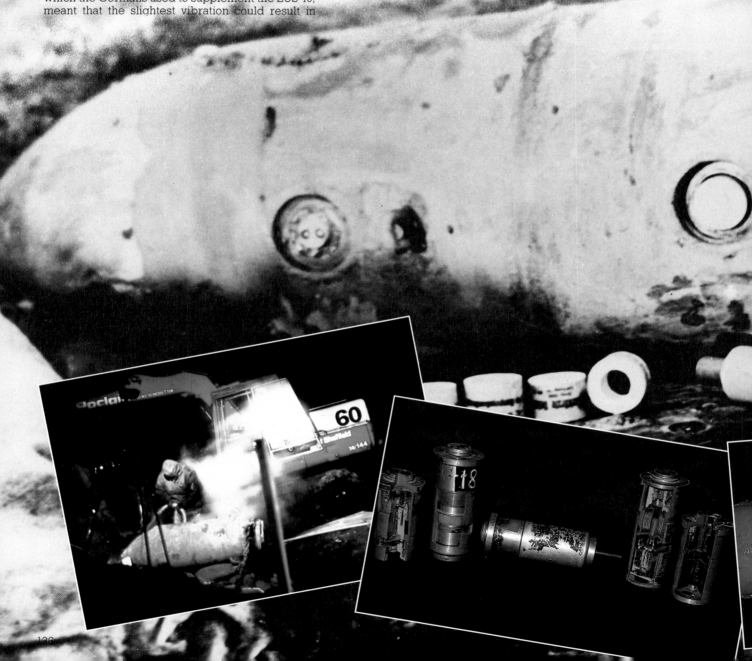

Although the officer in charge of a BDS shouldered the greatest risk when attempting to defuze a bomb, there were other dangers that took a heavy toll of the NCOs and sappers as they dug deep into the earth in search of their quarry. Bombs buried to a depth of 20ft were not uncommon, and on one site, in Hendon in north London, a bomb penetrated 60ft below ground level. In addition to the obvious danger of the shaft caving in, sappers had to be alert to the threat of carbon-monoxide poisoning. Bombs were often known to explode underground, impacting the surrounding soil and forming a cavity of deadly gas. With no discernible smell to betray its presence, this deathtrap would overcome a sapper, unfortunate enough to fall into it, within seconds. Another source of gas poisoning was the ammonia fumes given off by the aluminised powder filling inside the 'Hermann' 1000kg bomb. The huge size of this weapon meant that it invariably penetrated to a depth of over 20ft. Within the confined space of a bomb shaft, the fumes could kill almost immediately.

'A member of the BDS should be strong, unmarried and a fast runner'

During 1941, two devices emerged to counteract the threat of unexploded bombs, providing the Royal Engineers with a viable alternative to the more primitive methods they had previously employed. The Steam Fuze Discharger eliminated the charge within the fuze condensers by heating them, while the Brass Liquid Discharger performed the same function, except that this device used air pressure to force a solution of salt, benzole and methylated spirit past the condensers, thereby short-circuiting them. These two devices represented the first signs of victory for the BDSs over the German armourers, though one acute problem still remained. When dealing with a Type 50 fuze, some of which were highly sensitive, even the slightest vibration could activate the mechanism. There was no sure method to overcome this – the men of the BDSs had to rely on their attention to detail and a ready supply of steel nerve. It would be an injustice to say that the bomb disposers were fatalistic about their chances of survival, but the nature of their work certainly inspired a unique sense of humour. When asked what he thought the main characteristics of a bomb disposer should be, one man quipped: 'A member of the BDS should be strong, unmarried and a fast runner.'

As the battle of wits between the German armourers and the bomb disposers continued, even longer delayed-action fuzes were encountered by the Royal Engineers. It also became obvious that many of the bombs malfunctioned on impact, their clockwork mechanism halted until ominously restarted by the vibration of a sapper's shovel hitting the earth. Very soon, one phrase had become the catchword of many a BDS – 'Never trust a clock!'

In addition to free-falling bombs, the Germans used parachutes to drop a large number of mines into the harbours and estuaries around the coasts of Britain. Their magnetic fuzing system was intended to detonate the device on impact with any solid surface, and, though many malfunctioned, they still proved extremely awkward to disarm. Responsibility for defuzing these parachute mines was jealously guarded by the Royal Navy, though after a series of accidents when BDSs were present, the Admiralty agreed to instruct the Royal Engineers in the delicate technique of neutralising these devices. This training began in 1941, and coincided with the

TACKLING THE 'BUTTERFLIES'

An additional hazard confronting the Bomb Disposal Sections was the luminous yellow 'butterfly' bomb, used with increasing frequency by the Germans after 1942.
Each bomb weighed some 2kg, and was released from enemy aircraft in a 24-bomb container. An air-burst fuze would then destroy the container, releasing the butterfly bombs which would arm themselves in mid-flight. Once armed, the butterfly could not be defuzed and had to be detonated on site. However, since each bomb could contain either an impact, clockwork or anti-handling fuze, the problems of disposal were immense, and many sappers were killed by the explosion – not of the bomb they were working on – but of another lying close by. The butterfly bombs were employed by the enemy in saturation raids specifically targeted on the civilian population, and casualties were horrendous.
The task of clearing affected areas of the small but deadly bombs was enormous. For example, when a shower of butterflies fell on Grimsby, in the north of England, on 13 June 1943, No.3 Bomb Disposal Company, commanded by Major W.G. Parker, spent over three weeks clearing the devices. Whether lodged in attics, trees, or telegraph poles, or littering the streets of Grimsby, the bombs were tackled by the sappers. One officer, Lieutenant R. Sharp, disposed of over 40 butterflies in one day, despite having been treated for concussion only four days previously.

government's belief that German plans for invasion would soon be renewed. Defuzing parachute mines, gas bombs and 2500kg and 3000kg high-explosive bombs, was to be the exclusive responsibility of the BDSs should enemy plans become a reality, and a chilling directive to the bomb disposal organisation made clear the danger that this would present to the sections:

'All unexploded missiles will be dealt with as soon as possible as a matter of course, regardless of any safety period which it might be desirable otherwise to observe.'

Thankfully, the enforcement of this stark order never became necessary.

The slightest jar to the bomb case during this delicate process would trip the mercury switches and despatch him into oblivion

In 1943, the German armourers presented the bomb-disposal experts with yet another new problem – the 'Y' fuze. This was basically an improved Type 50 device, equipped with sensitive mercury trembler-switches, and was designed to detonate when the BDSs were attempting to disarm it – an elaborate booby-trap. Although the use of radiography equipment enabled bomb disposers to identify this fuze when it first appeared, there was no other way to disarm it other than by trial and error.

In January 1943 a 500kg bomb, armed with a 'Y' fuze, crashed into a Battersea warehouse, full of vital machine tools. Detonation on site was out of the question. The bomb had to be defuzed. The officer responsible was Major C.A.J. Martin, and his first task was to steam out the high-explosive filling – the slightest jar to the bomb case during this delicate process would trip the mercury switches and despatch him into oblivion. Martin worked for 24 hours before his labours were finally rewarded. The recovery of an intact 'Y' fuze enabled the experts to come up with a practical alternative to steaming out the explosive filling: by using liquid oxygen to freeze the fuze head, the batteries inside were rendered inert and the bomb neutralised.

A few days later, Major Martin had an opportunity to put this freezing method to the test on a bomb in the Old Kent Road in London. To his horror, the fuze

Type 17 fuze

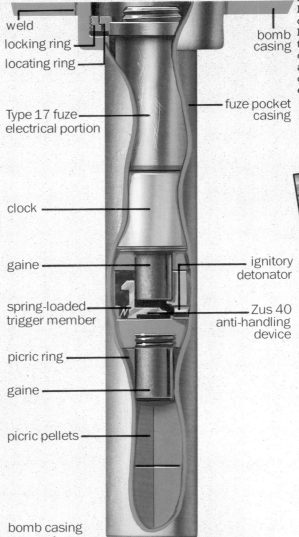

weld

locking ring

locating ring

bomb casing

Type 17 fuze electrical portion

fuze pocket casing

clock

gaine

ignitory detonator

spring-loaded trigger member

Zus 40 anti-handling device

picric ring

gaine

picric pellets

bomb casing

jammed inside the bomb case. Displaying the ingenuity typical of bomb disposers, Martin hit upon a bold plan to dribble liquid oxygen onto the fuze and remove it piece by piece. It was a method fraught with danger. If the oxygen came into contact with any exposed filling, immediate combustion would almost certainly occur, and one slip of Martin's hand could lead to the percussion cap striking the gaine – instant death. The operation, however, was a complete success and it led to the development of a device that could apply the cooling agent to 'Y' fuzes with a far greater degree of safety.

Once again, the bomb disposers had demonstrated their ability to keep pace with the technical advances of the German armourers. For his courage and devotion to duty, Major Martin was awarded the George Cross, and two of his colleagues, Major Hudson and Lieutenant Dean, were awarded the George Medal.

After May 1944, although German bomber raids had virtually ceased, the BDSs in London and the home counties were confronted by a monstrous new weapon – the V1 flying-bomb. In the early summer months, there were often up to 1000 V1s a week

Below: Sappers uncover a German bomb before the hazardous process of removing its fuze begins. Bottom left: While bombs in densely built-up areas had to be disarmed, bombs such as this one, which buried itself deep into the parade ground at RAF Hemswell, could be destroyed by a controlled explosion.

Above centre: Another victory for the Royal Engineers. A 1000kg bomb is loaded onto a truck to be taken away and destroyed. Right: In the claustrophobic depths of a bomb shaft, a Bomb Disposal Section gets to work on an unexploded German weapon in the bed of the lake in St James's Park, London. Above, far right: Despite the victory over Germany in 1945, the bomb-disposal work of the Royal Engineers was far from over. There are still a great many unexploded bombs around and every year a new crop of lethal relics from World War II comes to light. This photograph was taken in February 1976 and shows Major A.S. Hogben and WO2 Henton of the Royal Engineers getting to grips with a 1000kg bomb.

launched against Britain, and those that failed to explode upon impact presented the bomb disposers with three fuzes to disarm before the weapon could be safely transported to the 'bomb cemetery' for controlled detonation. Although the V1 did not incorporate an anti-handling device, the combination of two impact fuzes (one of which was spring loaded) and a clockwork fuze demanded the utmost care – even when separated from the bomb case, the booster-charges inside the fuze pockets contained enough explosives to kill anyone in a 10 yard radius.

Although the war in Europe ended in May 1945, the task of the Royal Engineers was far from complete. An enormous backlog of unexploded bombs had to be dealt with, in addition to the clearing of coastal minefields. The urgency of war may have disappeared, but the hazards remained, and in the two years leading up to May 1947 more than 100 officers and men lost their lives. In 1949 the General Service Medal was awarded to all ranks of the Royal Engineers engaged in bomb disposal and mine clearance.

THE AUTHOR David Esler is a freelance military writer who has contributed to a number of publications specialising in the history of World War II.

Popski's army of volunteers were hand-picked to perform crucial operations in the Desert and in Italy

ON THE NIGHT of 9 September 1943, advance elements of the British 1st Airborne Division slipped into the Italian port of Taranto, situated on the heel of the boot of Italy. On board was R Troop of Popski's Private Army (PPA), five jeeps under the command of Major Vladimir Peniakoff, or Popski as he was universally known. Its role was to act as an advanced reconnaissance force for the division: to ascertain the strength of both Italian and German troops in the area as well as to inspect possible landing grounds for the RAF in the low-lying ground between Taranto and Brindisi.

The political and military situation in Italy was extremely confused during this period, as the Italians had surrendered before Popski's arrival and so were nominally on the side of the Allies. The Germans, for their part, were outraged by what they considered treacherous Italian behaviour and ruthlessly took over those positions held by Italian forces. In southern Italy there were relatively few German troops, and consequently Popski and his men were able to dodge past the Germans and operate deep behind enemy lines.

The five PPA jeeps were standard-issue US vehicles but were modified to meet the special needs of the unit. As long-range capability was an essential requirement, seven four-gallon jerrycans of petrol were attached to racks on the outside of each of the vehicles, which, with the main tank, provided a

range of approximately 600 miles. On two swivels – mounted fore and aft – was the jeep's armament: two Browning machine guns, one of 0.3in calibre, the other 0.5in. Ammunition for these belt-fed weapons consisted of tracer, armour-piercing and incendiary rounds, fired in succession. Each jeep was crewed by two or three men, and their personal weapons consisted of Thompson sub-machine guns, M1 carbines, Colt automatics and an assortment of revolvers and knives. Spare parts, tools and compo-rations were stowed in any available space in and on the jeep. The tactical principles of the jeep-mounted PPA had been established in North Africa and were based on maximising the factors of firepower and mobility. In Italy the ability of a troop of five jeeps to climb near impassable tracks and then deliver a broadside from 10 machine guns proved invaluable on many occasions.

After disembarkation, the jeeps of PPA advanced inland towards Brindisi in order to test the attitude of the Italian armed forces towards the British. To his relief, Popski found them either friendly or apathetic, and while they were not prepared to take up arms against their former German comrades, they would not hamper the Allied advance. From the Italian Air Force, PPA learned of suitable sites for the RAF, despite the fact that the Germans had made a half-hearted attempt to destroy them. Popski reported his findings back to Divisional HQ and then drove on to Bari to start looking for the Germans.

Formed from members of No. 1 Demolition Squadron in October 1942, Popski's Private Army (PPA) fought throughout the North African and Italian campaigns, carrying out deep-penetration raids and reconnaissance tasks. The army's commander, a tough fighter of Russian blood, was Vladimir Peniakoff (right). Despite its small size, never more than around 120 men, PPA was able to hit the enemy hard, using the mobility and firepower of its jeeps to great effect. Above left: Men of PPA in North Africa. Corporal 'Jock' Cameron (sitting), a gamekeeper in civvy street, was Popski's gunner for much of the war. He died after an ambush in mid-1944, and was much mourned. Above: Popski (driving) and Private Yunes Yusef Abdallah in Tunisia. Yusef, a Senussi Arab, proved invaluable as an interpreter and was renowned for using an old umbrella to root out German mines.

PRIVATE

POPSKI'S PRIVATE ARMY

Beginning his war in the Western Desert with the Libyan Arab Force, Popski proposed that a small independent unit should be formed to work alongside the Long Range Desert Group (LRDG), specialising in sabotage behind enemy lines. During this early phase of the war 'private armies' such as the SAS, the commandos, the SBS and the LRDG flourished, and Popski's request was granted. In October 1942 he was given command of No. 1 Demolition Squadron (23 men all ranks), nicknamed Popski's Private Army by the then co-ordinator of special forces, Lieutenant-Colonel Shan Hackett. Raising his unit around two old comrades from the Libyan Arab Force, Bob Yunnie and Frenchman Jean Caneri, Popski chose a badge (above) in the shape of an astrolabe (an early navigational instrument) for his unit.

By the time PPA was operational in early 1943 the tide of war in North Africa had turned in the Allies' favour, with the Germans forced back to their stronghold on the Mareth Line in Tunisia. Along with other deep-penetration units, PPA helped find the route to outflank the line as well as conducting some other notable exploits in the final stages of the campaign. The war in North Africa over, there seemed few opportunities for the old 'private armies', but Popski had good contacts within the Eighth Army and so, instead of being withdrawn to Cairo and disbanded, PPA was allotted a new role in the invasion of Italy.

ARM

POPSKI AND HIS PRIVATE ARMY

Born Vladimir Peniakoff in Belgium in 1897, Popski was the son of wealthy parents of Russian extraction. Taught English at an early age, he was sent to study at Cambridge in 1914, but his university career was cut short by the onset of war. Instead of volunteering for either the Belgian or the British armed forces, Peniakoff enlisted as an artilleryman in the French Army as their entry requirements allowed him quick access to the front line; there he saw active service and was wounded. In 1924 he settled in Egypt as a businessman in the sugar industry. His interest in travel was stimulated by regular expeditions into the desert, an activity which ensured that he became proficient in the complex art of navigation in desert conditions.

A fervent admirer of the British way of life, he applied for a commission in the British Army after the outbreak of war in 1939, subsequently serving as a junior officer in the Libyan Arab Force. Finding little scope for his talents in this unit, he began to tag along on Long Range Desert Group (LRDG) patrols – it was then that he acquired his nickname of Popski – before forming his specialist unit. Popski was the guiding light and undisputed leader of his 'Private Army', which he guided through the latter stages of the North African campaign and during the war in Italy.

Although the force grew in size, from its original complement of 23 men in October 1942 to a peak of 80 men towards the end of the war, it was always small enough for Popski to impose his own special character on the unit. Especially so as Popski took the greatest care in picking his men; the vast majority of volunteers were rejected at the first interview. Popski looked for soldiers who were well trained in all the basic military skills, were highly capable cross-country drivers and, above all, were resourceful and showed initiative. Once accepted into the unit, the new recruit underwent a gruelling training programme, developing existing skills and learning new ones, most notably a proficiency in signals and demolition. Formal discipline was dispensed with: there was no saluting, no one was called 'Sir' (the men simply called their commander Popski) and there were no batmen or other types of military servant. Clothing and uniform were left to the men themselves (except that they were to be drawn from Allied stocks) and beards were optional, although during the war in Italy they became a privilege only for those who had conducted five or more operations. Popski had little time for paper-work – leaving that chore to his exceptionally efficient second-in-command, Jean Caneri – and equally he protected his men from what he saw as the petty restrictions of army red tape. Thus, for example, traffic offences forwarded to Popski were filed automatically in a waste-paper bin.

True military discipline was insisted upon, however, and any man who refused to obey orders, behaved badly on operations or who neglected his weapons and equipment was expelled from PPA and returned to his parent unit. The spirit and morale of the men remained at a consistently high level; they considered themselves a 'band of brothers', glorifying in their freedom from the conformity of the regular army and yet able to make their own special contribution to winning the war.

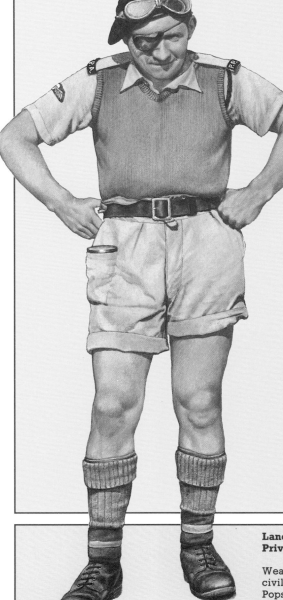

Lance-Corporal Locke, Popski's Private Army, Tunisia 1943.

Wearing KD shorts and shirt, and a civilian pullover, Locke typifies Popski's men in the field. His Royal Armoured Corps beret carries the PPA badge, and he wears para wings on his upper right arm.

Above: Popski (right) and his gunner, Corporal R.H. Cokes who succeeded 'Jock' Cameron, take time off from chasing the Germans out of Italy. On 9 December 1944 a PPA patrol of five jeeps, led by Popski, went to the rescue of a group of men from the 27th Lancers trapped in a farmhouse. In the ensuing firefight with two German companies supported by tanks, PPA loosed off some 25,000 rounds in 50 minutes, saving the situation. However, Popski was wounded and later had his left hand amputated. After hospitalisation in England, he returned to Italy in April 1945. Peniakoff was awarded the DSO for his part in the action. His artificial hand could be fitted with a variety of attachments including a rubber glove for ceremonial occasions. Below: PPA gunners blast away with a Browning.

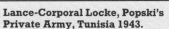

The 1st Airborne Division had set up a defensive perimeter around Taranto but, weak in artillery and other support arms, it needed accurate details of German troop strengths and dispositions in the immediate area before embarking on offensive action. Popski had gained a limited amount of information from simply ringing up local Italians who were friendly to the British, and who had some knowledge of the German forces. The German 1st Parachute Division was known to be in the area around Gravina, Altamura and Gioia del Colle, and although its strength was unknown, it was rumoured to have a near full complement. In order to make an accurate assessment, Popski decided to embark upon a reconnaissance in depth.

On the morning of 13 September Popski's Private Army set off due west from Bari and onto the Murge plateau, from the other side of which ran the main road from Spinazzola to Gravina, a route regularly

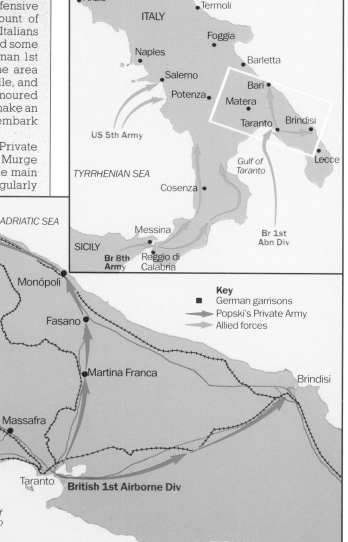

Jeep Reconnaissance
Popski's Private Army
September 1943

Key
■ German garrisons
→ Popski's Private Army
→ Allied forces

From 3 September 1943 onwards the Allied armies poured across the Straits of Messina and began their advance northwards. Six days later, the British 1st Airborne Division launched Operation Slapstick – a diversionary landing at Taranto. In the vanguard of the division was a small irregular formation commanded by Vladimir Peniakoff or 'Popski.' The strengths of the defending German forces in the area were unknown – and Popski's Private Army commenced jeep reconnaissance patrols.

frequented by German patrols. That night PPA jeeps crossed the road and, despite nearly blundering into a German convoy, they reached the shelter of the mountains to the west. The jeeps were concealed in a dark gully and Popski ordered his troop to rest. Although he had only a dozen men with him he was confident of results, placing complete faith in his men to ensure that the job was carried through.

While they rested and prepared their jeeps for action, Popski made contact with local villagers who, while being well-disposed towards the British, had little intelligence of German whereabouts to offer. After hours of discussion Popski realised he was getting nowhere, until one man informed him that he knew a staff officer in Gravina, a Major Schulz, who was responsible for buying supplies for the officers' mess. After further talks Popski decided upon a highly audacious plan to extract the necessary information, not from friends but from the Germans themselves.

Finding a workable telephone in a deserted railway station, Popski rang up Major Schulz. Popski later related their extraordinary conversation:

'Speaking Italian mixed with a few words of German I told him, with a great show of secrecy, that I was the quartermaster sergeant of an Italian Army headquarters in a town which had recently been evacuated by the Germans. I had, I said, the disposal of eight cases of cognac which I would like to sell if he would offer me a good price. We haggled a good deal about the sum. When we had finally come to an agreement I said that for obvious reasons I didn't care to deliver the goods by daylight. If he would wait for me in his office that night at 11 o'clock I would drive up with the drink in a small captured American car. Would he give the word to the control post on the Spinazzola road to let me through without asking questions?'

Although perturbed at the idea of buying stolen goods, Shulz couldn't resist Popski's bargain and so agreed to stay up to receive the cognac. Popski spoke reasonable Italian but at this early stage in the campaign his men did not, and so to minimise the risks of detection it was decided that just Popski and his taciturn gunner, Corporal 'Jock' Cameron, should drive into Gravina. After the war Popski was to claim that he was always careful to keep risks to a minimum, but this plan was daring to the point of foolhardiness; desperate for reliable information, Popski was prepared to try anything.

Popski and Cameron removed all their weapons and other military fittings from the jeep and then stowed away some compo-ration boxes, loaded with stones. Driving down the winding road towards Gravina the two men arrived at the German control post at 2250 hours. Tensing themselves for the prospect of discovery, they sighed with relief when the guard lifted the barrier and carelessly waved them on. The plan was working.

The jeep made its way to the town square and arrived outside Schulz's office dead on 2300 hours. Acting as casually as possible, Popski and Cameron each took hold of one of the cases and, walking past a sentry, made their way up the stairs to the office. Major Schulz lay dozing across his desk and when Cameron dropped his case on the floor with a thump, he looked up to see two British soldiers bearing down on him. Before Schulz could sound the alarm, Cameron smashed his rubber truncheon – a gift from SOE – down onto the luckless German's head. Knocked unconscious, Schulz slumped back into his chair, leaving Popski to go through the papers in his desk while Cameron continued in his task of humping the stone-filled cases of 'cognac'.

As he shuffled through the papers, Popski, to his great surprise and pleasure, found a document listing the ration strengths of the 1st Parachute Division, giving a detailed breakdown of the numbers and dispositions of the German troops facing the British 1st Airborne Division. Quickly snatching a few other supporting files, Popski and Cameron prepared to leave. As a consolation to the unconscious Schulz they left a bottle of whisky (quarter-filled) before regaining their jeep and slipping off into the night.

Popski realised that the venture had been an incredible stroke of luck, and once back in the safety of the mountains his radio operator quickly relayed the information back to the main force at Taranto.

From mid-1944 Popski and his men operated with the 12th and 27th Lancers. The Private Army would patrol through the countryside during the day (above) and then hole up for the night (top). During October Popski began to work with local partisan groups operating near Ravenna on the east coast of Italy. One unit, the 28th (Mario Gordini) Garibaldi Brigade, led by Arrigo 'Bulow' Boldrini, provided a 50-man group, under Ateo Minghelli, to fight, spy for and guide units of the Eighth Army. Right: Popski checks Minghelli's shotgun. Pushing northwards in early 1945, Popski and his army led the final advance into southern Austria where they met the first troops of the Red Army advancing from the east. A few months later, on 14 September 1945, Popski's Private Army was disbanded.

THE AUTHOR Adrian Gilbert has edited and contributed to a number of military and naval publications and is the co-author of *Vietnam: The History and the Tactics*.

SPECIAL HARDWARE

To carry out their undercover, small-unit operations, the Green Berets have put to the test a wide range of modern smallarms

THE US ARMY Special Forces, or Green Berets as they are generally known, are organised to work in small units, often behind the lines on clandestine missions. Apart from their extensive and sophisticated training, the key to their combat success and very survival in their shadowy role is the smallarms they carry. Reliability and stopping power are crucial, and in the years since their formation, the Special Forces have kept an open mind and an open eye for newly developed weapons to augment their armoury.

The Green Berets were among the first military forces to use the Ingram sub-machine gun (SMG) in its various forms. This small automatic was developed by Gordon Ingram, an ex-soldier who spent several years designing and producing a number of SMG models before meeting with success in the early 1970s with his Model 10. The Ingram is an extremely simple and robust weapon, little more than a stamped-steel receiver which houses a bolt, a barrel and a return spring. The 30-round box maga-

Page 148: While the Special Forces are equipped with the 5.56mm Colt Commando as a personal weapon (left), the 'base of fire' concept is retained in the form of the heavier calibre 7.62mm M60 machine gun, which is belt fed and has a high cyclic rate of fire (right).

In modern warfare, the use of a silencer to suppress the report of a smallarm is relatively rare. The other noises of battle will usually perform this task without the need for a muzzle attachment. But silencers play a vital role in the work of units such as the Special Forces, particularly when used in modern operations such as anti-terrorist work. Silencers can be fitted to pistols, rifles and sub-machine guns, provided that the velocity of the ammunition used can be reduced to below the speed of sound. This avoids the 'crack' of the bullet as it passes through the sound barrier.

On the silenced version of the Sterling sub-machine gun, for example, in order to reduce the velocity of the bullet, the gas pressure within the barrel is partially dissipated through a series of small holes drilled in the barrel. The diverted gases pass into a diffuser tube, fitted around the barrel, and then into an expanded metal wrap. The gases are then dissipated, partially through holes in the front barrel support on the weapon, and partially by returning into the barrel.

By the time the bullet exits from the muzzle, much of the column of gas has been broken up and the shot leaves the barrel at a subsonic velocity, followed by a silent flow of gas. Since 1945, a number of silenced versions of standard weapons have been produced for use by American forces, including the M16 and M21 rifles for use in the sniper role.

zine feeds in through the bottom of the pistol grip, a feature which is particularly appreciated by clandestine forces since it makes the weapon much easier to reload in the dark. When the magazine housing is situated elsewhere on a gun, it can be difficult to reload quickly and efficiently by touch alone, but incorporated into the pistol grip, the principle of 'hand finds hand' makes it almost impossible not to hit the housing at the first try.

The muzzle of the Ingram is threaded to accept a 'sound suppressor' or silencer. When used with the .45in Colt Auto Pistol cartridge, which has a muzzle velocity well below the speed of sound, the weapon is almost totally silent, and it then becomes extremely valuable for despatching sentries and outposts without alarming the main body of the enemy. The Ingram is also manufactured in 9mm Parabellum and .38in Auto Pistol calibres, though it is doubtful if the latter has ever been seriously used.

Prior to the advent of the Ingram, the Special Forces acquired a few Swedish Carl Gustav Model 45 SMGs which were also fitted with silencers. This particular weapon fires the 9mm Parabellum round, which has a higher muzzle velocity than .45in

One of the main requirements for units such as the Green Berets is the sniper rifle, and several models have seen service including the M21 sniping version of the 7.62mm M14 rifle (left). Above left: Two heavily camouflaged Special Forces personnel, armed with sniper rifles, stalk their prey during an exercise to develop skills for taking out enemy sentries. Top: The Swedish Carl Gustav Model 45 SMG. A silenced version of the weapon was produced for use with the Special Forces. Above: The compact and robust Ingram SMG has a threaded muzzle to accommodate a silencer, and a retractable stock.

ammunition, and, accordingly, silencing was less effective. Although the report of the gun was effectively muffled, the supersonic crack of the bullet could alert an enemy. Another silenced SMG, the British Sterling L34, has also seen service with the Green Berets, and it is thought that special subsonic ammunition has been used with it, reducing the velocity to a noiseless level.

While the silenced SMG is an extremely effective weapon for close-quarters, silent raiding work, there are times when a firearm with better range and

accuracy than the SMG is required. For this type of work, the Special Forces adopted a variety of silenced rifles, all fitted with sound suppressors developed by the Sionics Corporation. The standard 5.56mm M16 and 7.62mm M14 rifles were among the first to incorporate these silencers, but many less common weapons were also tried in the silenced form; among them were the M21 sniper rifle, an 'accurised' variant of the M14, and the .30in calibre Winchester Model 700, which is often used in the sniping role by other US armed forces. But the most

Below left: The Colt Commando version of the M16 assault rifle has a shortened barrel and telescopic stock for close quarters fighting and counter-ambush work. The Colt is fitted with a four-inch flash suppressor to compensate for the increased muzzle flash caused by the reduction in barrel length.

r increased firepower in bush and counter-ambush rk, the Special Forces ploy grenade launchers. e now obsolete 'blooper', M79 (below centre) has en replaced by the 'clip-on' 03 launcher which is unted beneath the barrel he assault rifle, providing trooper with a choice of e. Bottom: The 40mm enade, used with both apon types.

unusual of them all was the Remington Model 66, a nylon-stocked semi-automatic in .22in calibre. The Model 66 was totally silent in use, and proved to be extremely effective in action in Vietnam for striking down sentries and attacking patrols without giving any indication of where the hostile fire was coming from. It has been reported that one of these rifles was used by a Vietnamese agent to assassinate a North Vietnamese People's Mobilisation Minister in the middle of a public park in Hanoi in 1969; no-one was alerted by the shot, and until the body was examined in a hospital it was assumed that the victim had collapsed from a heart attack.

One unusual silenced weapon, developed experimentally by the Special Forces, was a highly modified version of the Colt M1911A1 automatic pistol with a silencer. The Colt used a 6.35mm blank cartridge, carried inside a dummy .45in cartridge case, which contained a piston, and in front of this piston was an eight-inch finned dart. On firing, the explosion of the blank drove the piston forward to launch the dart to a range of some 50yds.

On the more conventional level, the Green Beret's standard personal arm is his 5.56mm M16A1 assault rifle. The US Special Forces were among the first to adopt this weapon, which is a good deal lighter than the 7.62mm M14 and, since the lower calibre ammunition is also lighter, the individual soldier is able to carry more rounds with him on the battlefield. After the M16 had gone into production, Colt developed a shortened version, with a collapsible stock, known as the 'Colt Commando', and numbers of these were acquired for use by the Special Forces. While the Commando is a very compact and handy weapon, the shortened barrel does not permit the full ballistics of the cartridge to be developed and it delivers considerable muzzle blast.

Ambush and counter-ambush tactics are the stock-in-trade of the Special Forces, and for these rapid, high-firepower engagements something more potent than the normal rifle or SMG is often called for. The 40mm M79 grenade launcher is a

short, single-shot weapon which breaks open like a shotgun and is loaded with a complete round consisting of a grenade fitted to a cartridge case. The M79 uses an unusual propellant system known as the 'high-low pressure system'; the propellant charge is contained in a strengthened section of the cartridge case (the high-pressure chamber) and explodes inside this at high pressure. The gas created is then allowed to 'bleed' through vents into the outer body of the cartridge case (the low-pressure chamber) where it expands, drops in pressure, and thrusts the grenade out of the barrel at a muzzle velocity of 250ft per second. One of the main advantages of this system is that the launcher can be manufactured with a very light barrel, since the high-pressure element of the firing process is confined to the strengthened, inner section of the cartridge case.

The US Army developed a 'clip-on' grenade launcher in the late 1960s, known as the M203

A wide variety of grenades have been developed for use with the M79, including high-explosive fragmentation, shaped-charge anti-armour, smoke, incendiary and illuminating types. In addition, two special anti-ambush rounds were developed – one containing a charge of buckshot and the other a charge of 'flechettes'. Flechettes are small, finned darts, and the cartridge carries a plastic sleeve packed with these darts instead of the usual grenade. On firing, the sleeve splits and allows the flechettes to spread out from the muzzle of the launcher; although small, they have enormous penetrative and wounding power and are extremely valuable for a quick, all-round response to an ambush.

The only major drawback of the M79 in combat is simply that the man carrying it cannot carry any other weapon, except a pistol, with which to defend himself or engage in a firefight over longer ranges. To eliminate this problem, the US Army developed a 'clip-on' grenade launcher in the late 1960s, known as the M203, which can be attached beneath the barrel of the standard M16 assault rifle. In effect, this creates two weapons in one: the trooper carrying the combination can use the weapon as a conventional rifle or, without having to unload the 5.56mm ammunition magazine or make any adjustment to the rifle, can fire a grenade from the underslung launcher when a heavier density of fire is called for. Once the M203 had passed its trials, it became standard equipment with the Green Berets.

Another useful weapon for dealing with ambushes is the common shotgun, and several different models saw service with the Special Forces operating in Vietnam, since there was no standard military pattern available. The military authorities purchased different commercial riot guns, originally designed for police use, from various manufacturers as and when they were required. They were all basically the same type of gun, 12-gauge slide-action repeaters, since experience had shown this type to be capable of withstanding the rigours of military usage better than any other type. The Remington Model 870, Winchester Model 12, Ithaca Model 37 and Savage Model 77 were the most common.

The ammunition used with these guns was generally 00 Buck M19, a loading of nine lead balls, each of .33in diameter, inside a brass case. The propellant charge was such as to give the balls a velocity of 1100ft per second, and they had considerable

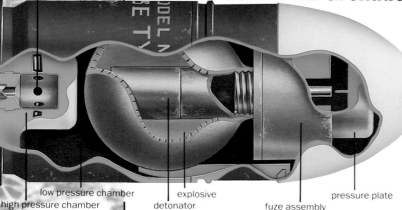

40mm HE Grenade

vent holes

low pressure chamber
high pressure chamber

explosive
detonator

fuze assembly

pressure plate

Winchester Model 12 12-gauge

Calibre 12-gauge
Length 102.7cm
Weight 3.8kg
Feed 6 shot slide-action

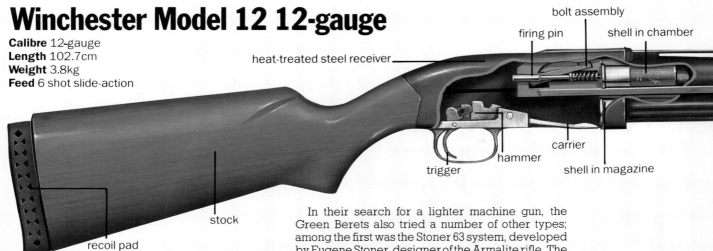

bolt assembly

firing pin

shell in chamber

heat-treated steel receiver

carrier

hammer

trigger

shell in magazine

stock

recoil pad

penetrative power. But nine balls spreading out from the muzzle meant that it was quite easy to miss a target, so to try and thicken up the lethal zone, the XM257 shot cartridge was developed, loaded with 27 No. 4 Buckshot of .24in diameter. Launched from the muzzle at 1325ft per second, these hardened shot have lethal effect to a greater range than the 00 Buckshot and provide a denser shot pattern. Flechette loadings have also been provided for use by the Special Forces but have proved to be somewhat erratic in use. Reports of penetrating body armour and steel helmets at ranges as great as 500 yds conflict with others that detail hitting men at much shorter ranges without seriously wounding them. Generally, it was found that the flechettes yawed in flight up to about 40yds from the muzzle, but after that they stabilised and were quite effective.

While clandestine, behind-the-lines operations, ambushing and small-unit raiding techniques are all important elements in Special Forces' work, their training is still basically that of an infantryman, with additional skills grafted on. Their tactics are also basically infantry, and the 'base of fire' concept is retained and provided for by the M60 machine gun. The M60 is a belt-fed gas-operated general-purpose machine gun, and has been in service since the early 1960s. As a tripod-mounted weapon it is excellent, but as a light one-man gun it is rather heavy. Special Forces were among the first to demand a reduced-weight version, which eventually appeared as the M60E3. The E3 variant has a permanently attached bipod, and a forward handgrip which allows it to be fired from the hip with some degree of accuracy.

In their search for a lighter machine gun, the Green Berets also tried a number of other types; among the first was the Stoner 63 system, developed by Eugene Stoner, designer of the Armalite rifle. The underlying concept of the Stoner system is that there is one basic receiver and mechanism on to which various barrels, stocks and feed systems can be fitted to build up almost any configuration from SMG, through various calibres of rifle, to general-purpose machine gun. The Stoner works by gas which operates a rotating bolt, and in machine-gun form the weapon weighs only 12lb unloaded. The weapon is belt-fed from a plastic magazine. Numbers of Stoner rifles and machine guns were adopted experimentally by Special Forces, the US Marines and the US Navy SEALs in Vietnam, and, as a result of their operations, several minor improvements were made to the general design. But the idea failed to catch on, and the system was eventually abandoned in the late 1960s.

The Belgian 5.56mm FN Minimi machine gun was also given a severe work-out by Special Forces, but they do not appear ever to have used it in combat.

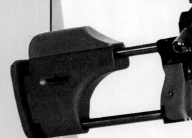

Above: The heavy-barrelled Stoner 63 light machine gun, mounted on a tripod.

Below: The M63A1 5.56mm rifle configuration of the versatile Stoner 63 system

magazine retainer   smooth-bore barrel   bead front sight

magazine cap

fore-end   tubular magazine

The Minimi, designated the M249, has now become standard in the US Army and Marine Corps and cannot be seen solely as a Special Forces weapon.

One of the most recent weapons to appear in the hands of Green Beret units is the .50in calibre sniping rifle. There has long been a requirement for an accurate rifle, capable of delivering a substantial effect at long range (ranges over 1000yds), and in 1983 a number of rifles in this calibre were developed and offered. To date, the only known .50in

Below: The Belgian 5.56mm FN Minimi machine gun. The Minimi has a cyclic rate of fire of 750-1000 rounds per minute and can be fed by a box magazine (shown here) or a 100 or 200-round belt.

calibre rifle that has seen use, in Grenada and Lebanon, is the RAI Model 500. The Model 500 is a single-shot, bolt-action weapon with a somewhat unusual action; on rotating the bolt and drawing it back, the entire bolt comes out of the gun. It is extremely short, little more than a breech plug with a handle. The cartridge is snapped into the extractor claw on the bolt and then inserted into the chamber and the bolt is rotated to lock. Inserting the bolt cocks the striker, and pressure on the trigger then releases it to fire the round. The barrel is anchored into the

receiver but is otherwise free to vibrate. There is a separate tubular fore-end which carries the bipod. A spring-weighted harmonic balancer, concealed within this tube, damps out barrel vibrations to improve accuracy, and the barrel is fluted to dissipate heat and add 'girder' strength. A muzzle brake is also provided to reduce the fierce recoil.

Reports on this weapon, and others of its class, vary: some speak of phenomenal accuracy at ranges out to 1600yds, while others are less enthusiastic. Much appears to depend upon tuning together the sights, the ammunition used, and the harmonic balancer to produce the optimum combination. But once tuned and zeroed correctly, this rifle could be very useful for delivering suppressive or interdictory fire against targets such as observation or command posts at ranges generally considered to be beyond the scope of effective smallarms fire.

The new 9mm weapon will provide considerably more stopping power then its 5.56mm predecessor

The armoury of such units as the US Special Forces is never static as the search for more efficient weapon systems continues and improved variants are adopted to replace weapons already in service. Currently, there are two new systems under development that may well see service with the Green Berets. The first of these, the Advanced Combat Rifle (ACR), is being considered as a replacement for the M16 and is being developed by the AAI Corporation of Baltimore. The ACR fires 5.56mm caseless ammunition and features a very advanced optical range-finding sight. The weapon provides the option of three modes of fire – fully automatic, three-shot burst and single shot. The ACR is scheduled to come into service in the mid-1990s.

For the SMG role, Colt are working on a new 9mm

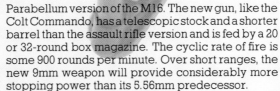

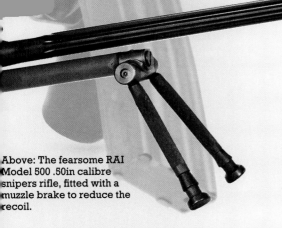

Above: The fearsome RAI Model 500 .50in calibre snipers rifle, fitted with a muzzle brake to reduce the recoil.

Parabellum version of the M16. The new gun, like the Colt Commando, has a telescopic stock and a shorter barrel than the assault rifle version and is fed by a 20 or 32-round box magazine. The cyclic rate of fire is some 900 rounds per minute. Over short ranges, the new 9mm weapon will provide considerably more stopping power than its 5.56mm predecessor.

Although still in the developmental stage, these weapons are likely to be put through trials with the Special Forces in the near future.

THE AUTHOR Ian Hogg is an authority on smallarms, modern weapon systems and equipment, and the technology of warfare.

COMBAT SHOTGUNS

The introduction of combat scatterguns into the armed forces reflected the need for a weapon which allowed sharp reaction, while retaining massive firepower and accuracy at short-to-medium range.

Their first use in the 20th century was during the Moro Insurrection in the Philippines, beginning in 1900. In response to the difficult terrain, the US military adopted the 12-gauge five-shot Winchester M1897 slide-action shotgun.

This weapon proved invaluable during the 'fleeting encounters' inherent in guerrilla warfare.

Modified for use during World War II, the M1897 was given a Parkerized finish and a stronger stock.

Supplemented by the Remington M11 and Ithaca 37, the Winchester again demonstrated its effectiveness in the jungle fighting of the Pacific campaign. These weapons were also used in Korea, providing the right balance of spread and penetration for close combat.

Vietnam saw the most widespread use of shotguns in any modern conflict, and the US Marines began issuing them in 1965. Preferring the more reliable pump-action types they had been using since 1900, a variety of models saw action. The most effective was the 12-gauge Ithaca M37 with a 20in barrel, capable of rapid fire. The Remington M10 and M11 were also used, along with the Winchester M1897 and M1912.

The Remington 870 Mark 1 was introduced into service in 1966. It has a seven-round tubular magazine capable of firing a wide range of ammunition. It was widely used by Special Forces during the Vietnam War, and often by SEAL teams.

SPETSNAZ

Little known but widely feared, Spetsnaz are the Soviet Union's elite forces, trained to a peak of fighting prowess for instant mobilisation under any conditions in the world

THE SOVIET UNION keeps the details of the special forces of its armed services under the strictest possible security. Just as, by comparison, minimal hard information is available concerning the activities of the US Central Intelligence Agency (CIA), there has been no official confirmation of data published in the West on the Soviet special forces, known as Spetsnaz. The only available source of information on Spetsnaz is found in the statements of such Soviet defectors as Viktor Suvorov, the pseudonym of a former Soviet Army captain who served in military intelligence. The revelations of these men can be used as a basis for speculations as to the size and functions of Spetsnaz, but it is difficult to go beyond the broadest description.

The special forces known as Spetsnaz act as the spearhead of the Soviet Army. They are controlled by Soviet military intelligence, the GRU. In wartime their main function is to destroy NATO nuclear missile bases, headquarters and communication centres, air defence installations, and other key military targets such as fuel pipelines. They are also tasked with assassinating military and government leaders in order to encourage panic in the civilian population. Other primary targets for sabotage are power stations, transportation systems and oil and gas depots.

Spetsnaz was virtually unknown until recently because of the effective cloak of secrecy with which the Soviets conceal their armed forces. But these units, considered by military experts to be the real elite of the Soviet armed forces, are increasingly seen as a major threat to Western security. Spetsnaz units are known to be fighting in Afghanistan, assassinating commanders of the Moslem Mujahidin and ambushing guerrilla columns in a bloody hit-and-run war in the mountains. Naval Spetsnaz units regularly

make secret landings along the Norwegian and Swedish coasts from mini-submarines to spy out coastal installations, map minefields and reconnoitre possible landing zones on NATO's vulnerable northern flank.

Special force units played vital roles in the Soviet invasion of Czechoslovakia in 1968, swooping down to seize Prague Airport in advance of the main Warsaw Pact invasion force. A joint Spetsnaz-KGB force was infiltrated into Kabul in December 1979 to pave the way for the Soviet invasion of Afghanistan.

There are 16 Spetsnaz brigades of between 1000 and 1300 men attached to each of the Soviet Army's 'Front' formations. There are also 41 independent companies of 115 men each. These are attached to each Soviet Army and consist of a headquarters unit, three parachute platoons, and support teams. There are four naval Spetsnaz brigades, one each with the

Below and right: While training in the Soviet Union, Spetsnaz teams adopt the uniforms of conventional forces; these personnel on infantry exercises wear the dress of the Red Banner Black Sea Fleet.

COUNTER-INSURGENCY IN AFGHANISTAN

The Soviet Army has committed Spetsnaz units in Afghanistan in a bid to curb Mujahidin guerrillas who, after five years of rebellion, have become increasingly adept in waging the kind of warfare used by their forefathers against earlier invaders, including the British.

The Spetsnaz teams are often integrated with other crack units such as airborne troops, and the Soviets make much use of Asian soldiers, such as Uzbeks, to infiltrate the tightly-knit, village-based communities. Small groups of between five and ten Spetsnaz men are helicoptered in to guerrilla areas, lie low on mountaintops to spot infiltration routes, and call in strikes by Sukhoi Su-25 Frogfoot fighter-bombers or the deadly Mi-24 Hind helicopter gunships. These deep-cover teams, often isolated in mountain caves for weeks, have proved highly effective in recent offensives in the Panshjir Valley. Nearly all of such operatives are officers or warrant officers who have trained in the Caucasus and Uzbekistan, areas which resemble the Afghan terrain.

However, the Afghan guerrillas have scored several victories against Spetsnaz. When a convoy led by Amin Bardak, a former Afghan Army colonel and a key guerrilla leader, was ambushed by 24 Spetsnaz men, a day-long battle ensued in which the Spetsnaz force was outflanked and defeated. When Soviet casevac helicopters arrived, one was downed by Mujahidin surface-to-air missiles. On another occasion, the Soviets sent two teams, dressed in Afghan robes, into the Panshjir Valley to kill guerrilla leaders. They were spotted, captured, and executed before hundreds of villagers.

Soviet Navy's Red Banner Fleets. These include paratroopers, midget-submarine units and two or three battalions of frogmen. All told, Spetsnaz strength in peacetime probably totals between 27,000 and 30,000 crack troops, many times the size of the US Special Forces formations which are only now being strengthened after the post-Vietnam War wind-down.

Spetsnaz training is the most rigorous in the Soviet Army and it has been claimed that many young soldiers have died on exercises. Selection begins when young men and women are drafted. Officers from special Spetsnaz training schools tour recruiting depots looking for tough, quick-witted youngsters, preferably those with language and sporting abilities. Usually about 100 are chosen for Spetsnaz. Over two months of intensive training that stretches them to their physical limits, the number of candidates is trimmed to 20. Those not selected are relegated to airborne or air assault regiments. After selection, the recruits are sent to training battalions for specialised training, including free-fall parachuting, use of explosives, and silent killing techniques. Since only the best become fully qualified and are then promoted to the rank of sergeant, there is always a surplus of capable men in Spetsnaz units, ensuring that combat losses, however heavy, will not weaken the lower command echelons.

Spetsnaz units are frequently mobilised without warning and airdropped into desolate regions such as the wasteland of Siberia

Most Spetsnaz soldiers are conscripts, as are many men of the Soviet Army. They serve for two years, during which their combat training is intense and unremitting. Half their time is spent in the field, often living rough in rugged terrain. A standard test is to send recruits on a 30km cross-country run – in gas masks. If one man rips off the mask to gulp down fresh air, his whole unit is sent back to base and told to start again. Spetsnaz units are frequently mobilised without warning and airdropped into desolate regions such as the wasteland of Siberia, often thousands of kilometres from their final rendezvous point. They are ordered to ski to their objectives, usually real Soviet installations, overcome the guards and secure the facility. The aim is to maintain the highest degree of combat-readiness, and they are expected to be able to move swiftly without back-up or supplies, and sometimes by improvising their own transport.

'Enemy' troops on these exercises are usually crack Interior Ministry, or MVD, soldiers or KGB troops. The exercises are deemed to be so realistic in simulating actual combat conditions that they often expose tactical deficiencies. The 'defending forces' are not briefed about the exercise and, as one specialist noted, the guards 'often find themselves being thrown around like dolls' by Spetsnaz men.

Spetsnaz forces are invariably dropped at night, always from transport planes, and usually from either extremely low levels or high altitudes to hone their parachuting skills for clandestine operations. They are usually dropped in small teams of between six and eight men – the formations they would adopt in wartime. Unlike other airborne units, Spetsnaz troops do not use heavy weapons or vehicles. In wartime they would be dropped up to

---

Soldier, Soviet Spetsnaz, 1980

The Soviet Union's special forces wear a variety of uniforms, to suit the conditions and requirements under which they are expected to operate. This soldier wears full camouflage overalls complete with hood, in a pattern designed for warfare in temperate climates. The trousers obscure his calf-length high boots, something of a throw-back to Russia's Imperial past, although Soviet troops consider them effective footgear in most combat conditions. On the waist belt is a web pouch for spare magazines and a bayonet/knife in a special scabbard, which, when used in conjunction with another similar scabbard, can be employed as wire cutters. Main armament comprises a 5.45mm AKS-74, featuring a folding stock and a plastic 30-round magazine. The AK-74 is the new small-calibre assault rifle which is the successor to the AK-47 series, upon which it is based. Supplementing the rifle is a PRI automatic pistol (carried on the waist belt in a black leather holster with spare magazine attached), also in the same 5.45mm calibre.

SPETSNAZ SPIES IN SCANDINAVIA

Scandinavia, a potential block to Soviet shipping lanes into the Atlantic, is regularly visited by Spetsnaz operatives. Naval commandos are known to slip ashore into Norway and Sweden to build up detailed dossiers on the defences on NATO's northern flank. It is suspected that among the men are Scandinavian defectors who are invaluable as infiltrators of their own countries. Naval Spetsnaz teams often operate in small groups attached to submarine crews. Alternatively, mini-subs are deployed from merchant ships or large deep-sea trawlers equipped as electronic surveillance vessels. With their large holds, which would normally carry fish, trawlers are ideal hosts for mini-subs and small raiding craft. One major target of the Baltic Fleet's infiltrators is the big Swedish naval base at Karlskrona. In 1984 the Swedes observed frogmen several times in the area, but none were caught. Divers were also spotted in the northern Stockholm archipelago. In recent years at least 150 clandestine landings are reputed to have been carried out by Spetsnaz units based in Kronstadt near Leningrad, and it is believed that the entire Swedish coastline from Haparanda to Malmo has been covered. Spetsnaz incursions have taken place along the Norwegian coast, where high cliffs and deep water make detection of submarines extremely difficult. Norway is a NATO member and a strategic component of NATO's northern flank. Sweden, though neutral, offers a route into Norway and, in the event of war, a Soviet force could use the Swedish route to attack vital Norwegian installations.

Above: Small teams of highly trained Spetsnaz frogmen would present a serious threat to Western marine installations in time of war.

500km behind enemy lines and would operate on their own until the main forces linked up with them.

Once a year, the best Spetsnaz units are assembled at the Soviet Army's main training centre near Kirovograd for a three-month burst of high-intensity training under the most realistic battlefield conditions. Their targets are real Soviet missile bases, military headquarters, and other key installations. The manoeuvres serve two purposes. They pit Spetsnaz against high-quality troops, and they foster those troops' capability to counter attacks by enemy special forces that would be ordered in to seize their installations in time of war.

In a recent exercise in the Soviet Far East, a Spetsnaz brigade was sent in to seize a nuclear weapons base. The commander of the 'defending force' formed his vehicles into an outward-facing ring around the base. When the alarm was sounded his drivers turned on their headlights, blinding the attacking sabotage teams and trapping them in a blaze of illumination. This tactic has now become standard practice at many Soviet command centres to counter sabotage raids.

Spetsnaz units also have special training centres in regions of the Soviet Union that closely resemble the areas of Western Europe they would infiltrate in wartime. The Baltic coast, for instance, is like northern Germany. To make training as realistic as possible, Spetsnaz brigades use accurate, full-scale models of key targets such as NATO installations and weapons systems. They employ inflatable models of Cruise, Pershing II and Lance missiles, and Mirage, F-16 and other fighter aircraft. The guards at these

Above: Officer cadets of the prestigious Suvorov Military College in Moscow. Most Spetsnaz soldiers are conscripts who have been selected from such establishments for their outstanding sporting and intellectual capabilities. Military and academic skills are then brought to a high level in order to prepare the men for their complex assignments. **Left:** Officer cadets work up to peak physical fitness.

installations wear NATO uniforms, to further simulate actual battle conditions.

Spetsnaz soldiers also regularly undergo simulated interrogation, using known Western techniques. They are dragged from their beds in the middle of the night and bundled into interrogation rooms manned by intelligence officers in NATO uniforms. These interrogations may last for days, during which the Spetsnaz men are stripped and left without food or water in damp, bare cells that are kept without light to disorientate them. Viktor Suvorov, the former Soviet Army captain who served in the GRU before he defected to the West, notes that, 'The lessons given to Spetsnaz soldiers are very instructive and long remembered.'

Sabotage and reconnaissance troops, such as Spetsnaz, are even more thoroughly trained than the airborne forces. Operations behind enemy lines are a key component in Soviet military strategy, and this accounts for the relatively large formations of special forces in the Soviet military establishment. Saboteurs are trained to operate in the harshest conditions with only the minimum of supplies of food and water. They are taught to pick locks and other 'techniques of bandit and burglar', as one former KGB officer put it. Frequently they are ordered to parachute into blazing forests, or in strong winds that would certainly lead to cancellation of the jump in the West.

It is reported that a key element of their training is the development of ruthlessness. Former KGB captain Aleksei Myagkov noted:

'Anyone who might betray their positions or prevent them carrying out their tasks must be killed, since they cannot take prisoners. Even women, children or old people who stumble on them in a wood must not be allowed to report their discovery. The saboteurs are told to kill without any pangs of conscience in order to do their duty. Any sentimental feelings must be disregarded and they must think of themselves as being above such "rubbish". The soldiers are encouraged to respect qualities of strength, boldness and cruelty.'

It has been claimed that this attitude extends even to their own comrades, and that they are ordered to kill their own wounded because they cannot take casualties with them or allow them to fall into enemy hands alive. Again, in wartime, if they spot a missile preparing to launch or an aircraft carrying nuclear weapons ready to take off they have orders to attack, even if it means certain death. Intelligence operatives who were deployed in Afghanistan with the Mujahidin said that Spetsnaz troops caught in an ambush killed 15 of their own casualties when it became impossible to lift them out by helicopter.

Normal Spetsnaz equipment includes a 5.45mm Kalashnikov assault rifle fitted with a silencer and flash suppressor, 300 rounds of ammunition, a silenced P6 pistol, a knife, six hand-grenades, a light grenade-launcher and a medical kit. Each team usually has at least one RPG-7D rocket-launcher. Units with special missions may also carry SA-7

Strela 2 surface-to-air missiles, mines and heavy explosives. Most units carry R-350-M burst-transmission radios that send messages in spurts of eight to ten seconds to prevent enemy scanners sensing them. If the men were dropped behind NATO lines they would probably carry NATO-issue weapons and wear NATO uniforms.

Spetsnaz officers and non-commissioned officers alike are highly versatile. Most know at least one foreign language, usually a Western European tongue as that region is the one in which most Spetsnaz units will operate in wartime. Many of these linguistically proficient cadres go through the Soviet Army's elite military academies and are taught specialised skills – intelligence techniques, communications, foreign policy, electronics and so on – for up to five or six years. Spetsnaz forces are so classified that officers and men wear the uniforms of regular regiments, usually the airborne. In Eastern Bloc countries they don the uniforms of auxiliary units, normally signals.

Outside the normal military structure, Spetsnaz is believed to have special units known as 'headquarters companies' or 'anti-VIP'. These highly secretive units, usually about 70-80 strong, are hard-core professionals who wear civilian clothes. They remain apart from regular Spetsnaz groups. These men and women are often described as assassins, for their task in war is apparently to eliminate the government or political and military leaders of their target country. Information on such units is naturally even less easy to obtain than that concerning the more conventional Spetsnaz groups; but it is reasonably likely that they exist.

Below left: A Spetsnaz soldier wearing protective eye goggles, aims his SA-7 Grail surface-to-air missile launcher. To fire the weapon the operator directs the tube through an open sight and takes first pressure on the trigger. A red light appears which will turn green when the weapon's infra-red seeker has locked on target, at which point he applies full pressure to the trigger. Below right: Soviet paratroopers prepare to enplane onto an Ilyushin Il-76 transporter.

Viktor Suvorov calls these hard-core agents 'cut-throats'. To conceal their existence, these highly secret units are detached from their parent brigades to Soviet Army military districts where they become 'athletics teams'. Even other Spetsnaz units may not be aware of the hit squads' existence, and Spetsnaz naval brigades have similar units.

They form boxing, wrestling, karate, shooting, athletics, skiing and parachute teams. All belong to the Central Army Sporting Club, or ZSKA. The KGB's 'sportsmen' belong to the rival Dinamo Sporting Club. As sportsmen, they are welcomed in the Western cities to which they travel. They hold many sporting records and Olympic medals.

Valentin Yerikalin of the Spetsnaz brigade attached to the Black Sea Fleet, which handles GRU operations in the Mediterranean and Turkey, was one of these 'sportsmen'. He won a silver medal for rowing at the 1968 Olympic Games as a member of the Soviet team. Years later he was assigned to Istanbul in a diplomatic post, where he was later arrested by Turkish police for attempting to recruit Turks for an undercover network run by the 'diversionary' Spetsnaz brigade attached to the Black Sea Fleet.

The 'sporting clubs' frequently visit the European capitals to which they would be sent in advance of any Soviet offensive. They learn to live in an unfamiliar environment, how to get around, and where to locate the target figures they would be sent to kill. Soviet strategists hold that the shock to national morale of attacks in the first days of a war on government ministries in Bonn, London, Brussels or Paris, with top politicians and industrialists being wiped out in their homes, would be devastating.

The 'anti-VIP' units are the only Spetsnaz operatives who are allowed to make contact with its network of agents throughout Western Europe. These are clandestine operatives, 'sleepers', sent in years before with established, respectable covers in all walks of life, often living in close contact with the targets they would sabotage in wartime.

Another principal task for the sleepers is to provide transportation and safe houses for infiltrated Spetsnaz operatives. These are usually located in isolated areas, near the sea or in mountains. Most would be equipped with deep underground bunkers able to withstand nuclear explosions, and would be well stocked with food, water and other supplies. The GRU maintains a large Spetsnaz group in East Germany, mainly because of the easy access it affords to West Germany, Belgium, The Netherlands and Britain. There are an estimated 150 sabotage groups trained to operate in Western Europe. All their members are fluent in English, French or German. As Suvorov has said: 'Spetsnaz is the sharpest and most effective weapon in the hands of the GRU's intelligence directorates.'

Admiral of the Fleet Lord Peter Hill-Norton, a former chief of Britain's Defence Staff, said that 1000 Spetsnaz operatives infiltrated into Britain, 'could make it very difficult for us to operate effectively' in time of war. In Spetsnaz, the Soviet Union has a powerful force of motivated and resourceful operatives. It is likely that Spetsnaz will play a highly significant part in any future Soviet military operation.

THE AUTHOR Ed Blanche is a journalist of the Associated Press who specialises in military subjects. He has written extensively on many aspects of the Soviet armed forces and on current Soviet military strategy worldwide.

CENTCOM

In 1981, the US Rapid Deployment Force was one man and some filing cabinets. Now CENTCOM can deploy more weight across the globe than Britain can across the Channel

THE ISSUES AT STAKE

In 1986 alone, the West imported 12 million barrels of oil per day from the Middle East. The prospect of this supply being cut off through the efforts of a third party is one of the main reasons for CENTCOM's continued existence. There are two further factors that pose a threat to the West – trade, and the unrestricted passage of vessels through the waterways of the Gulf region.

In 1985, US trade alone with the 19 countries in CENTCOM's sphere of operations amounted to well over 16 billion dollars. The whole region has a combined import and export trade valued at 197 billion dollars: trade that the Western world cannot afford to lose through Soviet domination of the area. There is also the question of the region's strategic waterways. More than 21,000 ships pass through the Suez Canal every year, carrying a staggering 10 per cent of the world's trade. In addition, the West must keep the canal open so that her warships may reach the Gulf area quickly in the event of a conflict. A long sea passage around the Cape of Good Hope would make a mockery of any pretensions to speedy deployment – aircraft may be able to move men and equipment in the first place, but the viability of a trans-global heavyweight punch depends on ship-borne re-supply. If the Straits of Hormuz were closed for any reason, two-thirds of all the Gulf region's oil would be denied to the West. And, if either the Bab el Mandeb Straits at the southern end of the Red Sea, or the Suez Canal itself, were closed, the remaining one-third of the West's oil supply could be lost.

THE RAPID DEPLOYMENT FORCE is dead; long live CENTCOM. When it was first created in 1977 under the command of General Paul Kelley, the United States' out-of-area (OOA) quick-reaction force was known as the Rapid Deployment Joint Task Force (RDJTF). However, it has since been incorporated into the US Central Command in an effort to give America's OOA forces a greater degree of political credibility and military clout. CENTCOM, to give the new organisation its usual nickname, is responsible for protecting Western interests in the oil-producing regions of the Arabian (Persian) Gulf in particular, and the Middle East in general. It is a massive force, capable of being deployed across the world with lightning speed. Indeed, from the point of view of America's European allies, CENTCOM's importance rivals that of European Command – the organisation that carries all US forces in Europe under its enormous umbrella.

CENTCOM's role, echoing the words of an American Civil War general, is to reach its objective 'firstest, fastest with the mostest.' When the call for deployment comes, this objective will more than likely be within the Gulf region. For the West, the importance of this area in terms of strategic military value and economic trade cannot be overestimated.

One of CENTCOM's main problems is that its area of operations comprises 19 countries that are spread across a region measuring 3100 miles long and 3400 miles wide. By comparison, in Europe NATO occupies one-third of the surface area but contains several times as many troops. To alleviate the difficulties inherent in co-ordinating troops over such an enormous area, General George B. Crist, the commander-in-chief of CENTCOM, travels nearly 150,000 miles each year – reassuring his allies of US commitment to the area and discussing contingency plans in the event of a crisis. CENTCOM depends on these allies, particularly Pakistan, Jordan and Oman, to augment the US combat force, provide airstrips and basing rights, and allow US aircraft to conduct over-flights into other countries.

CENTCOM's military strategy is based on the principle of 'coalition warfare'. Immediately following the call for deployment, local troops, reinforced by the Division Ready Brigade (DRB) of the 82nd Airborne Division, would join up and attempt to hold ground while the rest of CENTCOM prepared for the counter-punch. A key element in CENTCOM's planning is the series of exercises that takes place every other year in Egypt. Codenamed 'Bright Star', these exercises usually involve flying a battalion, some

times a full brigade, of paratroopers from the 82nd Airborne directly from their home in Fort Bragg to a drop zone in Egypt. Elements of the 101st Airborne (Airmobile) Division are then airlifted in, together with the unit's complement of Blackhawk helicopters. Up to this point, the majority of Bright Star exercises have involved Egyptian troops and a joint US/Egyptian command structure. Also present, however, have been small cadres of senior officers from member states of the Gulf Co-operation Council.

During the last few years, political relations between the US and the Gulf states have been somewhat reserved. This fact, combined with the danger inherent in any major deployment to the Gulf area by either of the two superpowers, has effectively denied CENTCOM the opportunity to run large-scale exercises in the region. With the exception of minor deployments of command teams, air-control teams

Page 161 : The 82nd and 101st Airborne Divisions can deploy by parachute and transport aircraft directly to the Middle East within 36 hours. Top: UH-60 Blackhawks see desert action during the Bright Star exercises in Egypt. Left: A para of the 82nd Airborne Division handles a Soviet-made AKMS assault rifle issued to an Egyptian counterpart. Far left: The US Marines wade ashore onto Egyptian soil during Operation Bright Star. Below: CENTCOM's AH-1 Hueycobras see action with the Rapid Deployment Force in Grenada.

and observers to exercises in Jordan, Oman and other small states, the US has kept a very low profile east of the Suez Canal. CENTCOM does have an ace up its sleeve, however. The Multinational Force of Observers (MFO) in the Sinai contains a small core of officers and men from either the 82nd or 101st Airborne Divisions. Among the varied tasks of these paras is that of gathering information on the current situation in the Gulf region. If the call for deployment goes out, this small cadre will act as a reception force for CENTCOM.

On the Special Forces front, CENTCOM possesses an almost embarrassing array of riches

CENTCOM is capable of putting over 290,000 men into the field, and its executive arm comprises four main elements drawn from the US Army, Navy, Marine Corps and Air Force. The army involvement revolves around the XVIIIth Airborne Corps based at Fort Bragg. This consists of the 82nd and 101st Airborne Divisions based, respectively, at Fort Bragg, North Carolina, and Fort Campbell, Kentucky. These two units perform the role of a fast-moving, quick-reaction force that is capable of deploying by parachute and transport aircraft directly to the Middle East. The 82nd Airborne Division is a heavyweight formation, despite its airportability. Its integral air strength comprises a battalion of AH-1 Huey attack helicopters and an air cavalry battalion equipped with UH-60 Blackhawk helicopters, while its offensive fire support is provided by a Sheridan tank battalion and four artillery battalions equipped with the 105mm Light Gun. The 101st Airborne has only three tank battalions and no armour, but can boast one attack and three transport helicopter battalions. Again, the Huey (soon to be replaced by the AH-64 Apache) and the Blackhawk represent the core of the aviation group, with CH-47D Chinooks fulfilling the medium-lift requirement.

The 9th Infantry Division (Light) is also assigned to CENTCOM and was created specifically for this role. It has a strength of 10,200 all ranks rather than the 18,000 of a normal 'heavy' infantry division, and its equipment has been designed for ease of movement. Like the 82nd, it uses the British 105mm Light

Gun rather than the older, more cumbersome M102 American howitzer; the former's longer range and greater mobility have made it the standard light artillery piece of CENTCOM's army component. The 10th Mechanized Division, a slimmer, lighter version of the traditional armoured division, provides the army with its heavy punch. Its 155mm artillery and M1 Abrams main battle tanks supplement the 105mm guns and Sheridan light tanks of the airborne and light divisions. The 197th Mechanized Brigade, together with the 6th Cavalry Regiment of the 1st Air Cavalry Division, make up the conventional army component.

On the Special Forces front, CENTCOM possesses an almost embarrassing array of riches. The newly formed US Special Operations Command at Fort Bragg, consisting of eight army Special Forces Groups, three Ranger battalions, Delta Force, two Special Operations Aviation battalions and four Psychological Warfare Groups, is at CENTCOM's disposal, together with US Navy, Marine and Air Force Special Operations Command (SOC) units.

The United States Marine Corps (USMC) provides the rest of the frontline fighting element, in a role complementary to that of the airborne and mechanised army troops. The USMC provides the approximate equivalent of five brigades of marines. The major element consists of a complete marine amphibious force (MAF). This is roughly equal in size to a division, and comprises three marine amphibious regiments of three battalions each, a complete air group and a force service support group. Including the 2500 sailors who man the necessary amphibious assault ships and landing craft, the 1st MAF, based at

Right: An M60 tank reverses out of a USAF C-5 Galaxy. Massive transports like the C-5 and C-141 give CENTCOM the capability to deploy rapidly in strength. The new C-17, which will replace some of the older C-130s, will give even greater flexibility. It will have the capacity and range of the C-5 but, like the smaller C-130, will be able to operate from improvised airstrips. Inset right: M1 Abrams main battle tanks supplement the Sheridan light tanks of the airborne and light divisions. Below left: This fast-attack vehicle is, in fact, a customised Beach Buggy. Below right: A tank is deployed in a low-level drop from a C-130, taking vital firepower to the heart of the action. Bottom: A C-5 Galaxy swallows a Blackhawk. The C-5 needs an enormous concrete runway – a dangerous dependence in times of conflict.

Camp Pendleton in California, has a strength of 52,000 all ranks. A marine amphibious brigade (MAB) is also attached to the MAF. This comprises three battalion-sized marine amphibious units (MAUs), an air wing (one A/F-18 Hornet fighter squadron and two AV-8B Harrier strike squadrons), and a brigade service support group. In addition, there may be up to five amphibious ready groups (ARGs) attached to the fleet. Each of these consists of an MAU equipped with integral transport helicopters. It was the 22nd MAU of the Mediterranean ARG, on its way to join the Sixth Fleet off Beirut, that took Pearls Airport in Grenada in October 1983.

The US Navy element of CENTCOM has its headquarters in Pearl Harbor, Hawaii. In the event of a call for deployment, whatever shipping is available in the area concerned will be used to support CENTCOM operations in the Gulf. The important element in the seapower equation is the pre-positioning of equipment for the marines at Diego Garcia, in the Indian Ocean. A fleet of 17 maritime pre-positioning ships (MPS) contains everything needed by the first MAB to reach the area. The supplies on board are intended to sustain the 'grunts' during the first 30 days of combat while the rest of the stores catch up.

A new concept for the USMC is embodied in the Landing Craft Air Cushion (LCAC), a large hovercraft that is capable of landing a company of marines, or alternatively two main battle tanks, after a high-speed transit from either a mother ship or a secure land base near the assault target. A total of 45 LCACs will eventually transform the corps' ability to mount MAB-sized assaults at high speed across the sort of distances normally covered in a cramped, uncomfortable and extremely vulnerable landing craft.

CENTCOM would be able to deploy men and equipment from the US to the Middle East within 36 hours

A total of 60 assorted amphibious cargo and assault ships are available to the US Marines. Many of these, of course, would not be available for deployment to the Middle East. However, even one Iwo Jima-class assault ship will carry six AV-8B Harriers, two CH-46 helicopters and 10 CH-53 transport helicopters. This lifting capacity would be sufficient to get an entire MAU onto the beach. Add to these assault ships the conventional carriers that would carry US Navy fighters and strike aircraft, and the offensive capability of the US Marine Corps reaches quite awesome proportions.

Perhaps the most important element in CENTCOM's ability to react hard and fast to a given threat is the United States Air Force (USAF). It is the USAF's tactical transports that would carry the 82nd and 101st Airborne Divisions to their destination during the initial stages of an emergency in the Gulf. The divisions' helicopters would either self-deploy in a series of long hops across the Atlantic, or be carried on board ship. Ideally, CENTCOM would be able to count on the use of a sizeable proportion of the USAF's transport force of 269 C-141 Starlifters, 70 C-5 Galaxies and over 500 C-130 Hercules. With the use of in-flight refuelling, these transport aircraft would be able to deploy men and equipment from their mounting bases in the US to a forward airhead in the Middle East within 36 hours. This is the time it takes most armies to distribute their mobilisation orders.

Integral to CENTCOM is an offensive air capability that comprises seven tactical fighter wings. F-4 Phantoms, F-14 Tomcats, F-16 Fighting Falcons,

Top: CENTCOM jeeps and trucks disembark from USS *Saginaw*. Right: Troops board USAF transports for a rapid deployment exercise. Bottom: A Blackhawk doubles as a logistical workhorse, keeping Rapid Deployment Joint Task Force personnel supplied in Grenada.

F-111s, A-7 Corsairs and A-10 Thunderbolts make up the fighter and strike element, with the EF-111 Electric Fox and EC-130 Hercules carrying out electronic reconnaissance. RF-4 Phantoms perform the role of tactical reconnaissance. Three Boeing E-3 Airborne Warning and Control System (AWACS) aircraft, permanently stationed in Saudi Arabia, monitor the western and northwestern shores of the Gulf. Interestingly enough, 60 per cent of the C-130s and all the RF-4s are operated by reserve crews, as are some 60 per cent of all the air force communications support systems. Although exact figures are unavailable, approximately 250 to 300 fighters are assigned to CENTCOM and controlled through the Commander USAF Central Command Air Forces; this is more than the Royal Air Force can field in the air defence of Britain.

It is a measure of the importance CENTCOM has placed on the rapid movement of men and equipment that the organisation is not entirely satisfied with the airlift and sealift capability it already possesses. General Crist's target is to be able to shift 66 million ton-miles per day (MTM/D) of men and equipment from the US to the Gulf by air alone. This would represent an enormous rapid deployment capability, and at present the USAF is capable of moving only 60 per cent of that requirement. A mixed force of Lockheed C-141 and C-5 transports, together with McDonnell-Douglas KC-10 tankers, are supplemented by the Civilian Reserve Air Fleet (CRAF). The latter comprises commercial cargo and passenger aircraft that have been earmarked for conversion into troop or cargo aircraft in the event of an emergency. These aircraft alone can carry nearly 12 MTM/D. A further 21 assorted Boeing 747s, Tristars and DC-10s will add another 3.2 MTM/D by the end of the decade.

The key to fulfilling the remaining 40 per cent of the airlift requirement will be the forthcoming C-17 transport aircraft, built by McDonnell-Douglas. Unlike the C-141 and C-5, it will not be confined to enormous concrete runways and will be capable of operating from improvised airstrips; this allows greater flexibility and, crucially, reduces CENTCOM's dependence upon unavailable or easily damaged permanent airfields in the region. The C-17 alone will eventually account for 43 per cent of CENTCOM's strategic airlift and another 60 per cent of the tactical airlift within the operational area.

For all this airlift capability, however, much of the heavy equipment and bulk stores must come by sea – up to 95 per cent of it in the case of a long deployment. CENTCOM's requirement for a fast fleet capable of loading and moving one million tons of cargo is now in sight, and 115 fast merchantmen and container ships (excluding the MPS based at strategic points around the world) are capable of moving nearly

three-quarters of a million tons of equipment, ammunition, food and stores at speeds approaching 30 knots. A series of major construction programmes has resulted in vital dock facilities and airfields being created in the Azores, Morocco, Egypt, Oman and Diego Garcia in order to support both CENTCOM and European Command.

CENTCOM has come a long way since the idea of a permanent OOA force was mooted in the Pentagon in the early 1970s. It was said as recently as 1981 that the RDJTF consisted solely of General Paul Kelley, an office at MacDill Air Force Base in Florida, and a collection of filing cabinets; this is no longer the case. CENTCOM is a highly flexible combat organisation that is capable of deploying more firepower across the world than the British armed forces could deploy across the English Channel.

THE AUTHOR Gregor Ferguson was a former editor of *Defence Africa and the Middle East* and has contributed to several other military publications.

THE THREAT

The traditional threat to stability in the Gulf region has been seen as the Soviet Union. In late 1979, when the US was preoccupied with the Iranian hostage crisis, the West and her allies were helpless to prevent elements of the Red Army from sweeping into Afghanistan. Caught with its eye off the ball, the US is determined not to allow a repeat of this situation.

The Soviets have designated Southwest Asia as the Southern Theatre of Military Operations (Southern TVD). Into this one area, comprising three military districts (Turkestan, North Caucasus and Transcaucasia), the Soviet Union has channelled 32 tank and motor rifle divisions and over 1000 combat aircraft. Appointed in July 1985, the overall commander in the Southern TVD is General Mikhail Zaytsev. He is a tough, highly respected commander, and is responsible for co-ordinating Soviet forces in Afghanistan, in addition to preparing contingency plans for the whole region.

So far, only aircraft bedecked in Afghan colours have been seen on the Pakistan border, but if the Pakistani Air Force's F-16 Fighting Falcons continue to shoot them down (an increasingly common occurrence), Zaytsev may unleash the new generation of fighters under his command. These include the Sukhoi Su-25 Frogfoot air-support fighter, the Su-24 Fencer fighter-bomber, and the Mikoyan/Gurevich MiG-29 Fulcrum and Su-27 Flanker air-superiority fighters. To back up this formidable array of airpower, Zaytsev can also call upon the latest generation of Soviet surface-to-air missiles, the SAM-8 and SAM-13.

Iran is seen as another major threat, one that is more immediate to the moderate Arab states such as Kuwait than that from the Soviet Union. The destabilising effect of an Iranian victory in the Gulf War could be enormous, with one state after another falling victim to Islamic militancy.

After being annexed in 1914, Cyprus was given full colony status in 1923. In 1931, as a result of widespread civil unrest, power was placed in the hands of the British governor.

In 1955, Cyprus had a population of 500,000 which was divided by loyalty to different states (Greece and Turkey), by language and by religion. The Greek Cypriots, led by Archbishop Makarios III and Colonel George Grivas, espoused 'enosis', or union with Greece. Although Grivas was truely committed to enosis, Makarios saw it as a means of achieving eventual independence for Cyprus. To this end, a campaign of violent insurrection was planned against the civilian population, the police force and the British garrison. Led by Grivas, EOKA began its terrorist activities in earnest on 31 March 1955. The programme of sabotage soon escalated into a series of assassinations which the poorly-equipped police force was incapable of preventing. A State of Emergency was declared on 26 November 1955.

Until the intelligence framework necessary for a counter-insurgency campaign could be erected, the large British garrison was forced to adopt a defensive role. Gradually, however, guerrilla activities were restricted. Operation Pepperpot in June 1956 eliminated half of EOKA's terrorists, and, over the next two years, the security forces went onto the offensive. Finally, a compromise was reached – Cyprus was granted independence, though Britain maintained a military base on the island. Cyprus was partitioned in 1974 in the aftermath of the Turkish invasion.

During the Cyprus Emergency, the British Intelligence Corps provided the security forces with the means to combat terrorism

THE EVOLUTION of intelligence networks worldwide has been so complex, and conducted in such secrecy, that the mention of them provokes a wide variety of responses. The military maxim 'Time spent in reconnaissance is seldom wasted', is in stark contrast to the comment of Malcolm Muggeridge (who served in the Special Operations Executive during World War II) 'Security is rather locking the stable door after the horse has bolted.' The popular 'James

Left: Armed with tear gas and batons, Military Police come to the aid of a young Cypriot injured during a student demonstration. Bottom right: Intelligence leads paratroopers to the discovery of a large, if somewhat primitive, weapons cache.

A QUESTION OF
SECURITY

During the Cyprus Emergency, 'I' Corps was called in to enable the 'active arm' of the security forces to mount counter-insurgency operations. Centre left: Suspects are rounded up during a spot-check in Nicosia. Below: Using the 'wanted list' as a reference, a British soldier examines identification papers.

Bond' image of intelligence operations is another type of response, though rarely is this view relevant to present-day security forces.

Within the modern British Army, understanding of the Intelligence Corps is equally varied, reflecting the range of tasks to which it is assigned. Any unit commander, faced with the sudden appearance of intelligence personnel, is likely to utter the universal sentiment, 'Here comes the 'I' Spy Corps.' The precise nature of intelligence work cannot, for security reasons, always be made known to the public or even to the armed services. One bemused 'I' Corps NCO, on discovering that his source reports were bypassing the local Army establishment and going directly to Downing Street, commented: 'Tell me, boss – just who the hell are we working for?'

Tactical intelligence – the use of information for combat and operational purposes – has undergone major changes during the 20th century. Originally associated almost exclusively with glamorous spies, such as Mata Hari during World War I, the increasing specialisation of warfare has spawned equally specialised intelligence networks, capable of adapting to the environment in which they are tasked to operate. During World War II, this process culminated in the detailed intelligence used in the preparation of Allied plans for the invasion of Normandy. After 1945, new factors came to the fore – terrorist and guerrilla insurgency – which further stimulated the development of Army intelligence. In Algiers, for example, the French Army established an information network in addition to the colonial administration. This played a significant role in breaking up the National Liberation Front in the Casbah prior to the Battle of Algiers in 1957.

The British Intelligence Corps, known as 'I' Corps, was formed in 1940, immediately after the Battle of France. Although it is similar to the G2 branch of the US Intelligence Corps and the Soviet GRU, 'I' Corps junior and senior NCOs enjoy a degree of responsibility and authority not shared by their American counterparts, while possessing nowhere near the manpower of the intelligence directorate of the Soviet Army.

'I' Corps is responsible for ensuring that the Army maintains a high level of internal security

'I' Corps is, therefore, a uniquely British answer to the problem of obtaining and supplying the intelligence that the armed forces in general, and the Army in particular, require in order to fulfil their roles. At the same time, 'I' Corps is responsible for ensuring that the Army maintains a high level of internal security – making it both poacher and gamekeeper. Since the Regimental March is based on the song *The Lincolnshire Poacher*, it is easy to assume where its heart really lies. However, both roles are equally important, indeed complementary, as it is far easier to prevent an enemy from gaining access to your secrets if you are aware of exactly what he wants – and how he intends to steal it.

The Intelligence Corps is composed almost entirely of officers and NCOs, most of whom are highly qualified in their fields. All possess quick and lively minds, coupled with an intense curiosity. Any private soldiers joining 'I' Corps are usually promoted to lance-corporal within months of completing their training, after which advancement to corporal and sergeant is expected to be rapid. Training for the Corps is extremely intensive and civilian entrants

The intelligence process encompasses a myriad of functions and tasks, operating concurrently, that blend into a coherent network.

The process begins with the collection of intelligence from 'sources'. 'Active' sources are those that are aware of their value, including prisoners, agents and informers. However, the majority of information is elicited from 'passive' sources, such as documents, newspapers, radio intercepts and the capture of enemy equipment. A person supplying information without being aware of doing so would also be classified as a 'passive' source. The distinction between active and passive sources can be extremely subtle, and the intelligence process seeks to evaluate both individually.

As information is collected, it passes upwards where it is first collated, and then interpreted before being disseminated to those people or organisations with 'a need to know' – not all and sundry. At any stage in the intelligence process re-tasking may take place, with additional information being requested by senior officers.

The flexible nature of 'I' Corps enables it to adapt its operations according to both the tasks expected of it, and local conditions. In the case of Cyprus, this meant starting an intelligence network virtually from scratch. Below: Field-Marshal Sir John Harding.

have found – to their dismay – that an understanding of the basic infantry role plays an important part. The philosophy behind this is that 'I' Corps personnel cannot operate effectively within an infantry formation unless they are reasonably competent soldiers, irrespective of the tasks expected of them. These vary from running an ops room to surveillance; organising personnel security programmes to taking part in long-range reconnaissance operations with special forces; and from running agents to being responsible for the unit transport. In general, the armed forces have a simple attitude towards 'I' Corps: 'You're the experts, so tell us what to do.'

Harding set up an integrated framework through which intelligence could be passed

When Field-Marshal Sir John Harding arrived as Governor to Cyprus on 3 October 1955, the colonial administration had already proved itself incapable of countering the military and political activities of EOKA, the National Organisation of Greek Cypriot Combatants. Despite growing signs of unrest, the intelligence infrastructure necessary to deal effectively with terrorism had not been erected. Harding was horrified to discover that secret cyphers were kept in a safe in the governor's lavatory – very quaint but hardly conducive to security. Determined to use the same tactics that General Sir Gerald Templar had employed in Malaya, Harding set up an integrated framework through which intelligence could be passed to the military, and to the Special Branch (SB) of the police force. Brigadier George Baker was appointed Chief of Staff and Director of Operations, and Chief Constable Geoffrey White was later brought in to preside over the reorganisation of the police force.

Initially, EOKA's cell structure and ruthless security, combined with the difficult terrain, severely restricted the success of counter-insurgency operations. With over 1000 potential assassins and saboteurs at its disposal, EOKA had no intention of engaging in open warfare, being content to carry out a carefully orchestrated series of attacks on military and civilian targets. In addition, EOKA's strong links with the Orthodox Church provided the terrorists with safe houses and weapons caches in monasteries scattered throughout the island. Eighty per cent of the civilian population refused to co-operate with the authorities and a State of Emergency was declared on 26 November 1955.

The British Army, having recognised that the spectre of terrorism can only be negated by an efficient intelligence network, tasked 'I' Corps with the job of providing it with the means to launch a counter-insurgency campaign. After 1956, the wholesale arrest, detention and interrogation of suspects, the infiltration of EOKA by defectors and pro-British Cypriots, and the discovery of EOKA documents, enabled the British security forces to inflict a series of crushing blows on the rural and urban organisation of the terrorists. Although failing to destroy EOKA, the intelligence process did restrict its activities – eventually leading to the announcement of a ceasefire on Christmas Eve 1958.

To illustrate how this intelligence network functioned during the Cyprus Emergency 1955-59, we will look at the organisation of the Travel Control Security unit (TCS), which was staffed by 'I' Corps officers and NCOs, followed by one of its operations.

Travel Control Security is an integral part of any

counter-terrorist permanent operation, for the ta of differentiating between nationalities, or bellig rents, is essential if the security forces are to distin uish between friend and foe. Basically, it is the mea by which all movement to and from a particular ar can be observed and, if necessary, interdicted. Cyprus, cordons and search patrols of varying tensity were set up around villages, airports, por towns and districts. Such methods, like the intel gence-gathering process itself, are on-going a complex, utilising all three service arms in additi to overseas information received from 'frien agencies'. It is not sufficient simply to mount sporac air or naval patrols backed up by spot checks a body searches. As an intelligence officer, you m be confident that your network of overt and cov sources will provide you with advance warning o potential threat to security. When is a suspect vessel due in? Its point of departure? Time of arriv It is your responsibility to provide the answers these questions by close monitoring of the intel gence process.

In collaboration with the army and the police, the duties of the TCS we threefold

On 8 July 1959, the TCS in Cyprus consisted of officers and 90 other ranks, plus four civilian cler The original unit had been an ERE (extra-regimen establishment), but under Harding the proviso h been made that as many 'I' Corps as possible shou be drafted in. All warrant officers and sergeants TCS had to be members of 'I' Corps.

TCS HQ was located in the police headquarters Thalassa, under the direct control of the Director of Operations, and equipped with good channels of communication to the Colonel of Intelligence and the Security Liaison Officer (SLO). It staffed and controlled five detachments: 51 (Mobile) based at Nicosia and responsible for deterrent operations along the coast; 52 based at Famagusta; 53 at Limassol; 54 at Larnaca; and 73, also based at Nicosia, and responsible for controlling the civilian airport.

In collaboration with the army and police, the priorities of the TCS were threefold. The smuggling of supplies and weapons to EOKA had to be prevented, the movements of people on the Cyprus Security Suspect List monitored, and the entry into the island of people on the Subversive List controlled. If any information relevant to these tasks came to light, the SLO and SB had to be contacted immediately. In addition, all travellers arriving in Cyprus from 'hostile' countries (the United Arab Republic, due to President Nasser's tacit support for EOKA, and any Soviet bloc country) were logged and reported.

The operation begins. Despite the three-year-old State of Emergency, EOKA terrorism is continuing to tie down the British garrison on Cyprus. 'I' Corps must maintain its vigilance. It

Intelligence Reorganisation Cyprus 1958

During the Cyprus Emergency, the Travel Control Security Section operated within an extremely flexible and effective intelligence system. Each senior 'I' Corps officer had a large department under his control. While the diagram shows a rigid chain of command, in practice there were numerous interchanges between the various elements.

Director of Operations

General Staff Officer I, Intelligence

Special Branch
The assigning of police activities to each particular district.

Central Registry
The storage of all intelligence files relating to Cyprus, classified under a personnel, subject and unit index.

Senior Intelligence Officer

Security Liaison Officer
Responsible for setting up channels of communication.

General Staff Officer II, Intelligence

MI5, SIS and other Intelligence Organisations

Combined Intelligence Unit
The vetting of all military personnel on active service in Cyprus, in addition to any dependants living on the Island.

Travel Control Security Section (TCS)

Intelligence Officer

Operations

Intelligence Officer
Dealing with sudden emergencies. This department had several brigades at its disposal in the event of an upsurge in terrorist activity.

Intelligence Officer
Responsible for the security of 'key points' such as police stations, observation points, likely civilian targets and army installations.

Static Section
Administration of the TCS, and the assessing of information in the early stages of the intelligence process.

Mobile Section
Free-ranging force, continually on alert, responsible for carrying out operations in the field, and for snap security checks on the army in Cyprus.

...eophanis Agamemnonas.
...illeas.
...Theodoros Elia.
...ANOU, Georghios.
...nnis Georghiou.
...os Vissou.
...icos Lambrou.
...9ES, Panayiotis, Achilleas.
...LOS, Ioannis Kyriacou.
...Andis Pyripidou.
...8ES, Costas Christoforou.
...Kyriakos.
...Nicos.

RISTOFI, Napoleon.
35, NATA, PAPHOS.

is 0930 hours at TCS HQ in Thalassa. The Director of Operations has called an urgent meeting. The SLO explains that, according to information received from 'friendly' agencies, a caique (small vessel) is due into Limassol carrying a supply of explosives and ammunition. The caique has not sailed directly from Athens, and has picked up its cargo from one of the countless islands in the Aegean Sea. Its name is unknown, but intelligence believes that it will arrive sometime today. In addition, a suspected terrorist has arrived in Nicosia having flown in from London. Although travelling on a Canadian passport, the man is a Greek national and a known associate of EOKA leader Colonel Grivas. Intelligence fears that a major act of sabotage or assassination is planned, as the suspect has an extensive background in booby traps and demolitions. The TCS must unearth both caique and assassin. First the man.

The Security Control Officer's diary at Nicosia's civil airport has an entry relating to the suspect, dated the previous day. An alert immigration official was intrigued as to why a Canadian businessman would come to Cyprus, and had smelt a rat when the man spoke perfect Greek with a mainland accent. The suspect has given an address in Limassol, and 253 Field Security Section, responsible for security in the Limassol area, are alerted that a possible terrorist has entered their district. Military units are

171

placed on standby and 253 begins to tap its overt sources in the civilian population. The Special Branch is also contacted, since any subsequent operation has to involve the civilian authorities.

Meanwhile, sources in the dock area are being approached in an attempt to verify intelligence information regarding the caique's arrival. The Royal Navy is tasked to supply details of all such craft that have arrived within the past 48 hours.

The address that the suspect has given is found to exist. Although the occupants appear to be law abiding, 'I' Corps records reveal that they are cousins of a well-known EOKA gunman, and of an Orthodox priest who has been outspoken in his support for Archbishop Makarios, the political leader of the organisation. An immediate raid is advised, a joint TCS/SB operation.

Inside the house, a family protests its innocence, denying that any stranger has stayed there. However, 253 have an informant who lives on the other side of the street. Although given to wild flights of fancy in the past, the informant needs no prompting to describe a man who, disguised as a local farmer, left the house early that morning in an old Ford. Piecing together the leads, TCS believes that his destination is one of the Orthodox monasteries high in the Troodos mountains, southwest of Nicosia. Not all of the monks are necessarily sympathetic to the EOKA cause, and, back at TCS HQ, intelligence officers establish that there are only three monasteries within a day's drive of Limassol that could be deemed totally safe as refuges for EOKA terrorists. It is

Above left: Following the ambush of an army unit by EOKA, the local villagers are subjected to a thorough search.
Below: General Grivas is rumoured to have moved his base to the mountains around Limassol; the area is scoured for hidden weapons and ammunition.

The most common home-made bomb favoured by EOKA was a closed metal pipe packed with dynamite (left), and the terrorists had no qualms about using school-children (above right) to throw the device. A four-second fuze was even installed to prevent the victim from taking cover. Above left: Officers from 'I' Corps have reassembled this motorbike in an effort to track down the bomb's maker. Their conclusions will be used as forensic evidence. Following Operation Pepperpot in June 1956, EOKA was forced to disperse from its bases in the Troodos mountains (below).

decided to raid each one in turn, having established Observation Posts (OPs) in the event of a hurried departure by the suspects, once they realise that there are extensive troop movements in the area.

Meanwhile, the search for the caique has reached a satisfactory conclusion. Only six caiques had arrived in Limassol from a non-Cypriot point of departure, of which four were well known to TCS as being captained by EOKA sympathisers. Working on the assumption that such an important cargo would be entrusted to an innocent-looking vessel, it was decided to carry out spot checks on the remaining two – but only cursorily. If either caique was carrying explosives, the effect of passing a spot check would, it was hoped, make the crew confident of unloading their cargo unhindered. However, as soon as the patrol boat was seen approaching the second vessel, much of the cargo was hurriedly thrown over the side. Nevertheless, there were sufficient quantities of subversive literature left on board to make an arrest, and the following day Royal Navy divers would attempt to recover the abandoned cargo.

By 1800 hours the following day, OPs have been established outside the three monasteries, and RAF helicopters have been deployed to provide transport for Army units carrying out the raids. 'I' Corps have provided the 'active arm' of the military with the necessary information, and soldiers are on station ready for the operation. Although a search of the first monastery comes up empty-handed, one of the OPs reports three men leaving the second – driving up into the mountains in an old Ford. Immediately, a small detachment of infantry is flown by helicopter to initiate a roadblock, while others are deployed to cover the suspects' flanks. Upon being stopped, the three men are so surprised at discovering soldiers so high in the mountains that they offer little or no resistance.

Although all three are on the 'wanted' list, the main suspect appears to have vanished into thin air. The search will continue, hopefully exerting sufficient pressure for the assassin to abandon his assignment. With his presence widely publicised on the island, TCS expect him to make a quiet exit from a deserted beach. If this is the case, it will probably be the last that the British authorities will hear of him.

Back at Nicosia, 'I' Corps has another problem on its hands – a schoolboy has been apprehended in the act of throwing a home-made bomb. Instead of the normal 12-second delay fuze, this explosive is equipped with one of only four seconds. Questions: where did the bomb come from, and is it the handiwork of any known terrorist? Since one of 'I' Corps' chief informants has just been shot in the back, should the Army and police anticipate a fresh outbreak of bombing? Who, or what, will be the terrorists' next objective, and how can their strategy best be combated? These are the questions that the Chief of Staff will be asking the following day – somehow, 'I' Corps will have to come up with the right answers.

THE AUTHOR Nigel Foster was a member of the British Army's Intelligence Corps. Following training at Lympstone, he was attached to 3 Commando Brigade.

COMBAT SKILLS Of The Elite

ESCAPE AND EVASION

Below: In the thick Vietnamese jungle it was easy for combat patrols to become separated from their units. Evasion of the enemy took great care and one man lighting a cigarette could jeopardise an entire group if an enemy force downwind noticed its scent.

The development of conventional warfare and counter-insurgency operations has been characterised by a growing tactical need for greater individual and unit dispersion. This requirement naturally increases the chances of your unit becoming isolated from friendly forces. A sudden massing of enemy forces may cut off your unit entirely, or, alternatively, you may become separated from a patrol and find yourself alone behind enemy lines. Your first priority in this situation should be to carry out your original assignment. Only when this has been accomplished does your primary objective become that of rejoining friendly forces. Successfully reaching your own lines will depend on your ability to perform three tasks: to survive off the land with only limited resources, to move across terrain without being observed, and to effect an early escape should you fall into the hands of hostile forces.

If you are captured, try to focus your mind on an escape plan as early as possible – the chances of success will reduce the longer you wait. A prisoner's rations on the battlefield are unlikely to be sufficient to sustain your health, let alone afford you the opportunity to build up reserves of energy. Moreover, your ability to withstand any mistreatment or lack of medical care will rapidly diminish the longer you are held captive. It is only during the early days of imprisonment that your powers of reasoning and your morale will remain at their peak – do not wait until they fall to a low ebb. Bide your time if necessary, but seize any opportunity that arises.

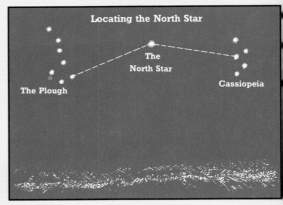

Locating the North Star

The North Star

The Plough

Cassiopeia

Other factors will also contribute to the importance of an early escape. If you have been captured during or after a fierce battle or firefight, the enemy will probably be confused and disorientated. Artillery or air strikes screaming down on his positions may add to the chaos of battle and give you the chance to steal an advance on your captors. For the first few hours of your capture you will be in the hands of frontline troops, rather than the prison guards positioned further to the rear. Good soldiers do not always make careful prison guards, and they may be too distracted by their own casualties and the need to maintain defensive positions to keep a close eye on you. Watch out for, and exploit, any lapse in their scrutiny. For the moment, at least, you will be reasonably acquainted with the surrounding terrain and the approximate deployment of your own forces. The location of inhabited areas, water sources and suitable lying-up positions may be known to you. Later, after several days of hard trekking as a captive, the surrounding country will become totally unfamiliar.

Given the endless number of possibilities, there can never be any specific rules for effecting an escape – you will have to rely on your natural instincts and ability to improvise. If the planned escape is to take place from a prison camp, however, a great deal of organisation and attention to detail will be essential. Approach the escape plan as you would any military operation, seeking always to narrow the margins for error.

Once the escape has been effected, your cardinal rule should be to get as far away as possible. This may

In hilly or mountainous terrain, avoid using ridges that increase the danger of your being silhouetted. Change direction on a downward slope after crossing a skyline, and make constant checks behind to ensure that you are not being followed. Enemy cordons should be relatively easy to breach under the cover of darkness, provided you locate the position of the sentry nearest you. Silence and careful observation are the keys here – listen for the routine sounds of sentry relief, and then pass as near to the guard as is safe.

If you can, make your silhouette as similar as possible to that of the local inhabitants of the area, or those of enemy sentries and soldiers, particularly their headgear. It is possible that individual guards will not be expecting enemy presence in their vicinity and, if one spots you, there may be a moment of hesitation while he decides whether to fire. This provides you with an opportunity to throw him off-guard. It is a very good idea to learn such a phrase as 'Don't shoot, you bloody fool' in his language, for use in this type of situation. It may sound a little simplistic, but this technique has been used to great effect by special forces teams throughout the world.

Any lying-up position (LUP) that you establish must be well concealed from the ground and air, with access to water if you intend to leaguer for more than one day. Make sure that the site has only one good approach route, and position a sentry if you are in a

involve a distance of several miles; at other times, just a few yards. Approach the problem with the same amount of care that you would if you were a member of a lost patrol.

Pinpoint your location as accurately as possible, using the sun, stars or any known landmarks. In the northern hemisphere, the sun will be due south at mid-day. If you have a watch, hold it horizontally with the hour hand pointed at the sun. Then draw an imaginary line from the centre of the watch through the 12: true south is midway between the hour hand and the 12. This procedure will indicate true north in the southern hemisphere. At night, use the Plough constellation to locate the North Star. If you have studied these and other methods of navigation, you are much less likely to become totally disorientated in unfamiliar terrain.

Ninety per cent of your evasive movements should be restricted to the hours of darkness, but do not become over-confident just because you cannot see or hear the enemy. One sniper with an infra-red sight may be silent, but he will also be deadly. Rivers are one possible means of escape, but avoid the large ones as they will probably be watched. Never move along roads, and only cross them immediately after a vehicle has passed and only if you have a positive fix on the location of any sentries. The vehicle's lights will temporarily dazzle any soldiers nearby and facilitate your safe crossing.

Above: When you are crossing hilly country there are precautions that you can take against being spotted by the enemy. Always run a ridge some yards below its crest, taking care to travel on the far side of known enemy positions, and never allow yourself to be silhouetted against the sky. Above right: If enemy forces in your area oblige you to lie up for a while, make sure that you have access to water, otherwise a raging thirst will bring the risk of you betraying your position while attempting to slake it.

Navigating with the sun

Northern Hemisphere

Southern Hemisphere

True South

True North

sun

3

12

6

9

9

12

6

3

Hour hand

group of more than two. Cover your tracks when moving on: bury all refuse and remove every trace of your presence – your own lines may be several days' travel away, and you cannot afford to give the enemy any clue as to your whereabouts.

The secret of successful escape and evasion lies in your determination to avoid capture, to resist enemy intimidation if captured, and to seize every opportunity to reach friendly forces. In addition to the techniques of navigation, stealth and survival in the field, you will need to draw on all your resources as a combat soldier to evade the enemy. Cover, concealment, the passing of obstacles, the use of silent weapons, health precautions and cautious patrolling – these are all basic to survival behind enemy lines.